SIBERIA:
Problems and Prospects for Regional Development

SIBERIA

Problems and Prospects for Regional Development

Edited by ALAN WOOD

CROOM HELM
London ● New York ● Sydney

©1987 Alan Wood
Croom Helm Publishers Ltd, Provident House
Burrell Row, Beckenham, Kent, BR3 1AT

Croom Helm Australia, 44–50 Waterloo Road,
North Ryde, 2113, New South Wales

British Library Cataloguing in Publication Data

Siberia: problems and prospects for regional development
 1. Siberia (R.S.F.S.R.)—Social
 conditions
 I. Wood, Alan
 957'0854   HN530.S5
 ISBN 0-7099-3655-9

Published in the USA by
Croom Helm
in association with Methuen, Inc.
29 West 35th Street
New York, NY 10001

Library of Congress Cataloging in Publication Data

ISBN 0-7099-3655-9

Phototypeset by Sunrise Setting, Torquay, Devon
Printed and bound in Great Britain
by Billing & Sons Limited, Worcester.

Contents

Introduction

The word Siberia has several connotations. The definition used in this book is one commonly accepted in the West: all of the USSR east of the Urals and north of the Central Asian republics — what in Soviet parlance would be West Siberia, East Siberia, and the Far East. This region has many astonishing features. It is not just a large slice of territory: if it were an independent state, it would very easily be the largest country in the world. The 'subcontinent' of Asia, as the territory occupied by India, Pakistan and Bangladesh is sometimes described, is less than one-third of its size. Thus it is perhaps even more astonishing how little is known about it outside the USSR. It only has land frontiers with China and the Mongolian Peoples Republic (and North Korea, for 15 kilometres), and no doubt partly for this reason it has made little direct impact on the outside world. Yet its name is known to everyone, not because of its size, or its riches, or its beauty, but because of its history as a place of exile and incarceration. Relative inaccessibility and bad press have effectively stifled knowledge.

This book seeks to redress the balance in some small measure by providing the reader of the late 1980s with some background, and with an up-to-date summary of the most important current developments. The background is both geographical and historical. Denis Shaw, in his geographical outline, touches on the elements of the physical and biological environment, as well as human factors like population dynamics; and his message is that the dreadfulness of Siberia has been much exaggerated. Similarly Alan Wood shows that Siberian history is not an unmitigated record of hardship and suffering. If Academician Okladnikov's *Istoriya Sibiri* in five volumes (Leningrad, 1968–69) were available in English, this would not have to be stressed; but as Wood points out, there is no major history of Siberia in a Western language.

The other chapters in the book are more directly concerned with the current situation. If the importance of Siberia to the USSR is seen as providing a storehouse of raw materials, then Theodore Shabad and David Wilson contribute up-to-date statements on economic resources in general, and oil and gas in particular. Siberia produces at present two-thirds of the

1

country's oil and over half its gas — and these two fuels between them account for over half of Soviet hard currency earnings. If one considers the wider energy situation, Siberia is even more predominant, with over 80 per cent of Soviet potential oil reserves, 90 per cent of gas reserves, and over 90 per cent of its coal reserves (though one must concede here that the Tunguska and Lena coal basins, which appear huge in Soviet atlases, remain 'largely hypothetical, inaccessible, and unexploited', in Shabad's words). In other mineral resources, Siberian nickel, platinum, cobalt, diamonds, tin, and gold are all vital to the national economy, and in some cases, put the USSR at or near the top of the world league for production.

Fundamental to the exploitation of minerals and fuels is a transport system. Robert North discusses the evolution of the Siberian system and examines particular aspects of it. One feature which has much more than domestic significance is the development of a container land-bridge between the Far East and Western Europe. This is already carrying freight of the order of two million tonnes a year, and expansion by a factor of three by 1990 is hoped for. This could have wide repercussions on world trading patterns. There is interesting speculation, too, on the future of Arctic navigation along the north coast of Siberia. One particular major transport development, the Baikal-Amur Railway (BAM) is accorded separate treatment in a chapter by Violet Conolly. This gigantic and very difficult project will not be fully completed for several years.

A final group of three chapters considers factors in Siberian development directly affecting the outside world. John Erickson surveys the military and strategic dimension, adopting a primarily historical perspective to explain the 'Pacific shift'. Stuart Kirby is concerned with the relation between Siberia and its Far Eastern neighbours, China and Japan, and examines present and potential economic interaction. Finally John Stephan looks at the wider picture of Siberian involvement with the rest of the world, setting out a whole range of prospects from which the new Soviet leadership must make a selection.

This broad and balanced survey raises in our minds, as it should, all sorts of questions. How does Siberia, with over 28 million inhabitants, relate to the rest of the country, which is smaller but contains 246 million people? To what extent do its natural riches compensate for its sparse population? Is Siberia really a colony, or even an empire, its colonial or imperial status disguised by contiguity with the mother country? The nineteenth century Russian historian Yadrintsev thought that it was, as have others since. It is now easy to visit some parts of Siberia: Novosibirsk, Irkutsk, Khabarovsk, and the Trans-Siberian Railway are open to tourists. The curious can go and have a look for themselves.

The book owes its existence to the energy and persistence of the historian Alan Wood of the University of Lancaster. He is also the moving spirit behind the British Universities Siberian Studies Seminar, to which almost all the contributors belong. The Seminar meets at roughly annual intervals, and is inter-disciplinary in character. It seeks to enlarge and publicise knowledge of this immense landmass. Anyone wishing to participate in this process is welcome to write to the editor for information. Earlier in this century the Norwegian Fridtjof Nansen was fired by the same enthusiasm. He travelled across Siberia, from north-west to south-east, and named the book he wrote about it *Through Siberia, the Land of the Future*. The epithet would be equally appropriate for the present volume.

Terence Armstrong
Cambridge

Editor's Notes

(i) 'Siberia' for the purposes of this volume designates the entire territory of the USSR east of the Ural mountains to the Pacific coast, and from the Arctic Ocean to the Chinese and Mongolian borders. It comprises the three major economic planning regions of the Russian Socialist Federated Soviet Republic, viz. West Siberia, East Siberia and the Far East (including the island of Sakhalin). Although current Soviet usage makes a distinction between the first two and the third, the term Siberia is used here to mean the whole area traditionally and historically known by that name. The capitalised forms 'West Siberia' and 'East Siberia' are used when referring to the economic/administrative region; 'western Siberia' and 'eastern Siberia' are used in a looser, mainly geographical sense.

(ii) Euphony has been sacrificed for uniformity throughout all the chapters by retaining the Russian terms for the territorial–administrative subdivisions within the Union Republics and Autonomous Republics (ASSRs) of the USSR, thus: *oblast*, *okrug* and *krai* (rather than region, district and territory). This is done in order to avoid ambiguity where the English terms are used in a more general sense.

(iii) Transliteration of Russian names and technical terms is based on the Library of Congress system with minor adaptations. Thus the letters *ia*, *iu* and initial *e* are rendered as *ya*, *yu* and *ye*; '*i kratkoe*' is given without the diacritical hook, thus *i*; and representation of the 'soft sign' has been omitted throughout.

(iv) Thanks are due to Jean Dowling and Clair Jarvis of the Geography Departments of Birmingham and Lancaster Universities for preparing the maps in chapter 1 and chapters 2 and 4 respectively; also to the secretarial staff in the Department of History, University of Lancaster, for furtive help with typing and preparation of some tables.

(v) Any inquiries concerning the British Universities Siberian Studies Seminar, out of whose activities the idea for this book emerged, should be addressed to the editor, Department of History, University of Lancaster, UK, and not to the publishers.

(vi) The views expressed in the following chapters are those of their respective authors. No attempt has been made to impose any uniform editorial 'line', save that of addressing the triple theme of Siberia's 'progress, problems and perspectives'. Consequently, there may be detected differing nuances and shades of opinion among the interpretations of the individual writers. If this stimulates further research and debate, then the book will have served a useful purpose. On the other hand every effort has been made to maintain consistency of convention and presentation throughout. Any remaining flaws or infelicities which have escaped the editor's attention must be considered his responsibility.

Alan Wood
Lancaster

The Contributors

Terence Armstrong was formerly Reader in Arctic Studies at the Scott Polar Research Institute, University of Cambridge, and is an internationally recognised authority on the history, geography and development of the Soviet North. Among his extensive publications in this field are *Russian Settlement in the North* (1965) and *Yermak's Campaign in Siberia* (1975).

Violet Conolly has been described as 'the leading authority on Siberia in the English-speaking world'. She was for many years head of the Soviet research section at the British Foreign Office, and from 1964 to 1966 Hayter Research Fellow at the University of London. Her two best-known books on Siberia are *Beyond the Urals* (1967), for which she was awarded the medal of the Royal Central Asian Society, and *Siberia Today and Tomorrow* (1975).

John Erickson is Professor and Director of Defence Studies at the University of Edinburgh. One of the West's leading experts on East-West military affairs, he is the author of many books and articles including *The Soviet High Command* (1961), *The Road to Berlin* and *The Road to Stalingrad* (1975–83).

Stuart Kirby is Professor Emeritus, Aston University, Birmingham, and Senior Associate of St Antony's College, Oxford. He spent many years in the Far East and was formerly Professor of International Economics at the University of Hong Kong. His published works include *The Soviet Far East, Russian Studies of China, Russian Studies of Japan* and the Economist Intelligence Unit's Special report, *Siberia and the Far East* (1985).

Robert North is Professor of Geography at the University of British Columbia, Canada. He is a specialist in Soviet and East European transport and communications policy on which he has written widely. His major study on *Transport in Western Siberia: Tsarist and Soviet Development* appeared in 1979.

Theodore Shabad was until his death Editor of the influential New York-based journal, *Soviet Geography*. He was for some time the *New York Times* correspondent in Moscow and has authored, edited and co-edited many works on Soviet economic resources, including *Basic Industrial Resources of the USSR*, *Soviet Natural Resources in the World Economy* and (with Victor Mote) *Gateway to Siberian Resources (the BAM)*. Tragically, Ted Shabad died suddenly of a heart attack as this book was going into print.

Denis Shaw is Lecturer in the Department of Geography, and an Associate member of the Centre for Russian and East European Studies, University of Birmingham, and has written widely on the geography, including historical geography, of the Soviet Union. He is co-editor of *Soviet and East European Transport Problems*, *The Soviet Union*, and co-author (with Judith Pallot) of *Planning in the Soviet Union*, published by Croom Helm in 1981.

John Stephan is Professor of History at the University of Honolulu, Hawaii, and Director of the recently established programme for the study of the Soviet Union in the Pacific-Asian Region (SUPAR). He has written extensively on the Soviet Far East and Pacific regions, including *Sakhalin: a History*, *The Kuril Islands* and *The Russian Fascists*. He is also co-editor (with V.P. Chichkanov) of *Soviet-American Horizons on the Pacific* (1986).

David Wilson is Lecturer in Soviet Geography in the School of Geography, University of Leeds. He is one of Britain's foremost experts on Soviet energy policies and the author of the Economist Intelligence Unit's *Quarterly Energy Review: the Soviet Union and Eastern Europe* and also of the EIU's report, *Soviet Energy to 2000*. His book, *The Demand for Energy in the USSR*, was published by Croom Helm in 1983.

Alan Wood is Lecturer in Russian History at the University of Lancaster, Convenor of the British Universities Siberian Studies Seminar and editor of its occasional publication, *SIBIRICA*. He has written numerous articles on Russian and Soviet history and is co-author (with John Massey Stewart) of *Siberia: Two Historical Perspectives*. At present he is completing a study of tsarist penal policies in Siberia.

1

Siberia: Geographical Background

Denis Shaw

'As I approached the frontiers of Siberia I began to give
way to groundless, though perhaps natural apprehensions;
and indeed as I neared such a supposed scene of cruelty and
misery, I became completely agitated. Hitherto Providence
had protected me, but although I felt thankful for the past,
I could not but be concerned for the future, reasonably
doubting how, where, and when, my pilgrimage would
end'.

Captain John Dundas Cochrane, R.N., 1823.[1]

The 'groundless apprehensions' felt by the British naval
commander John Dundas Cochrane as he entered Siberia in the
summer of 1820 have been experienced by many other travellers
before and since. The remoteness of that land, the harshness of
its environment, and its uncomfortable associations with hard
labour and exile, promote strong and often negative images even
today. The current labour shortage in Siberia, for example, and
the high wages that must be paid to persuade people to work in
many areas, are a reflection of this public image. The purpose of
this chapter is to suggest that, in terms of the natural
environment at least, the image is often exaggerated. Siberia is a
huge land and conditions vary greatly across it. Statements
regarding the unpleasantness of the natural environment are
often over-generalisations which take little account of the way
that environment varies locally.

For the purposes of this book, Siberia is that territory of the
Soviet Union within the Russian Federation which lies to the east
of the Urals. Thus defined, Siberia extends all the way from the
Urals to the Pacific and occupies about 13 million square

kilometres, which is 60 per cent of the entire territory of the USSR. This means that Siberia is approximately one and one-third times the size of Canada, one and half times that of the United States, and four times the size of India. The countries of Western Europe are dwarfed by Siberia. The United Kingdom, for example, is more than 50 times smaller.

From the point of view of physical geography, Siberia has little meaning. Its western boundary, the Ural mountains, is merely part of the conventional dividing line between Europe and Asia. Describing 'the mighty barriers which divide Europe from Asia', Captain Cochrane noted that 'the ascent and descent are so nearly imperceptible that, were it not for the precipitous banks everywhere to be seen, the traveller would hardly suppose he had crossed a range of hills'.[2] Socially, however, the Captain did mark a difference, noting that the Siberians were more civil, more cleanly dressed and more hospitable than the European Russians. Indeed, so hospitable were they that the Captain was able to renounce 'the hackneyed and unsocial custom of paying for food'. The Captain also noticed differences in flora and fauna as he crossed the Urals and related an old story 'that mice taken from one side to the other will not survive'.[3]

Siberia's northern boundary is provided by the Arctic sea coast and the off-shore islands. To the south are the border with the Kazakh Republic and the international frontiers with Mongolia, China and North Korea. This southern boundary has fluctuated considerably over the past few centuries. To the east, according to the definition adopted by this book, Siberia extends to the Pacific Ocean. In Soviet thinking, however, it falls far short of the Pacific.

In the administrative sense, Siberia also has little meaning at the present time. As noted later, only at certain periods of its history has Siberia been a single administrative unit. It does, however, have real significance in public perception, and Moscow-based administrators and politicians have often had to cope with manifestations of regional feeling. On the whole, perhaps, like Metternich describing pre-unification Italy, it is best to think of Siberia as a 'geographical expression'.

CONCEPTS OF SIBERIA

The uncertainty regarding Siberia's boundaries relates to the different usages of the term in history. The origins and meaning of the word have been matters of considerable disagreement among etymologists. It seems that the word was first used with reference to western Siberia by Iranian writers at the end ot the thirteenth century and on a Catalonian atlas in 1375. In the Russian sources a disputed reference occurs in the chronicles for the year 1407 when it is recorded that 'tsar' Shadibek killed 'tsar' Tokhtamysh 'in the land of Sinbirsk'. A more dependable reference is made by the 'Arkhangelgorod chronicler' for 1483. In this year a Muscovite force commanded by Fedor Kurbskii and Ivan Saltyk Travin crossed the Urals, moved down the river Tavda and 'past Tyumen' to 'the land of Siberia' where they did battle. They then returned to Russia by way of the Irtysh and 'the land of Yugra' on the lower Ob.[4]

At this early period, then, the term Siberia referred to an area of western Siberia, and most probably to the town of Isker or Sibir located on the river Irtysh. This was the centre of the Tatar khanate of Sibir which first acknowledged Muscovite supremacy in 1555 and was conquered by Yermak in the 1580s. However, before the final conquest and incorporation of Sibir into Muscovy, Ivan the Terrible already claimed the title of 'Sovereign of all the Siberian lands' (from 1554) and 'of all Siberia' (from 1563).[5]

In the early seventeenth century the cartographic inventory known as *The Book of the Great Map* was still distinguishing between Sibir located along the middle Irtysh river, and the lands along the lower Ob inhabited by the Khanty and known as Yugra. As Russian control spread to the east, however, more and more of the new territories were embraced by the term Siberia. This tendency may have been fostered by the early administrative importance of Tobolsk founded in 1587 close to the old Tatar capital of Isker (Sibir) and soon assuming various administrative duties with respect to other 'Siberian towns'.[6] The inclination to think of Siberia as a distinct and definite territory, to be distinguished from European Russia or 'Rus', was also encouraged by the attempts of the Russian government to keep tight control over the fur trade. Early in the seventeenth century a special section responsible for Siberian affairs appeared within the Kazan palace chancellery, the department of the government which administered various south-eastern and eastern regions. This office became the independent Siberian chancellery (*Sibirskii prikaz*) in 1637, and oversaw all the new territories lying to the east of the Urals. By the middle of the century, the idea that the term Siberia described all Russia's possessions in the east seems to have been firmly established. Thus such significant sources as the *Inventory of Siberian Towns and Forts*, probably compiled before 1640, the celebrated map of Siberia by Peter Godunov with accompanying text (1667), the *Plan of the Siberian Lands* and accompanying inventory (1672), and the *Atlas of Siberia* by S. Remezov (1701) all had a wide geographical brief. The same was also true of such volumes as the *History of Siberia* written by Yurii Krizhanich about 1680, and the *Description of the New Lands or Siberian State*, probably compiled in Moscow around 1686.

The boundaries of Siberia were given a stricter definition by Peter the Great. In 1708 he created the new province (*guberniya*) of Siberia stretching all the way to the Pacific, but also containing Vyatka and Solikamsk regions to the west of the Urals. The latter were transferred to Kazan Province in 1726. The capital of the new Siberian Province was Tobolsk but because of the problem of distance Irkutsk Province was made virtually independent in 1736. The *Sibirskii prikaz* operated intermittently until 1763. Under Catherine II's provincial reforms, Siberia was further subdivided, but once again attained some measure of administrative unity in the first half of the nineteenth century, most notably in the workings of the Siberian committee after the Speranskii reforms of the 1820s.

From the very beginning of Russian penetration into Siberia the territory had been the object of exploration, both official and unofficial. In the reign of Peter the Great such work was given a scientific basis, and scholars were soon joining explorers in the task of gathering geographical information. To this they added the goal of synthesising and generalising their findings in works of topography and of systematic description. Thus such scholars as I. K. Kirilov, S. P. Krasheninnikov, G. F. Müller, G. W. Steller, J. G. Gmelin, P. S. Pallas, I. I. Lepekhin and I. F. German greatly added to the store of knowledge concerning Siberia and, incidentally, to the popular understanding of its extent and character. The eighteenth century also witnessed attempts to make sense of the varied and complex geography of Russia in the exercise of regionalisation, often on a physical basis. This pioneering work received further development in the nineteenth century. Hence in such regionalisation proposals as those by K. F. German (1815) and K. I. Arsenev (1818 and 1848)

Siberia is recognised as a distinctive region with its own peculiar characteristics in physical geography. However, such schemes were hindered by contemporary ignorance concerning the natural environment and it fell to such later scholars as P. P. and V. P. Semenov-Tyan-Shanskii, V. V. Dokuchaev and L. S. Berg to make proposals on physical and human regionalisation by which the great variety of landscapes within Siberia might be understood.

When Russia occupied what is now the Kazakh Republic in the middle of the nineteenth century, geographers began to distinguish between Siberia on the one hand and Russia's newer Central Asian dominions on the other. Regional descriptions of the period generally draw the boundaries between these two areas to correspond with those of provinces. On the other hand, as the various frontier adjustments were made with China further east, the new acquisitions in this area came to be regarded as integral parts of Siberia. Now more than ever it was clear that the term Siberia was no more than a geographical convenience used to describe a substantial portion of Asiatic Russia. As the new physical geography made abundantly clear, this huge area had no real environmental unity.

Under the Soviets the term Siberia has been used in a more restricted sense than was common under the tsars. In the scheme of economic regionalisation adopted in the late 1930s, Siberia was divided into three regions: West Siberia, East Siberia and the Far East. The boundary between the last two regions was defined according to administrative convenience, while that between West Siberia and Kazakhstan corresponded with the Union republican frontier demarcated in 1936. In 1961 the system of economic regions was revised, and in 1963 the Yakut ASSR was transferred to the Far East. Since that time, in official parlance, the term Siberia has been used to refer only to the West and East Siberian economic regions. In this narrow sense Siberia extends neither to the Pacific in the east nor fully to the crest of the Urals in the west. It occupies only about half of the territory defined above (see Figure 1.1).

However, by no means all Soviet scholars are content with this narrow definition. Physical geographers such as L. S. Berg and his followers have proposed regional classifications based upon a multiplicity of environmental characteristics. In such schemes the Siberian regions invariably include territories consigned by economic regionalisation to the Far East. Similarly, when the 22-

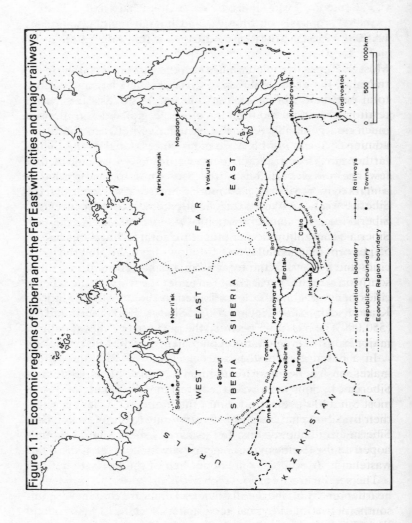

Figure 1.1: Economic regions of Siberia and the Far East with cities and major railways

volume geographical survey *Sovetskii Soyuz* was published in the late 1960s, the Yakut Republic was included in the East Siberia volume on the grounds that its geographical characteristics were closer to that region's than to those of the Far East.[7]

LANDSCAPES OF SIBERIA: THE INHABITED ZONE

Most Siberians live in the south, in a zone whose west-east axis is traced by the Trans-Siberian Railway. Thus 93 per cent out of a total population of 28 millions live in only 40 per cent of the territory. In actual fact the degree of population concentration is much greater than these figures suggest since the more populated administrative regions contain many empty areas. As a rule, the farther north one travels from the Trans-Siberian Railway, the fewer people one is likely to meet. It is also the case that there is a marked population bias towards the south-western parts of Siberia, west of Lake Baikal. Thus the southern parts of West Siberia and the southern portion of Krasnoyarsk *krai* in East Siberia occupy about 15 per cent of the total territory but contain 55 per cent of its population.[8] It follows from this that the larger cities and industrial concentrations are also located towards the south of Siberia. Particularly important in this regard are the cities of Novosibirsk (1.3 million in 1979), Omsk (1 million), Krasnoyarsk (796,000), Vladivostok (550,000), Irkutsk (550,000), Barnaul (533,000) Khabarovsk (528,000) and the major industrial region around Novokuznetsk (541,000).

In a description of the landscapes of Siberia, therefore, it makes sense to begin with a discussion of those areas where most Siberians live and work. Here, after all, are the landscapes which most Siberians actually see and in the context of which most of their lives are spent. They are also the landscapes most visitors to Siberia are likely to experience. By beginning in this way it is hoped to dispel the popular misconception of Siberia as an arctic wasteland.[9]

The southern part of West Siberia constitutes the agricultural heartland of the Siberian territories (Figure 1.2). Here, on the southern part of the great geographical feature known as the West Siberian Plain, lie a series of three very flat and fertile lowlands based on extensive glacial lake beds. These three lowlands are known as the Ishim Steppe, the Baraba Steppe and the Kulunda Steppe, and their agricultural importance is derived

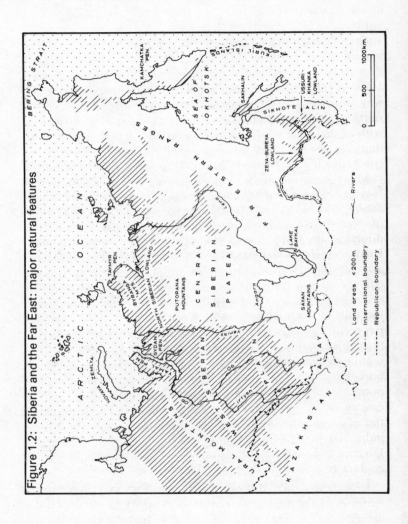

Figure 1.2: Siberia and the Far East: major natural features

from their fertile loess-like loamy soils. The lowlands correspond with the interfluves between the main northward-flowing rivers which drain the region: the Tobol, the Irtysh and, to the east, the Ob and its tributaries. The Trans-Siberian Railway cuts right across this important belt which displays a varied landscape of agricultural land, forests (birch, aspen, poplar with some spruce and fir) and lakes. South of the railway is found a mixed agriculture of spring wheat, corn, sunflowers, and some other drought-resistant crops together with cattle- and sheep-raising. However, in this direction the rich chernozems gradually give way to poorer chestnuts, solonchak and solonets soils. To the north of the Trans-Siberian is a zone some 150 kilometres deep with a mixture of arable farming (spring wheat, flax) and dairying. North of this again, the farmlands are gradually succeeded by coniferous forest, swamp and poor leached soils.

Many of the most important industrial cities of Siberia (Omsk, Novosibirsk, Novokuznetsk, Barnaul, Kemerovo and Tyumen) are located on the southern part of the West Siberian Plain. East of Novosibirsk, the Trans-Siberian runs north-east in the direction of Tomsk, thus skirting the industrially important Kuzbass region which lies to the south between two ridges which are extensions of the Altai mountains. In this basin, among the cities, coal mines and associated industries, one finds an urban-oriented agriculture of vegetables and fruit. Bypassing Tomsk, the railway then runs due east to Krasnoyarsk on the Yenisei river. Here the area of agricultural fertility has been narrowed by the spurs of the Sayan mountains, situated in a complex of inter-secting ranges just to the south, and the poor acidic soils of the boreal forest to the north. This agricultural strip, based on poorer soils than the black earths further west, extends as far as east as Taishet. Dairying and the cultivation of spring wheat are the main agricultural activities. Krasnoyarsk itself is a major industrial city dependent upon hydroelectricity from the Divnogorsk plant on the Yenisei river, and also on the brown coal from the surrounding Kansk-Achinsk coalfield.

East of the Yenisei the traveller encounters a very different scenery from that which is typical further west. One finds an altogether more rugged topography with folded-and-fault block mountains interspersed by broad intermontane basins to which settlement is largely restricted. Between the ridges of the Sayan and adjacent mountains, for example, are found a series of basin-like lowlands, often of agricultural and some industrial importance. An example is the Minusinsk Basin on the upper Yenisei, a triangular lowland centred on the two cities of Abakan and Minusinsk. Here a large industrial complex is being developed based upon hydroelectric power. Such basins are frequently subject to drought and are characterised by steppe-like vegetation with some forest, especially on the wetter slopes. The black earth and chestnut soils are cultivated for grain and are also used for grazing. Grazing also characterises the more suitable slopes of the southern mountains.

Between Krasnoyarsk and Irkutsk the Trans-Siberian Railway runs to the south-east through a deep tectonic trough separating the Sayan mountains to the south-west and an irregular ridged landscape to the north-east which is in effect a southward extension of the Central Siberian Plateau. Here and in the valleys to the east of Lake Baikal there is some cultivation but grazing is especially important. Dairying and vegetable growing are found near the cities.

The highland scenery becomes especially marked in the region around Lake Baikal where the parallel ranges are oriented south-west to north-east. This pattern is caused by downfaulting and uplifting whereby uplifted blocks alternate with rift valleys or grabens. The major rift valley is that occupied by the remarkable Lake Baikal itself. It is believed that this particular valley was formed some 25 million years ago. The lake, which is noted for its great beauty and unique ecology, is about 636 kilometres long and has the greatest depth and the largest volume of any fresh-water lake in the world. Mountains approach the shores of the lake on all sides and the building of the Trans-Siberian along the southern shore involved some quite difficult feats of engineering. This is also a region of considerable seismic activity. The seismic zone extends well to the north-east of the lake to affect the route of the new Baikal-Amur Mainline Railway which is being built through the mountains of this inhospitable area.

East of Lake Baikal the Trans-Siberian threads its way through the south-west north-east trending mountain ranges whose heights usually do not exceed 1,500 metres. Eventually it reaches the valley of the Amur where it runs close to the Chinese frontier. In Amur region and the Khabarovsk and Maritime territories of the Far East, the highland areas are somewhat more dispersed than further west, giving rise to broader lowlands. These include the Zeya-Bureya Plain along the Amur river, an alluvial lowland which is the most important agricultural district in the southern part of the Far East. Further east is the Ussuri-Khanka lowland, a broad tectonic trough stretching from the south coast of Maritime *krai* by way of Lake Khanka and the Ussuri valley (including part of north-east Manchuria in China) and down the lower Amur valley to the sea. These Far Eastern basins often have fertile soils with a distinctive mixed forest vegetation, but they suffer from a short growing season and marshy conditions, especially in the lower Amur valley. Moreover, winter temperature inversions and summer frosts sometimes restrict cultivation to valley slopes. The grazing of dairy and beef cattle is generally important with some cultivation of grains (spring wheat, oats, buckwheat, barley) and of industrial crops (soya beans, sugarbeet, flax, hemp, and sunflowers). The Khanka lowland is particularly noted for the variety of its crops.

The Ussuri-Khanka lowland and the lower Amur valley are bounded to the east by the well-folded Sikhote-Alin mountains and there is little coastal plain in this area. Across the Tatar Strait, however, lies the long, thin island of Sakhalin, characterised in its lower two-thirds by two parallel mountain chains and an interior valley. Some grain and root crops are cultivated and dairy cattle raised in the more favoured districts such as on the southern tip of the island and in the lower part of the interior valley, but Sakhalin is best known for its lumbering industry, based on its spruce-fir forests, and for its oil production.

With an average population density of nearly twelve persons per square kilometre, Maritime *krai* is something of a population outlier in terms of Siberian settlement. Settlement in the Far East is particularly concentrated in the Ussuri-Khanka lowland and lower Amur valley (Vladivostok, Khabarovsk, Komsomolsk-na-Amure), in the Zeya-Bureya Plain, and on the lower part of Sakhalin. To the west lie many thinly populated districts with islands of denser population around such cities as Chita, Ulan Ude and Irkutsk. Only west of Krasnoyarsk is the zone of more continuous settlement to be found.

LANDSCAPES OF SIBERIA: THE EMPTY ZONE

The regions considered so far constitute the settled heart or 'ecumene' of Siberia. To the north of this narrow strip of territory lies the vast wilderness whose harsh character has endowed Siberia with the forbidding image known worldwide. Much of this northern region is situated within the coniferous forest or boreal forest belt (*taiga*) which stretches from the Urals to the Pacific. This, of course, does not imply that the whole of this huge area is actually covered by trees. The boreal forest is in fact a mixture of forest, swamp, natural pasture, meadow and other types of landscape. The soils are poor, acidic podsols, usually unsuitable for cultivation, and swamp or permafrost conditions inhibit settlement. Population densities are therefore low. In places where conditions improve or there are promising resources, outliers of settlement occur. A handful of railways and roads penetrate the *taiga*. A good example is the new Baikal-Amur Railway currently being constructed to connect Bratsk and Ust-Kut, on a branch line from the Trans-Siberian at Taishet, to Komsomolsk in the Far East (see Figure 1.1). Plans call for the eventual setting up of significant population centres along this route to exploit the many resources found in the region. The expense and other difficulties of developing this remote area will however be significant (see Chapter 6). A further railway is now being built to connect the Baikal-Amur Railway with the city of Yakutsk in the heart of north-east Siberia. This will undoubtedly greatly improve access to the north-east, but the area is even more remote than the Baikal-Amur zone.

Far to the north, as the Arctic Ocean is approached, the *taiga* gradually peters out to be replaced by the barren, treeless tundra. Conditions in this arctic territory are even more unfavourable for human settlement than those in the *taiga*. Here again settlement depends upon useful resources such as minerals, or reindeer pastures which can be used by the native herders. In the Far East the mountainous terrain has the effect of extending this tundra zone well to the south.

The empty zone of Siberia can be divided into three regions in terms of structure and relief. To some extent these regions have been encountered already. They are the West Siberian Plain stretching from the Urals across to the valley of the Yenisei; the Central Siberian Plateau; and, beyond the broad lowland of the Lena Basin, the fold mountains of the Far East (see Figure 1.2).

The *West Siberian Plain*, which extends all the way up to the Arctic Ocean, is one of the largest areas of flat land in the world. It has been inundated by the sea several times in recent geological history, and poor drainage is still a major characteristic of the region. South of the Siberian Ridges, which are a series of east-west running heights dividing the plain into two, is the vast Vasyugan swamp occupying the zone in which the Ob and Irtysh meet. Here are found the middle Ob oilfields whose exploitation had been rendered especially difficult by the swampy conditions and the annual spring floods. Temporary corduroy roads have had to be laid down and the expense of building more permanent roads has been considerable (see Chapter 4). The spring floods, which most seriously affect the broad river valleys, are encouraged by ice-jams on the lower portions of the rivers situated to the north, but the interfluves are also frequently badly drained, and the plain is dotted with many thousands of lakes of disparate origins.

To the north of the Siberian Ridges is a swampy lowland that reaches towards the Arctic Ocean. The Gulfs of Ob and Taz, an extensive estuary system which penetrates far inland, divide the coastal regions into a series of peninsulas (Yamal, Taz, Gydan) with a morainic hilly terrain (except for their coastal terraces and dunes). This hostile tundra region is the site of the rapidly developing West Siberian natural gas field.

Apart from the tundra in the north, the predominant vegetation on the plain is coniferous forest, with a poor larch cover in the northern part, interspersed with extensive sphagnum marshes, grading into spruce, cedar, birch and then fir to the south. As a resource, however, the timber stand suffers from the harsh climate, swamps and permafrost soils, and better stands are found on the slopes of the Altai mountains to the south-east as well as in the Urals and areas further west.

The great rivers of West Siberia, the Ob, Irtysh and Yenisei are used for navigation and the generation of electric power. There have also been plans to use part of the water in the Ob-Irtysh system in a diversion scheme to benefit the arid parts of Central Asia. Thus far, however, the costs and environmental consequences of such proposals have seemed prohibitive.

East of the Yenisei valley is the second major region of Siberia, the *Central Siberian Plateau*. This is an enormous upland area, generally 500–700 metres in height, based upon a stable Precambrian shield, one of the oldest formations in the Earth's crust. The irregular upland rises to 1,700 metres in the Putorana mountains in the north-west. The plateau has been dissected by numerous river valleys which in places take the form of deep gorges with many rapids and waterfalls. The plateau edges are usually steep, especially to the west where an escarpment runs along the edge of the Yenisei valley.

The northern slopes of the Putorana mountains fall steeply to the North Siberian lowland, an east-west oriented plain which runs between the Lena Delta and the West Siberian Plain. Beyond this lowland is the Taimyr Peninsula, jutting northwards into the Arctic Ocean to form the northernmost tip of the Siberian mainland. The peninsula is dominated by the Byrranga mountains, rising to an elevation of 1,146 metres.

The harsh landscape of the Taimyr Peninsula and the adjacent coastlands is characterised by tundra, which also occurs on the higher slopes of the Putorana range. The North Siberian Plain has a mixed vegetation of poorly developed trees and bushes with typical tundra grasses and moss. This is thus described as forest-tundra. Further south, on the Central Siberian Plateau, coniferous forest is usual. The common species are the Siberian and Dahurian larch, which are tolerant of the severe climate and permafrost soils, with cedar, spruce and fir becoming more widespread to the south. Pine species are found on sandy soils.

Great resources of coal are believed to underlie part of the Central Siberian Plateau and the Lena Basin to the east, but they will be difficult to mine in view of their remoteness and the hostile environment. Human activity is generally restricted to reindeer-herding, hunting and the mining of some valuable minerals including diamonds. Far to the north, just under the western slopes of the Putorana mountains, is the nickel-copper-platinum centre of Norilsk (population 180,000, 1979).

The Lena-Vilyui-Aldan lowland separates the Central Siberian Plateau from the fold mountain systems further east. The lowland is covered by conifers but seasonal droughts also encourage the growth of wide areas of steppe grasses. In spring ice-jams on the lower portion of the Lena river induce extensive flooding. The Lena Delta is covered with tundra vegetation which also extends eastwards along the marshy coastlands of the Arctic lowland. However, in the central and upper portions of the Lena valley the environment is somewhat kinder and around Yakutsk there exists a significant area of northern agriculture which has pioneered the cultivation of hardy strains of wheat, rye and barley.

The fold mountain systems of the Far East, constituting the third major region of Siberia, are very complex and need not be detailed here. Only rarely do they extend above 2,000 metres in altitude but because of the northerly latitude and severe climate, arctic conditions are generally to be found on their upper slopes. Varieties of coniferous trees dominate the lower slopes and intervening valleys, but the larch is the most common species in view of the harsh climatic and soil conditions. In some areas seismic and volcanic activity is important, the latter especially characterising the Kamchatka Peninsula and the long chain of the Kuril Islands. Human settlement is naturally very restricted in this forbidding land and there is little agriculture. The working of some valuable minerals (gold, tin, mercury, tungsten), fishing, hunting, reindeer-herding and some lumbering constitute the main economic activities. As already noted, the economic prospects are somewhat better further south in the Baikal-Amur Railway zone where lumbering, coal mining and mineral working, as well as the exploitation of natural gas and other resources, may be encouraged by the advent of the new railway. However, over the greater part of the far north-east, distance and a rigorous environment constitute major barriers to economic development.

CLIMATES OF SIBERIA

It would not be too much to argue that the severity of Siberia's climate is probably the only fact about Siberia which has made any real impact on the popular imagination. It is a fact that has already been alluded to on more than one occasion above. Like many popular notions, however, this is by no means the whole truth about Siberia. As already noted in this chapter, the population of Siberia is not insignificant, and the agricultural economy of the south-western regions bears witness to the fact that here at least the growing season is sufficient to sustain reasonable cultivation practices. The purpose of this section is to explore the nature of Siberia's climates in greater depth.[10]

A number of features of Siberia's geography help to endow its climate with its own distinctive character. The first and most obvious is its position on the Asian landmass, resulting in many regions being far from the climatically moderating influences of the world's oceans. The continentality of the climate is further enhanced in the winter by the fact that the Arctic Ocean and adjacent parts of the Pacific are frozen. The influence of the Pacific is also reduced in winter by the Asiatic high which encourages offshore winds. Mountainous terrain along the southern boundary of the Soviet Union effectively cuts off possible incursions of warm, moist air from the Indian Ocean and nearby seas.

A further factor influencing Siberia's climate is its relatively northerly latitude. Much of it is situated above 50°N, which puts it in similar latitudes to Canada. The southern and more settled portion, however, is not especially far to the north when compared to Western Europe. Thus Novosibirsk (55°N) is only marginally south of Copenhagen or Edinburgh. This is however well to the north by Canadian standards: Novosibirsk is some way north of Edmonton (53°34'N) and just south of Thompson, Manitoba (55°45'N). Irkutsk, at 52°18'N, is located at approximately the same latitude as Birmingham, England, whereas Vladivostok (43°06'N), on the southern tip of Maritime *krai* in the Far East, is about as far south as southern Oregon, Boston (Massachusetts), and Marseille, France.

Siberian winters are long and cold. The dominating winter feature is the Asiatic Maximum or high, the high pressure system which centres on north-west Mongolia and the Tuva ASSR. Two ridges extend from this system; one north-east into Yakutia and towards the valleys of the Kolyma and Indigirka, and the other westwards towards the European USSR. Paul Lydolph has argued that the conception of an integrated high-pressure cell given on weather maps is in fact an illusion, since what appear on maps are sea-level equivalents.[11] Since much of the land surface in the eastern parts of Siberia is elevated, the actual weather experienced may not always be influenced by high pressure. Pressure systems look very different at the 850-millibar level. Nevertheless, the characteristic pattern over wide areas of central and eastern Siberia in winter is the trapping of isolated pockets of very cold air under temperature inversions in intermontane basins. This gives rise to clear, calm and extremely cold weather over many of the lowlands and valleys of the region.

Winter conditions over central and eastern Siberia contrast with those in much of western Siberia. Here, to the north of the high pressure ridge extending westwards across northern Kazakhstan, the influence of the Icelandic low is felt. Cyclones may sweep in across Scandinavia, the Baltic and the Barents Sea, and thus along the Arctic coast, or alternatively from around the southern tip of the Urals and thence northwards through the Ob Basin. Winter weather here, therefore, tends to be much cloudier and stormier, although less cold, than that further east.

The zone of low pressure extends along the Arctic coast as far east as the Lena Delta. In winter cyclones sometimes travel south-eastwards along this route into the Lena valley and then on into the Sea of Okhotsk, thus bringing storms and snow to the region. Much of the Far East, however, experiences the cold, stable winters associated with high pressure conditions.

The Siberian spring tends to be delayed until the snow melts in April or even May, but then temperatures rise very quickly. By contrast, the autumn is longer and temperatures fall more gradually except, perhaps, in the far north-east. Summers are short but often rather warm for the latitude, the main exception being the north coast. The temperature range between summer and winter is therefore considerable. On the coasts of the Far East summer temperatures are cooled by the ocean and also by the monsoon regime which brings considerable cloud and rain into' many areas. In many parts of Siberia the short growing seasons are not infrequently interrupted by summer frosts.

Table 1.1 indicates weather data for many of the main cities of Siberia, and for parts of the north. The low winter temperatures are evident everywhere. The characteristic tendency is for temperatures in January to fall towards the east and north-east to reach the extremes of cold to be found in north-east Siberia. Here in the interior valleys enormous temperature inversions build up in winter under high-pressure influences. At Verkhoyansk, for example, January temperatures average −48.9°C and minima of −68°C (−90°F) have been recorded. At Oimyakon in the upper Indigirka valley, at rather higher elevation (740 metres), minima of −71°C have been experienced. Fortunately for the residents of these regions, the air tends to be stable in winter and so there is little wind-chill. In summer, similar conditions of continentality and air stability lead to considerable heating. Thus July temperatures at Verkhoyansk average 15.3°C, giving an annual temperature range of 64°C. However, oceanic influences have a slightly moderating effect upon temperatures along the coasts.

Table 1.1 illustrates the fact that even Far Eastern cities such as Vladivostok and Khabarovsk have rather cold winters and cool summers despite the proximity of the Pacific Ocean. Far Eastern coasts suffer the effects of offshore winds in winter which result from the high pressure conditions inland. Only a few points along the coast are unaffected by sea ice. In summer the coasts are cooled by the ocean and the effects of the summer monsoon.

Table 1.1: Climatic data for selected Siberian cities

City	Temperature (°C) Mean-January	Mean-July	Mean annual precipitation (mm)	Annual snow cover (days)	Frost-free period (days)	Fog (days)
Barnaul	−17.7	19.6	464	164	116	52
Irkutsk	−20.9	17.5	458	162	94	103
Khabarovsk	−22.7	21.0	569	156	159	18
Krasnoyarsk	−17.4	19.9	419	150	119	18
Novosibirsk	−19.0	18.7	425	168	120	27
Okhotsk	−24.5	11.9	378	199	107	48
Omsk	−18.9	19.5	325	157	115	37
Ostrov Dikson[a]	−27.5	3.6	266	253	44	92
Salekhard	−24.4	13.8	464	233	94	43
Surgut	−22.2	16.8	492	205	102	
Verkhoyansk	−48.9	15.3	155	223	69	52
Vladivostok	−14.7	17.5	721	80	187	81
Yakutsk	−43.2	18.8	213	205	95	59

Note: a. Situated off the coast of the Taimyr Peninsula.

Source: Paul E. Lydolph, *Climates of the Soviet Union. World survey of climatology*, vol. 7, (Elsevier, Amsterdam, 1977), pp. 365–427.

Comparisons with California, or even British Columbia are therefore misplaced.

Annual precipitation declines across Siberia as one moves towards the east. Beyond Yakutsk and Lake Baikal, however, it starts to rise again, although the detailed picture depends upon the local topography. The Pacific littoral has high precipitation generally. In West Siberia, precipitation falls off also as one moves south, and semi-arid conditions are approached as one reaches the frontier with Kazakhstan. Droughts are not uncommon in this region. Seasonally, there are considerable variations in the amounts of precipitation received in Siberia. Generally speaking, since low-pressure conditions predominate in summer the maximum occurs in July, or August towards the north and the Far East. Needless to say, it is unfortunate for agriculture that maxima should occur late in the growing season, especially since spring and early summer drought is common in the interior basins of East Siberia and the Far East.

The summer monsoon regime brings much precipitation to coastal areas in the Far East. The precipitation is associated with cyclones which travel in a north-easterly direction across the region. At the surface, the easterly airflows under the warm fronts bring considerable rainfall to the eastward-facing slopes, while valleys in the lee of such slopes receive far less. However, towards the north, both annual and summer precipitation are reduced by the colder air. The peninsulas and islands off the east coast of the mainland have a maritime climate in which the precipitation maximum tends to occur late in the year but in which annual precipitation is often more evenly spread. Once again, the windward slopes are generally much wetter than more sheltered areas. Autumn precipitation in the maritime parts of the Far East sometimes comes about as a result of the after-effects of typhoons which have travelled north-eastwards from Japan.

Mean annual snowfall follows a pattern similar to that of precipitation as a whole. On the southern part of the West Siberian Plain, it exceeds 100 cm per year and is even greater in parts of the Altai and Sayan mountains. It then falls away towards the north and east to less than 50 cm along the Arctic coast and over much of eastern Siberia. It increases again towards the Pacific margins. The distribution of snow cover is rather different since the depth of snow is a product of both snowfall and the frequency of thaws. The greatest depths are generally found around latitude 63° or 64° and exceed 80 cm in the middle Yenisei valley. In the southern basins of East Siberia and the interior Far East the poor snow cover facilitates deep freezing of the soil in winter and also freeze and thaw at the beginning and end of winter. This is very detrimental for wintering crops.

Almost the whole of Siberia and the Far East is covered by snow by the end of October and the snow begins to disappear during April. Along the Arctic coast however, the snow often lasts until well into June. Practically the whole region, therefore, experiences more than 160 days of snow cover per year, and the Arctic coast up to 280 days.

Patterns of fog vary considerably over Siberia according to the differing causes at work. In summer advection fog is a frequent visitor to the Arctic coasts as a result of onshore winds carrying fog, which has been formed over the cold seas, on to the land. Elsewhere, in the early winter before rivers and lakes freeze, steam fog occurs as a result of cool air from the nearby land passing over the warmer water surfaces. In the depths of winter, ice fog is a common problem over large parts of eastern Siberia. This may be caused by the injection of moisture from settlements into the extremely cold surface air which then freezes into ice crystals. Intense temperature inversions may trap such fogs above Siberian cities for weeks at a time during winter. Finally, along the Pacific coasts, the cold northerly currents and floating sea ice induce frequent periods of fog, mist and cloud, especially in the early and middle parts of the summer period.

In the cold Siberian winters winds can make conditions particularly uncomfortable and even hazardous. Wind especially characterises the coastal areas in view of the fact that pressure gradients are accentuated there by land and sea differences. The Arctic coasts in particular are frequently smitten by severe wind-chill for this reason. At Salekhard, for example, close to the gasfields of north-west Siberia, January temperatures average −24.4°C but the wind often effectively makes it much colder. Conditions on the gasfields are therefore especially unpleasant at this time of year. Further south on the oilfields severe wind-chills are less frequent, but eastwards along the Arctic coasts of East Siberia and the Far East wind-chill factors can reach temperature equivalents of −125° to −135°C. High winds in winter are also very common along the Pacific coast. In many places, winter winds average 7–8 metres per second (15–20 miles per hour) and are frequently much stronger. Even Vladivostok, on the southern tip of Maritime *krai*, experiences winds in December and January which average more than eight metres per second.

POPULATION AND LABOUR SUPPLY

Earlier sections of this chapter have already commented on the basic patterns of settlement in Siberia. Nothing need be said here concerning the native peoples, which constitute only a small minority of the population. This subject is touched on briefly in Chapter 2. The present section is more concerned with recent population trends and the current labour shortage.

The population of Siberia and the Far East has grown considerably during the Soviet period: from 11.6 million in 1926 to 28 million at the last census in 1979. Natural increase has been responsible for a proportion of this, but there has also been much eastward migration. The early Bolsheviks declared themselves in favour of eastern development and of exploiting the rich resources of Siberia. These sentiments were to a certain extent realised during the subsequent five-year plans and the wartime shifts of industry and population away from the western frontiers. Between 1939 and 1959 the population of the entire region grew by 36 per cent and its share in the total Soviet population increased from 8.6 to 10.8 per cent. Since then, however, progress has been less certain. The controls upon population movements, and the forced labour policies of the Stalin era were gradually relaxed from the 1950s and there was a move towards more positive incentives to migration. Yet the new policies were unable to attract and retain labour in the required numbers. Wage differentials, for example, often failed to compensate for increased costs of living in Siberia and discriminated against certain groups. The northern territories also lost their special differentials in 1960. The 1960s therefore witnessed considerable labour turnover and out-migration in many areas. Policies were amended from 1968 and have recently been rather more successful. Thus, between 1970 and 1979 East Siberia and the Far East were areas of above average total and urban population growth. In the Far East, rural population also grew during the same period. On the other hand, West Siberia remained a region of below-average population growth and of rural depopulation. Overall, Siberia continued to experience population increase, although it was outpaced by certain other regions. Thus, whereas it contained 10.8 per cent of the Soviet population in 1959, it only had 10.7 per cent in 1979.

The successes of Soviet migration policies in the 1970s were especially marked in pioneering regions undergoing rapid resource development. In the northern part of Tyumen *oblast*, the Yakut ASSR, and certain other remote areas, population increase from 1970 to 1979 far exceeded national averages. Of course, the population bases in these regions are small and migration was not the sole factor behind the increases. But credit should also go to official migration policy.

The failure of Siberia to attract sufficient labour, and the tendency towards high labour turnover, has long been a cause for concern. Since the population base of the Soviet Union continues to be in the west, and the resource base is increasingly in the east, Siberia's labour shortages are a matter of national importance. Failure to develop Siberian resources could have considerable repercussions on the Soviet economy. Enough has been said in this chapter to suggest some of the problems. The unattractive natural environment of many areas is clearly one problem. Siberia's negative image, inherited from history, is another.

Scholars of Siberia have also pointed to other, perhaps more easily rectifiable, causes of the Siberian labour shortages. Despite the wage differentials, Siberians must often endure standards of living which are little better, perhaps even worse, than those in European locations. The tendency in many Siberian cities is for housing space allocations and housing quality to be lower than the USSR urban average. In 1979, for example, *per capita* living space in Novosibirsk was 8.6 square metres and in Omsk only 8.3, compared with a USSR urban average of 8.6. Both of these are large and well-established cities. The situation in the new towns is often much worse.

An analysis of Siberian cities by Ye. N. Pertsik pointed to another characteristic problem: the predominance within Siberia of relatively small towns with narrow economic bases.[12] Most such towns are vulnerable to economic change and have restricted employment opportunities for young people. One suspects that the monopoly power of a few industrial ministries in such places also reduces the incentive to supply adequate housing and services. A case in point is the new city of Angarsk in East Siberia where, according to one analysis, the local oil refining and petrochemical association employs almost half of the industrial personnel and owns over 40 per cent of the housing.[13] A handful of large industrial concerns owns most of the housing and services in the town. Competition for labour produces great unevenness in the allocation of housing and other facilities and the local government authorities are powerless to ensure co-ordinated development. Large bureaucratic bodies like industrial ministries centred in Moscow find it easy to ignore local needs. Consequently, disillusioned young people move away, the birth rate falls, and labour shortages ensue.

Conditions may be worse in the pioneering frontier regions. One study of the housing situation in Tyumen *oblast*, the area which embraces most of the oil and gas fields of north-west Siberia, indicated that *per capita* living space in the region's towns was worse than that for West Siberia as a whole, which in turn was worse than that for the entire RSFSR. The situation was especially unsatisfactory in many of the northern new towns where living space averaged only 85 per cent of the level for Tyumen *oblast* as a whole, and only 74 per cent of the officially approved norms. Rather similar problems occur in terms of the servicing of the housing (i.e. with running water, hot water, central heating, and sewage disposal). Here again a number of the northern towns had poor provision. In 1979, for example, only two per cent of the housing in Salekhard was fully serviced and over half was unserviced.[14]

Problems of the new towns of Siberia have been examined elsewhere by Violet Conolly.[15] She concludes that the Soviet reliance upon new-town development by industrial ministries leads to many difficulties which could have been avoided by a more co-ordinated planning approach. Clearly, the Soviets are determined to exploit the remote resources as quickly and as cheaply as possible and have a tendency to skimp on infrastructure where not absolutely necessary. The high costs of providing housing and other facilities in remote and environmentally difficult regions are obviously an important constraint. Hence there is now considerable reliance upon temporary contract labour working tours of duty in the remote regions. In more settled parts of Siberia, answers to the labour shortages may be found in seeking greater labour productivity and in developing capital- rather than labour-intensive industry. Finally, a general Soviet emphasis on conservation and new technologies may also serve to temper the demands being made on Siberia's resources.

CONCLUSION

This chapter has attempted to give an account of the environmental diversity of Siberia. The overall impression is one of difficulty from the point of view of human settlement, but not perhaps of the insuperable obstacles which loom so large in the popular imagination. After all, the climate of the south-western and more settled part of Siberia is not dissimilar to that of the Prairie Provinces of Canada. Like those provinces, south-western Siberia has not always seemed to be the most desirable place in which to live, and yet like them it has a large and growing population. Indeed, it should be added that this part of Siberia is more densely settled and has more big cities than the Prairie Provinces. This might be a consequence of Soviet development policies and the presence of local resources such as Kuzbass coal. There is also the fact that south-western Siberia is contiguous to the historic core of Russian settlement west of the Urals, whereas the Prairie Provinces are separated from metropolitan Canada by the great mass of the Canadian Shield. Whatever the differences and similarities, however, the central point is that the environments of these two areas are certainly conducive to human settlement and agricultural exploitation.

Comparison between Siberia and western Canada can also be instructive in other respects. In Canada, for example, only the width of British Columbia and the Rocky mountains separate the prairies from the Pacific Ocean and the thriving metropolis based on Vancouver. In Siberia the distance from, say, Krasnoyarsk to the Pacific is much greater and there are the vast spaces of East Siberia and the Far East which intervene. Here, even in the southern parts, agriculture and settlement are restricted by severe winters and mountainous terrain. Moreover, as noted above, the coastal climate of the Far East cannot be compared with that of British Columbia. Vladivostok has never, therefore, been the magnet that Vancouver has been to many Canadians, and the Soviet Far East has been far more peripheral to its country's economy. On the other hand, north of the zone of settlement in both western Canada and Siberia lie huge areas of wilderness with extremely harsh environments but promising significant natural resources. These two regions may thus experience important new developments in the future.

In conclusion, then, in Siberia's case as in that of western Canada, it is important to distinguish between the more clement and settled parts of the territory, and the harsher periphery. In the future, parts of the Siberian periphery may be further incorporated into the settled zone, but environmental constraints will probably always be significant. Yet the present chapter has argued that the seeming unattractiveness of Siberia to migrants cannot necessarily be put down to climate; living standards, housing and other factors are also important. If these problems could be overcome, then the more temperate portions of the territory could conceivably change their image. The others will presumably retain that of a hard if challenging environment for human endeavour.

NOTES AND REFERENCES

1. Captain John Dundas Cochrane, R.N., *A Pedestrian Journey* (The Folio Society, London, 1983), p. 79.
2. Ibid., p. 82.
3. Ibid.
4. V. A. Nikonov, *Kratkii toponomicheskii slovar* (Mysl, Moscow, 1966), pp. 379–80; D. M. Lebedev, *Ocherki po istorii geografii v Rossii XV i XVI vekov* (Izdatelstvo Akademii Nauk SSSR, Moscow, 1956), pp. 28–30.
5. Nikonov, *Kratkii toponomicheskii slovar*, p. 380.
6. O. N. Vilkov, 'Tobolsk — tsentr tamozhennoi sluzhby Sibiri XVIIv' in O. N. Vilkov (ed.), *Goroda Sibiri* (Nauka, Sibirskoe otdelenie, Novosibirsk, 1974), pp. 131–69.
7. *Sovetskii Soyuz. Geograficheskoe opisanie v 22-kh tomakh: Vostochnaya Sibir* (Mysl, Moscow, 1969); *Dalnii Vostok* (Mysl, Moscow, 1971).
8. i.e. Altai *krai*, Kemerovo, Novosibirsk, Omsk and Tomsk *oblasts*, Tyumen *oblast* (excluding Yamalo-Nenetskii and Khanty-Mansiiskii national *okrugs*) and Krasnoyarsk *krai* (excluding Taimyr and Evenki national *okrugs*). The most densely populated regions of Siberia (Kemerovo, Novosibirsk and Omsk *oblasts*, plus Altai and Maritime *krais*) occupy seven percent of the area and have 44 percent of the population.
9. L. S. Berg, *Geograficheskie zony Sovetskogo Soyuza* (2 vols., OGIZ, Moscow, 1947, 1952); N. A. Gvozdetskii and N. I. Mikhailov, *Fizicheskaya geografiya SSSR: Aziatskaya chast* (Mysl, Moscow, 1970); Paul E. Lydolph, *Geography of the USSR*, 3rd edn (Wiley, New York, 1977); S. P. Suslov, *Physical geography of Asiatic Russia* (W. H. Freeman, San Francisco, 1961).
10. The standard English-language climatology is: Paul E. Lydolph, *Climates of the Soviet Union. World survey of climatology*. vol. 7 (Elsevier, Amsterdam, 1977).
11. Ibid., pp. 8–11; Lydolph, *Geography*, p. 402.

12. Ye. N. Pertsik, *Gorod v Sibiri* (Mysl, Moscow, 1980).

13. 'Otraslevye i regionalnye problemy sotsialnogo planirovaniya', *Chelovek i obshchestvo*, vol. 17 (1978), pp. 42–55.

14. L. I. Gubina, 'Obespechennost zhilem naseleniya Tyumenskoi oblasti i problema zakrepleniya kadrov' in *Problemy razvitiya Zapadno-Sibirskogo neftegazovogo kompleksa* (Nauka, Novosibirsk, 1983), pp. 217–23.

15. Violet Conolly, 'New Siberian towns: plans, motivation, problems, progress', *SIBIRICA* (Lancaster, 1983), pp. 5–17.

2

From Conquest to Revolution: The Historical Dimension

Alan Wood

No such thing as a comprehensive history of Siberia exists in English or any other Western language. There has been published, however, a variety of works of solid scholarship dedicated to individual, isolated chapters of this as yet unwritten chronicle which analyse and illuminate disparate aspects of the territory's conquest and exploration and of its social, economic and political development. Reference will be found to many of these in the footnotes throughout this volume. There is, too, at a less academic level, a large number of accounts written by foreign travellers in Siberia, from the seventeenth to the twentieth century, whose eye-witness reports of the country range from the fascinating to the banal. All of this, however, does not add up to a quantitatively impressive body of scholarship or source material, and the lack of a major study of Siberia's epic past still represents a fairly large lacuna in the Western historiography of Russia as a whole.

The situation in Russia itself is of course quite different. An enormous literature, both pre-revolutionary and Soviet, covers the entire history of Siberia from palaeolithic times to the most recent past and is being voluminously augmented every year by cohorts of historians delving productively — like their colleagues in the extractive industries — into the huge untapped resources of both central and provincial archives.[1] As Stuart Kirby has recently written: 'The Russian literature specifically on Siberia would fill a large modern library, the non-Russian at most a few shelves.'[2]

Given the territory's enormous size and economic importance, and the integral role it has played in the fortunes of Russian state and society — from the slaying of the first sable to the sinking of the latest oil-well — what is surprising is not of course the wealth of material in Russian, but the relative dearth of interest and industry on the part of Western historians. Even Siberia's notorious reputation as a vast penal colony inhabited by thousands of criminals and political prisoners has not until recently attracted any serious scholarly attention outside the Soviet Union. This sinister side of Siberia's record apart, the whole history of the region's discovery, colonisation and development is still wide open for investigation.

While most of the contents of this volume concentrate on Siberia's recent progress, current problems and future perspectives, the present chapter is intended not simply to give a potted narrative of the region's historical evolution, but rather to consider a few of the controversial issues of her remoter, pre-revolutionary past, and to locate the subject-matter of the following chapters within a more extended historical context.

RUSSIAN CONQUEST AND EARLY SETTLEMENT

For present purposes the story of Siberia's pre-Russian antiquity is largely irrelevant, though it is not of course without its own intrinsic importance. It is, however, more the preserve of the anthropologist and the archaeologist than of the modern historian. What is clear is that the many tribes, civilisations and peoples, both nomadic and sedentary, which inhabited Siberia in earlier centuries had developed a rich pattern of independent cultures which were neither European nor wholly Oriental in their provenance. Emphasising the specificity of pre-modern Siberian civilisations, the late A. P. Okladnikov has dismissed both the 'Eurocentric' and the 'Asiacentric' approaches to the study of Siberian native culture as 'reactionary', and quotes with approval the conclusion of the nineteenth-century Siberian regionalist writer N. M. Yadrintsev, that 'it is indisputable that in these regions there must have developed a distinctive, original culture'.[3]

At the beginning of the thirteenth century, the whole of southern Siberia was overrun and incorporated into the vast Mongol Empire, its peoples becoming the tribute-paying vassals of the Great Khan. With the disintegration of the Golden Horde in the late fifteenth century a number of independent khanates were established including Kazan, Astrakhan, and later *Sibir*, otherwise known as Isker, on the river Irtysh. It was this relatively tiny principality which was destined to bequeath its name to a territory covering over half of the Russian Empire and one-twelfth of the planet's land surface. During the reign of Ivan the Terrible (1537–84) these Mongol, or more properly Tatar, khanates fell to the military superiority of the recently consolidated and still vigorous Muscovite state — first Kazan, the gateway to the Urals, in 1552, and then Astrakhan, lower down the Volga, in 1556. For the time being Sibir itself remained unmolested, partly because its rulers prudently decided to pay annual tribute to the Russian tsar, and partly because at that time the Muscovite government had in all probability no concrete plans for a further eastwards expansion into what was still a remote and hostile *terra incognita*.

This is not to suggest that the lands lying immediately to the east of the Urals were totally virgin territory as far as Russian penetration was concerned. As early as the eleventh century merchants and hunters from the independent trading city of Novgorod had moved in a northern arc into the upper parts of western Siberia — then known as the 'Yugran land' (*Yugorskaya zemlya*) — in quest of valuable peltry either through direct hunting, trading or the imposition of fur tribute (*yasak*) on the local native tribes, mainly the Uralic-speaking Voguls and Ostyaks (present-day Mansi and Khanty). Moscow's conquest of Novgorod at the end of the fifteenth century and the consequent take-over of her defeated rival's Yugran colonies meant therefore that she already had a valuable trans-Uralian entrepôt well before the more dramatic thrust against Sibir in 1582, from which Russia's annexation and settlement of Siberia is traditionally dated. (It is thus interesting to note that Moscow's very first commercial interest in Siberia was geographically located in the very region — i.e. north-west Siberia and the lower Ob — from which the bulk of her most recent wealth in oil and natural gas has flowed; see Chapter 4.)

After a period of bloody dynastic rivalries within the ruling clan, the new khan of Sibir, Kuchum, finally ceased paying tribute to Moscow in 1571 and was probably involved in instigating a series of anti-Russian rebellions and raids into Muscovite territory at about the same time. Soon afterwards, the powerful Russian merchant family of the Stroganovs, which owned enormous territorial and commercial interests all along the Urals, was authorised by a series of royal charters to fortify their eastern boundaries and mount military expeditions against the rebellious Siberian tribes. It is in this context that the celebrated Cossack *ataman* and freebooter, Yermak Timofeevich — sometimes extravagantly described as the Russian Cortez or the Russian Pizarro — makes his portentous appearance in the annals of Russia's conquest of Siberia. The historical controversy surrounding the exact chronology and the actual provenance of the instructions which led to his campaign need not detain us here.[4] The distinguished Soviet historian R. G. Skrynnikov has, on the basis of fresh archival evidence, concluded that Yermak and his band of Cossacks, probably acting as agents for the Stroganovs, launched their initial onslaught against Kuchum's Siberian khanate in 1582.[5] The campaign was not an unqualified success. Although Kuchum was forced to abandon his capital (Isker), the Cossacks soon lost control and Yermak himself was later drowned during a skirmish on the river Irtysh (1585), dragged down, we are told, by the weight of his armour which was a personal gift of the tsar. The widely differing posthumous evaluations of Yermak as either a heroic pioneer of Russia's manifest Siberian destiny, or else as merely a marauding and bloodthirsty robber bent on plunder, nicely reflect the later and broader historical debates over the very nature and quality of Russia's conquest, or assimilation, of Siberia as a whole, an issue to be discussed below.

Kuchum, for his part, continued a courageous guerrilla campaign against the Russian occupying forces who followed in Yermak's wake until his final defeat and death in 1598. His descendants continued the struggle well into the seventeenth century, but what resistance there was to the renewed Russian advance was quickly overcome, and by dint of superior firepower and the construction of an interconnecting network of fortified outposts (*ostrogi*) and settlements, Russia's military, political and commercial presence in Siberia was now permanently established and vigorously enforced. Not only the minor khanate of Sibir, but now the whole vast continent of northern Asia lay at Moscow's feet. What had originally begun as the private enterprise of Cossack conquistadors and merchant adventurers now had the full and determined backing of the Muscovite state.

Russia's eastward advances were remarkably swift and her new domains equally swiftly consolidated. By the 1640s her trailblazers and troops had already reached the Pacific littoral and founded the garrison of Okhotsk from where the maritime route lay open to Kamchatka. The astonishing speed of this trans-continental anabasis was facilitated by a variety of factors. The terrain and climate (described in Chapter 1) were not wholly dissimilar to that of European Russia, and by the skilful use of Siberia's river systems (see Chapter 5 for their contemporary importance) and interfluvial portages a steady eastwards progression was maintained by extending and consolidating the interlacement of fortified stockades which formed the basis of future towns and served initially as the military-administrative centres from which the Russians imposed their authority on the indigenous Siberian peoples.[6] The latters' bows and arrows were no match for Russian gunpowder and shot, and in any case, inured as they were to their vassal status under Mongol suzerainty, it was probably no hardship for them to switch their payment of the *yasak* from the Mongol khan to the Russian tsar. 'In this sense it may be said,' according to George Vernadsky, 'that the Russians inherited their Empire from Chingis-Khan.'[7]

Just how quickly and systematically Moscow established its control over the territory once the *Drang nach Osten* had begun can be demonstrated by plotting the foundation dates of some of the major fortresses and future cities — Tyumen (1586), Tobolsk (1587), Mangazeya (1601), Tomsk (1604), Yeniseisk (1619), Bratsk (1631), Yakutsk (1632), Okhotsk (1647) and Irkutsk (1661). The major motive behind this — as behind many another — imperial venture was an economic one. It was above all the quest for fur, in particular the luxurious and coveted sable, which drew the Russian trappers and traders, closely followed or accompanied by military and administrative personnel (*sluzhilye lyudi*), deeper and deeper into the *taiga*, initially teeming with the unfortunate fauna which for many years provided the principal trading commodity for Russia's internal and external markets. Just how valuable was this 'soft' Siberian gold is illustrated by the following calculation quoted by Raymond Fisher. In 1623 two black fox skins were valued at 110 rubles. For this, the owner 'could have purchased more than fifty acres of land, erected a good cabin, bought five good horses, ten head of cattle, twenty sheep, several dozen fowl, and still have had almost half his capital left over'.[8] If the game was profitable for the individual huntsman, so it was for the state. Again, Fisher estimates that in the seventeenth century, i.e. before the fiscal reforms of Peter the Great, the fur business accounted for as much as ten per cent

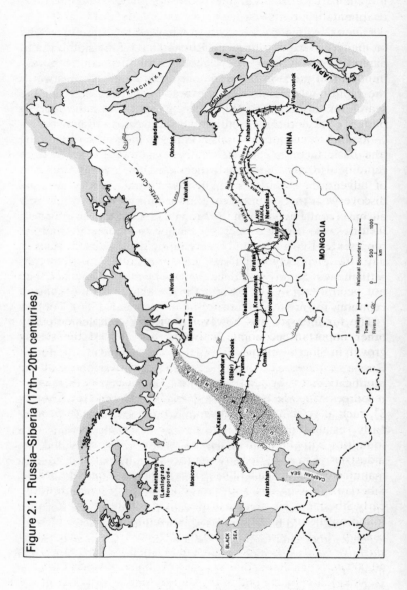

Figure 2.1: Russia–Siberia (17th–20th centuries)

of total state revenue — not an inconsiderable proportion, which more than justified the administrative energies and expenditures devoted to its promotion.[9]

Given these figures it is small wonder that the 'fur fever' lured so many private entrepreneurs and state officials to seek and exploit these new sources of wealth. Nor is it surprising that over-hunting and the lack of modern conservation awareness led to the rapid depletion of natural stocks and the more extensive search for fresh killing fields. This ever-widening and repeated pattern of exploration, exploitation and exhaustion of resources — leading to further exploration etc. — is, according to Fisher, 'the basic factor' which, more than any other, explains the rapidity of Russia's eastward advance across Siberia. The spirit of adventure, scientific curiosity, territorial imperatives, the discovery of other natural riches and sheer imperial prestige may all have contributed to the process, but the major motivating factor was unquestionably the economic determinant represented by fur. In later centuries too, as indeed at the present day, the physical discomforts and disincentives to voluntary settlement in Siberia would hardly have been overcome had they not been offset by the prospect of considerable material and economic reward for both state and individual.

The fur industry was however obviously complemented by other important economic activities, and indeed the steady growth in Siberia's population figures during the early period of Russia's expansion can hardly be explained with reference to the ramifications of the fur trade alone. The discovery of mineral resources with which Siberia is so richly endowed (see Chapter 3), such as gold, silver, lead, iron, copper and mica, led to the early establishment of industrial enterprises, mines and foundries with their attendant workforces. The metallurgical industries were of course particularly important in the manufacture of ordnance and other military *matériel*. The fabled Siberian salt-workings, too, served a necessary function in the early Siberian economy, particularly high-quality deposits being found on the upper Irtysh at the beginning of the seventeenth century. In 1626, according to P. P. Yepifanov, 'six hundred *sluzhilye lyudi*, Cossacks, Tatars and Ostyaks extracted around 40,000 *puds* of salt and delivered it to Tobolsk in boats' (1*pud* = 16.38 kg), and by the end of the century similar workings of the precious commodity had been developed throughout Siberia — their product being used not only in the preservation of foodstuffs but also as a medium of exchange and remuneration.[10] In addition, the Siberian transport and communication system required a considerable labour-force —for example in the construction of river- and sea-going boats, and in manning the extensive overland animal-draught transport and haulage network. By the mid-seventeenth century many towns and settlements had their own 'transport workers' quarter' (*yamskaya sloboda*) inhabited by hundreds of coachmen, drivers, farriers and their families who were responsible for keeping Siberia's provisioning, merchandise and human traffic in motion.[11]

However, by far the largest category in the Russian population of Siberia during the early period of its settlement was represented by military personnel (*voennosluzhilye lyudi*). The Soviet historian, N. I. Nikitin, calculates that it was not until the early eighteenth century that the peasant population of Siberia was equal to that of the military servitors — and the vast majority of the former was concentrated in the relatively small Verkhoture-Tobolsk agricultural region. Elsewhere, particularly in the far north, in the south-west, in Transbaikal and in the major towns — Tobolsk, Tyumen, Tomsk, Nerchinsk and Yakutsk — service personnel far outnumbered the rest of the population groups, despite the fact that military commanders constantly complained about insufficient troops (*malolyudstvo*). The vast majority of the *voennosluzhilye lyudi* were made up of common Cossacks originating from European Russia, particularly those provinces closest to the Urals, who, apart from their military duties, also engaged in agriculture and a variety of trades and crafts. Military records reveal that among the civilian occupations of the Siberian Cossacks were included millers, leather-, silver-, gun- and blacksmiths, carpenters, soap-makers, tailors and glaziers, not to mention the butchers, bakers and even candlestick-makers. In this way the 'rude soldiery' of Siberia contributed much to the civic development and economic diversity of the territory.[12]

According to P. A. Slovtsov, in 1662 the Russian and other immigrant population of Siberia stood at 105,000 out of an overall total of 393,000. One century later (1763) the Russian population massively outnumbered the native peoples (420,000 and 260,000 respectively), and by the time of the major census in 1897 Russian Siberians numbered almost five million, in comparison with only 870,500 natives. Even more spectacularly, by 1911 the Russian element had nearly doubled to 8.4 million while the indigenous peoples only marginally increased to 973,000.[13] In both pre-revolutionary and Soviet historiography there have been many attempts to analyse the population dynamics of Siberian settlement from European Russia, some of them muddied by ideological presuppositions dictated by the prevailing political climate. Western scholars, too, notably Armstrong, Coquin and Treadgold have made valuable contributions to the subject.[14] The basic question seems to boil down to this: was Russia's penetration and colonisation of Siberia the result of state-sponsored and government-directed initiatives, or did it owe more to the spontaneous movement of the Russian people migrating freely and voluntarily to fill up the huge vacuum across the Urals in search of wealth, land, or freedom from an oppressive central government? Allied to this is the crucial question of the nature and quality of the Russian conquest in its effects on the Siberian native peoples, 'the litmus paper of Siberian historiography', as it has been called.[15]

On the matter of migration and settlement, what is perfectly clear is that this complex phenomenon is not reducible to a single, all-embracing formula which will satisfactorily explain the process *in toto*. Different factors operated at different times and in different places. In a recent survey, David Collins has drawn together the results of the Russian historiography to demonstrate convincingly that what might hold good for north-west Siberia does not necessarily apply in the more fertile south, while in Yakutia and the far east the picture alters yet again. In one case the principal attraction was fur, in another, land, and in yet another the major determinant was the need to establish fortified (and hence populated) defence lines to protect important trade and communication routes against the encroachment of hostile neighbours. Despite the variety of circumstances, Collins is persuaded that there is much in favour of the thesis that a leading role was played in the colonisation process by the fortress towns, the establishment of which *preceded* the wider settlement of a particular region. Contrary to the spontaneous, mass peasant-migration theory promulgated by nineteenth-century regionalist historians and subscribed to by some eminent Soviet scholars, notably V. I. Shunkov, this view suggests that, fur-hunters apart, it was the *sluzhilye lyudi* or state servicemen who arrived first in any large numbers, established military control, and then engaged in non-military activities which created conditions favourable for further civilian settlement.[16] This interpretation is certainly consistent with the case put forward by Nikitin (above).

However, in the final analysis the argument over 'which came first, the *muzhik* or the militia?' becomes a circular one, and it may not simply be a matter of avoiding the issue if one agrees with the conclusion of N. V. Ustyugov that 'government-directed and 'free' colonisation [of Siberia] are two parallel, mutually dependent and closely connected processes which are impossible to understand one without the other'.[17] What is certainly indisputable is that, contrary to a popular misconception, the compulsory settlement of Siberia by common criminals and political offenders exiled by judicial or administrative order played a very minor and almost entirely negative role in the history of Siberian colonisation. The major factors were always a combination of state service, voluntary migration and — problems of gross sexual imbalance notwithstanding — the process of natural procreation.

NATIVE PEOPLES

Although there is no chapter in this volume devoted specifically to the condition and status of Siberia's non-Russian native peoples, a few words should be said in this historical survey concerning the sensitive issue of the impact of Russia's presence in Siberia on its original, autochthonous inhabitants. The differing evaluations of the character of Yermak's expedition, referred to above, in a sense epitomise the long-standing controversy over the relative benefits — or disastrous consequences — of the victorious newcomers' treatment of the various non-Russian nationality groups (*inorodtsy*) with whom they clashed during their inexorable eastwards advance. To put the question succinctly, was Russia the bearer of a superior civilisation bringing with her the benefits of economic progress, advanced technology, agriculture and Christianity to a primitive patchwork of backward and mutually belligerent tribes; or was she merely a rapacious plunderer, viciously exploiting the natives, literally holding them hostage to a fortune in fur, and bringing only brutality, bad liquor and pathogenic bacilli which in some cases resulted in creeping genocide? Certainly the most enlightened and civically conscious writers of the nineteenth-century Siberian regionalist school (*oblastniki*) inclined to the latter view. N. M. Yadrintsev in particular assembled a good deal of statistical material to support his contention that the Russian conquest of Siberia, at least as far as the natives were concerned, was simply the result of a ruthless campaign of military subjugation and even extermination of the indigenous peoples and cultures by naked force, totally unmitigated by any of the supposed benefits of an allegedly superior civilisation. It was a process that was marked by extortion, rapine and mindless cruelty. Even where the state purported to safeguard the interests of the natives, this was, according to Yadrintsev, motivated purely by selfish fiscal considerations aimed at preventing any decrease in the tax- and tribute-paying capacities of the subjugated races. Consequently, a genuine concern for the wretched plight of the aborigines — squeezed and humiliated by their Russian overlords for 300 years — formed an important part of the *oblastniki*'s regional programme. It was their objective not only to guarantee such residual rights as the *inorodtsy* possessed and rescue them from gradual extinction, but also to improve their material circumstances and integrate them fully into the further civic development of their homeland. This, of course, was part of Yadrintsev's major thesis that Siberia was, after all, only a colony of European Russia and therefore its people obviously suffered from the familiar range of exploitative and parasitical practices common to all imperial regimes which batten on their colonial possessions.[18]

Variations on this theme continued into the early Soviet period and occupied a central place in, for example, S. V. Bakhrushin's negative assessment of Russia's impact on the Siberian natives. More recent Soviet historiography, however, has attempted to square the ideologically sound criticisms of tsarist colonial practices with what is regarded, from a nationalist point of view, as the beneficial consequences flowing from the inevitable, historically predetermined 'fusion' of the Russian and Siberian native peoples. It is notable, for instance, that words like *zavoevanie* (military conquest) and *pokorenie* (subjugation or 'taming') have been increasingly replaced with less emotionally charged words such as *sblizhenie* (drawing together) and *osvoenie* (assimilation) in describing the process of consolidating Russia's dominant presence among Siberia's lands and peoples. This phenomenon, moreover, was not merely fortuitous, but, to quote a typical recent source, 'governed by the laws of historical development' (*ne sluchainym, a istoricheski zakonomernym sobytiem*)[19]

It is in fact impossible to deliver a single, clear-cut judgement which would satisfactorily resolve the issue. There is no doubt whatsoever that in many areas the treatment of the indigenous peoples at the conquerors' hands was inhumane and catastrophic, often leading to the disappearance of whole tribes. This was the result of a variety of factors including physical destruction in an unequal military conflict; the practice of hostage-taking which regularly denuded villages of the ablest hunters, chieftains and shamans; the abduction of native women and children; the introduction of virulent alien diseases such as smallpox, leprosy and syphilis; forced labour and conscription into military service; and famine resulting from over-exploitation and depletion of natural food resources.[20]

On the other hand, whether its motives were purely mercenary or not, the tsarist government did take many positive steps to try to protect the natives' legitimate interests, though it was often unable to enforce the various measures in practice. In contrast to the West Europeans' treatment of the South and North American Indians, official policies of *deliberate* genocide were never pursued; genuine attempts were made to incorporate native leaders into the administrative structures of the territory; there was no sustained programme of enforced Russification or even christianisation; and there was a good deal of voluntary intermarriage. Tribal organisation and social, judicial and religious customs were not grossly interfered with, and as long as the natives remained docile (which by and large they did, once conquered) and kept the *yasak* flowing in, they were for the most part left to pursue their traditional ways of life. The Russians, moreover, brought with them superior tools and weapons which gradually replaced the more primitive implements to positive effect on the domestic tribal economy, and in certain areas the introduction of settled agricultural techniques greatly supplemented the traditional sources of nutrition. While some of the smaller and weaker peoples undoubtedly dwindled or even disappeared either through destruction or assimilation, others, like the Ostyaks and the Yakuts, flourished and multiplied under Russian rule, as the 1897 census figures make clear.[21] During the last century of the Russian Empire, the Siberian nationalities were governed according to the theoretically enlightened legislation of Mikhail Speranskii which sought in a positive sense to reconcile the policy of leaving the traditional patterns of Siberian native culture undisturbed while gradually drawing the various ethnic groups into a proper appreciation of the virtues of Russian economic, social and political practices. Thus it was hoped that there would develop a process of what Marc Raeff describes as 'organic Russification'.[22] Legal enactments and administrative reforms passed in far-off St Petersburg, however, did little in real terms to alter or ameliorate the familiar pattern of Russo-aboriginal relations already established over the previous two centuries.

Under Soviet rule, there is no doubt that the minority peoples have benefited in many important respects from government policies which have significantly enhanced their social and cultural well-being. Thus, for example, most of the killer diseases have been eradicated; literacy levels, educational opportunities, the social and economic status of women, housing standards and social services have all markedly improved, as have population figures — though the native peoples now constitute only four per cent of the total population of Siberia.[23] The cost of this progress, however, has been the steady erosion of many ancient cultural values, religious traditions and age-old socio-economic relationships under the impact of centrally imposed ideological and organisational norms. Even so, the combined effects of collectivisation, urbanisation and overall 'sovietisation' have not resulted in the total extirpation of separate national identities, but have in many ways brought about the successful inosculation of individual minority interests with the overarching uniformity of the Soviet social and political system. This view is shared by leading Western and Soviet ethnographers. Caroline Humphrey, for instance, in her major study of Buryat collective farmers, gives many examples of traditional customs and rituals being syncretised with official Soviet values and practices,[24] and S. S. Savoskul of the Soviet Academy of Sciences' Institute of Ethnography, writing about the impact of urbanisation on the 'little' peoples of the Far North, concludes that 'urbanisation performs a dual function: on the one hand it stimulates the integration of the Northern peoples with other peoples of the USSR and their participation in the formation of a new historical community — the Soviet people — and on the other hand it promotes the consolidation of their nationality and the growth of national consciousness'.[25]

THE EXILE SYSTEM

No résumé of Siberia's historical record, however sketchy, would be complete without some mention of the system of exile, forced labour and compulsory settlement for which the territory is notorious. Indeed, apart from the equal notoriety of its climate (which Denis Shaw qualifies somewhat in Chapter 1), the image of Siberia as a huge penal settlement, a remote place of banishment for Russia's social misfits and political dissenters is what most readily springs to many people's minds at the mention of the place. To some extent of course this sombre reputation is a deserved one, and right from the time of Ivan the Terrible to the Stalinist 1930s millions of common criminals, political offenders, religious dissidents, prisoners-of-war, social rebels and even innocent children have dragged themselves along Siberia's *via dolorosa* into a life of permanent suffering and pain. What attention has been paid by Western and Russian émigré writers to Siberia as a land of exile has tended, largely for political reasons, to concentrate on what has happened in the Soviet period, with little or no attempt to examine the historical background in a proper scholarly manner. Indeed, there have been some misinformed attempts to dismiss the pre-revolutionary exile system as hardly a punitive institution at all.[27] What follows, therefore, deliberately focuses on some aspects of Siberian exile before the revolutions of 1917, with only a few concluding remarks on the more recent period, which has been widely covered elsewhere.[28]

The growth of the Siberian exile system went hand-in-hand with Russia's conquest and consolidation of power over the region, and as early as the seventeenth century it was already well-established as a central feature of the tsarist penal system. Two popular misconceptions, however, must be dispelled. Firstly, as mentioned above, exiles and deportees only made up a very small proportion of the population of Siberia — in the nineteenth century only about six per cent. Secondly, political exiles, i.e. state criminals banished for anti-government activities, subversive ideas, or suspicion thereof, only accounted for a tiny proportion (just over one per cent) of the exile population itself.[29] The overwhelming majority of those sent to Siberia were either common criminals sentenced by the courts for a broad range of often violent crimes or else unfortunate victims of the widespread practice of 'administrative exile'. In fact the greatest number of all the people exiled to Siberia were sent there without benefit of any judicial process by the fiat of police and government agencies or else by various social institutions and communities which had the right to expel their unwanted members and have them committed by administrative process to banishment in Siberia — a system which was throughout its existence subject to massive abuse.[30]

In the seventeenth century many contemporary sources, as well as later commentators, agree that exile to Siberia was a positive phenomenon, often replacing the more barbaric forms of aggravated capital punishment commonly practised in mediaeval Muscovy while at the same time adding to the stock of Russian working and service personnel in the new territories. Moreover, a genuine attempt was made in the earlier period to fit the experience or capabilities of the deportees both functionally and geographically to where they could be of most benefit to the state's purposes. The number of exiles diminished somewhat during the first quarter of the eighteenth century as Peter the Great preferred to redirect convict manpower into his enormous military and civilian construction projects in European Russia. However, in the second half of the century figures began to increase substantially for two main reasons, one indirect, the other direct. Firstly, Empress Elizabeth's *de facto* abolition of the death penalty for criminal offences in 1753 meant that many who would otherwise have been executed were now sent for life into forced labour (*katorga*) in Siberia or elsewhere. Secondly, the same ruler's decree of 1760 granted the serf-owning nobility the right to hand over their insubordinate or unproductive peasants to the state authorities to send to compulsory, permanent settlement in Siberia. While the primary purpose of this legislation was one of colonisation and manpower provision, the huge discrepancy between the large numbers involved and the hopelessly inadequate administrative, supervisory, transport, distribution, settlement and supply networks ensured that the whole business was a disaster from beginning to end. The Siberian exile 'system' at this time had nothing systematic about it. It was utterly chaotic, corrupt and calamitous in its social, demographical and penological consequences.

Nor did Speranskii's well-intentioned legislation of 1822 do much to put the operation, as he declared, 'on a more orderly and businesslike foundation'. The Exile and Convoy Regulations, part of his Siberian administrative reform package, which were planned to make the system more humane, efficient and productive were from the outset fouled not only by the familiar drawbacks referred to above, but also by a massive, unforeseen increase in the numbers involved which heavily overburdened an already overworked and undermanned distribution and settlement apparatus. Far from adding in a positive and constructive manner to the further colonisation of Siberia, the exile operation only succeeded in inflicting untold damage on the social fabric of the region, and seriously impeded its more rapid civic development.

The reasons are obvious. Although, as stated, the ratio of the exile to the free population was so low, the effect of their presence was nevertheless traumatic, and out of all proportion to their numbers. The bulk of the exile population was made up of the worst criminal elements of the Empire and the wretched human detritus of the oppressive tsarist social and political order. Murderers, rapists, arsonists and bandits were accompanied by wastrels, vagrants, fornicators and petty thieves into a vicious circle of misery, flight, recidivism and further retribution which remained a permanent and debilitating incubus on Siberian society. The administrative and constabulary personnel were woefully inadequate to keep proper surveillance and control over this shifting mass of uprooted humanity, and there existed a state of almost constant hostility, even warfare, between the exiles and the old inhabitants of Siberia (*starozhily*). Towns and villages alike were permanently plagued by marauding gangs of escaped convicts and itinerant brigands who preyed on the settled population through a mixture of begging, looting and abduction of Siberia's already-scarce womenfolk. The gross disproportion between the sexes had always been (and in some areas still is) a serious problem in Siberia, but this was obviously aggravated by the steady stream of thousands of predominantly male, predominantly young, and predominantly unconscionable outlaws from European Russia. Consequently the exile population was responsible not only for the large majority of all crimes, particularly violent crimes, committed in Siberia, but also for the distressingly high levels of abduction, rape, prostitution, homosexuality, bestialism and venereal diseases which in some areas were practically endemic.[31]

Small wonder, then, that the abolition of the exile system had first priority among the demands of the Siberian intelligentsia and even the more progressively minded of the region's senior officials. However, despite the pressure of public opinion — local, national and international — and despite a sympathetic government inquiry followed by an Exile Reform Law of 1900, the practice of punitive banishment to Siberia for both criminal and, increasingly, political offences remained in existence until the revolutions of 1917 when it was formally abolished by the Provisional Government. There , of course, the tragic story did not end, and during the first two decades of Soviet rule Siberia continued to swallow up millions more victims of the social, economic and political policies of the new regime. Many of the vast new construction, mining and engineering projects in Siberia during the first five-year plans were built under the direction of the Main Prison-Camp Administration (*GULag*), and by the efforts of countless convict labourers and exiles, many of whom managed to survive, later adding the record of their experiences to the long, grim repertoire of Russian prison and exile literature and perpetuating the region's melancholy, if misleading, reputation as a 'vast roofless prison'. Though it is no longer the mass phenomenon that it was historically, exile to Siberia (as well as to other places in the USSR) is still retained as a sanction available under the provisions of the Soviet Penal Code.[32]

SIBERIA BETWEEN REFORM AND REVOLUTION: 1861–1917

One of the paradoxes of Siberia's history is that while it was acquiring its reputation as a place of imprisonment and exile, for many people it simultaneously represented a land of escape and freedom from the constraints of serfdom, officialdom and religious persecution in European Russia. However, even the boundless opportunities provided by the regions' agricultural, mineral and other natural resources could never be properly exploited while the daunting obstacles of distance, climate and shortage of supplies remained. In addition, before the emancipation of the serfs in 1861, the problems of geographical and social mobility within the Empire were compounded by the legal restrictions which were inherent in the quasi-feudal relationships of pre-reform Russia. However, towards the end of the nineteenth century, the combined effects of the abolition of serfdom, the spectacular population explosion and consequent land-hunger in the central provinces, together with the construction of the trans-Siberian rail-link between European Russia and the Pacific facilitated the more energetic settlement and economic development of the region. Furthermore, Russia's recent annexation of the Amur and Ussuri regions from China, largely on the initiative and insistence of Eastern Siberia's ambitious Governor-General, N. N. Muravev, and confirmed by the treaties of Aigun (1858) and Peking (1860), meant that the government had an extra incentive both to consolidate the presence it had now established in the Far East and to promote the region's development. Thwarted in its territorial ambitions in this area in the late seventeenth century on running up against the highly organised Chinese Manchu Empire, the Muscovite authorities had turned their attention perforce to the north and north-east. Now, after two centuries, and in response to increased Western imperialist activities in northern China, Russia had finally established herself not only as an Asiatic, but also as a great Pacific power.[33] The foundation of Vladivostok — 'Lord of the East' — in 1858, and the sale of Alaska to the United States in 1867 constituted an unequivocal signal, and symbol, of the new orientalism. (The long-term strategic ramifications of this far-eastern presence and of the Soviet Union's more recent relations with China, Japan and the countries of the Pacific Basin are examined in Chapters 7, 8 and 9).

It was, however, mainly the western provinces of Siberia which benefited from the increasing rate of free migration and settlement in the wake of Alexander II's reforms. Between 1861 and 1895 750,000 new colonists migrated there and established successful large-scale farming enterprises along the southern tract. As most of the land in Siberia technically belonged to the state or the crown, serfdom had never taken root in Siberia, and it was obvious even to foreign travellers that the Siberian peasantry was usually more prosperous and their farms — partly in response to labour-shortage — more highly mechanised than in European Russia.[34] The building of the Trans-Siberian Railway, started in 1891 and finished in 1904, helped, among other things, greatly to accelerate the rate of peasant migration across the Urals on an unprecedented scale. This movement, one of the most spectacular migratory shifts in history, has been thoroughly examined by Donald Treadgold, and there is consequently no need to rehearse the details here.[35] Suffice it to say that between 1896 and 1914, peaking during the period of Stolypin's agrarian reforms (1906–13), more than four million peasant settlers arrived in Siberia and turned it into one of the Empire's major agricultural regions, dairy farming and butter production being particularly important factors in the region's economy.[36] Cereal farming also increased enormously, more than doubling its acreage in some districts. Thus, between 1905 and 1913 Tomsk district alone increased its area of sown land from 1,455,000 to 3,544,000 *desyatinas*; and of this total, figures for land under wheat were 641,000 and 1,851,000 *desyatinas* respectively (one *desyatina* = 2.7 acres or 1.09 hectares).[37]

Not only agriculture, but also industry expanded steadily during this period, stimulated of course by the laying of the Trans-Siberian Railway and significantly financed by the influx of foreign capital into the economy. In comparison with European Russia, however, Siberia still remained very much an underdeveloped region, producing only about two per cent of the nation's industrial output, and at the time of the 1917 revolutions containing an industrial working class of about half-a-million. Notwithstanding these relatively small numbers, Soviet historians naturally emphasise the leading role played by the Siberian proletariat in the revolutionary upheavals in the early years of the century, and the steady growth in the influence of early Marxist Social Democratic organisations.[38] There is, indeed, some justification for this view. It was, for example, the massacre of striking workers at the Lena goldfields in eastern Siberia that sparked off the wave of industrial revolutionary activity which swept Russia until temporarily halted by the outbreak of World War I; and the government's own policy of exiling ever-mounting numbers of political activists, trade unionists and strikers throughout this period only served to widen and deepen the geographical, organisational and ideological influence of the revolutionary movement. By seeking to isolate them from their party comrades and their class support in the industrial centres of European Russia, the government only ensured that the most far-flung corners of its Empire were well-stocked with a cohort of trained, committed activists constantly on the *qui vive* for revolutionary opportunities and the chance to disseminate their political message even in the most difficult circumstances.[39]

Well before the advent of the Russian Marxists, however, there had been no lack of disaffection in Siberia toward the policies of the central government, and not just among the ranks of political exiles, though these were certainly an influencing factor. There has already been more than one occasion in this chapter to refer to the work of N. M Yadrintsev as a representative of Siberian regionalism (*oblastnichestvo*) in the latter half of the nineteenth century. During the 1860s, a number of young members of the intelligentsia, including Yadrintsev, returned to their native Siberia after studying in the heady, radical atmosphere of post-emancipation St Petersburg. There they began to turn their thoughts towards the advancement of their homeland's interests and to tackling its many malaises which they saw as a direct result of the territory's colonial status. Apart from a variety of intellectual stimuli — notably the writings of the Siberian populist historian, A. P. Shchapov — which fostered the growth of a regional self-consciousness, Soviet writers also point to economic factors such as the growth of capitalist relations and the development of a powerful merchant community in Siberia with strong economic and fiscal grievances against the central government which treated Siberia merely as a source of raw materials and a profitable market for the manufactured products of European Russia.[40] As well as resentment at this 'economic yoke of Moscow over Siberia', dissatisfaction with the corrupt practices of St Petersburg-appointed officials, a deep hatred of the exile system, demands for the improvement of cultural and educational opportunities in the region, and a sympathetic concern for the plight of the Siberian natives, added fuel to the fires of a growing movement in favour of some form of regional autonomy.[41]

Not all of the *oblastniki* were by any means supporters of the complete political severance of Siberia from metropolitan Russia, but nevertheless a skeletal programme of regionalist demands gradually developed which in its more extreme form did call for the formation of an independent, separate Siberian republic (to be renamed Svobodoslavia) or at least some kind of equal, federative status for the region on the lines of the United States of America. In 1866 an abortive uprising of Polish political exiles around the shores of Lake Baikal, coupled with an equally abortive plan to spring the exiled revolutionary, N. G. Chenyshevskii, from confinement and install him as president of the new Svobodoslavia, was ruthlessly crushed and its leaders executed.[42] All hopes that the rebellion would attract widespread support among broader sections of the Siberian population and that a revolutionary tide would surge westwards and liberate the entire country from tsarist tyranny were dashed, and throughout the remainder of the century the Siberian regionalists largely contented themselves with promoting the cultural, social and educational welfare of the territory and eschewed the more radical aspirations of the earlier period.

Among modern Soviet scholars controversy still exists regarding the political orientation and class characterisation of the Siberian regionalist movement. Some writers, notably S. S. Sesyunina, regard them as 'bourgeois nationalists' or even as precursors of the Siberian 'counter-revolution' of 1918–21, whose battle-cries found no resonance among the broad masses of the Siberian workers and peasants.[43] Others, such as the distinguished historian, S. F. Koval, place them firmly among the ranks of the 'revolutionary democrats' of the 1860s and see them as a genuine manifestation of the radical temper of the decade.[44] To the present author it seems that the regionalists' proven links with both Russian and Polish political exiles, the explicitly anti-government tenor of their views and their aspirations for 'national liberation' from tsarist imperialism favour the latter view. It is certainly true that towards the turn of the century they abandoned their maximalist demands and concentrated on a more moderate, reformist programme, but this hardly qualifies them for the reactionary or counter-revolutionary label that has been applied to them — except on a very narrow, sectarian definition of what is revolutionary and what is not.

When revolution did actually break out in 1917, Siberia became the broad stage for a long, bloody and complex struggle between many different contending military, political, regionalist and nationalist forces before Soviet power was finally established from the Urals to the Pacific in 1922 with the Red Army's occupation — or liberation — of Vladivostok and the departure of the last Japanese interventionist troops. The history of this bitter internecine conflict is of course impossible to summarise satisfactorily at this juncture, and is in any case treated in its military aspects by John Erickson in Chapter 7. At all events the political victory of the Bolsheviks in October 1917 and their eventual military victory in the civil war opened up a momentous new chapter in the history of Siberia, an opening which Soviet writers often refer to as 'the third discovery' of Siberia.[45]

CONCLUSION

It is to various aspects and results of this new 'discovery' that the following chapters are mainly devoted. Despite the impressive economic and social achievements — in industry, communications, urbanisation, education and scientific research — Siberia is still very much a pioneering region with many traditional problems of the old frontier territory to be confronted. The physical geography and climatic conditions still create formidable technical and engineering, as well as human, problems. The transport and communications networks, described in Chapter 5, are still fraught with all kinds of difficulties, though of course enormous progress has been made — most spectacularly with the building of the Baikal-Amur Railway (the BAM; see Chapter 6) and the all-year-round opening-up of almost the entire length of the Arctic sea-routes with nuclear-powered icebreakers. The population has multiplied rapidly over the past few decades, numbering at present almost 30 millions, although the bulk of the population gain has been contributed by the 'new' pioneering areas in the oil- and gas-fields and in the BAM zone. Elsewhere, population decline, skilled manpower shortage, high labour turnover, as well as out-migration continue to be a headache to both central and provincial planning authorities.

Academician T. I. Zaslavskaya and her colleagues at the Academy of Sciences' prestigious Institute of Economics and Organisation of Industrial Production in Novosibirsk have recently identified and quantified a range of impediments to Siberia's further social development, including slow transition to labour-saving technologies; inefficient organisation of labour; unjustifiable (in Siberia) legal restrictions on extra earnings; insufficient educational facilities; poor provision of basic food products including meat, fruit and vegetables; thinly-spread medical and recreational amenities; inadequate housing standards; and a generally low standard of living in comparison with national and republican figures.[46] Given these circumstances it is not surprising that job turnover is so high. In a 1984 survey conducted among urban workers in West Siberia over 40 per cent indicated that they were considering changing their jobs and/or migrating. Nor was it found by the same researchers that the higher wage levels in Siberia were sufficient compensation for the local higher cost of living.[47] The very process of planning to cope with some of these and other economic problems is, moreover, often bedevilled by bureaucratic inefficiency, competing (even conflicting) sectoral interests in the political and administrative hierarchy, arguments over spatial resource allocation and a recurring incongruity between micro- and macro-economic development priorities.[48]

Nevertheless, the overall achievement has been remarkable. As early as the 1920s, decisions were taken by the new regime about the economic development of Siberia which were translated into concrete reality during the first two five-year plans (see Chapter 3). In particular the formation of the huge Urals-Kuznetsk coal and metallurgical Combine and the Norilsk mineral industries provided the economic base for Siberia's considerable contribution to the Soviet war effort during World War II. At the onset of war in 1941 Siberia's productive capacity was rapidly augmented by the wholesale shift of over 300 entire enterprises from the threatened or occupied western regions of the USSR. Seventy-eight mainly machine-building plants were relocated in East Siberia alone, and Siberia as a whole continued to be a major arsenal providing vital military *matériel* throughout the conflict: for instance, between 1941 and 1945 the Siberian aircraft industry produced more than 59,000 fighter planes for the Soviet airforce. (For further details on the Siberian war effort, see Chapter 7.)

This necessarily hasty and makeshift process of industrial relocation meant that re-adaptation to the post-war peace-time economy was rather difficult and slow. However, during the period of Khrushchev's leadership in the 1950s there was a massive injection of human, financial and scientific resources into Siberia in a deliberate drive to harness and exploit the country's fabulous natural wealth. The Virgin Lands campaign, the building of the Bratsk hydroelectric station and the establishment of the Siberian Branch of the USSR Academy of Sciences at Akademgorodok near Novosibirsk were all three major symbols of the new eastwards orientation in official thinking. The impetus was maintained throughout the sixties and seventies, the most crucial factor then being the discovery and exploitation of West Siberia's seemingly inexhaustible deposits of oil and natural gas (see Chapter 4). The laying of the BAM and the new Territorial Production Complexes along its route, the tremendous publicity and propaganda surrounding its progress and the grandiose projections for its contribution to the national

57

economy also argued of the government's continuing commitment to the further development of Siberia.

There is, however, much debate in the Soviet Union today as to whether this policy should continue to be as highly 'prioritised' as it has been in recent years. Should budgetary provision for the expansion of Siberian productive capacities be maintained at the expense of the western and central regions of the country? Has the potential of the BAM in exploiting the resources of the Soviet Far East and in stimulating greater East-West trade been exaggerated? John Stephan analyses some of the international ramifications of the various arguments in Chapter 9, while Theodore Shabad concludes his chapter on economic resources (Chapter 3) by raising a tantalising question mark over Mikhail Gorbachev's commitment to the future development of the eastern regions.[49] The new General Secretary of the Communist Party has certainly not been slow in familiarising himself with the situation in Siberia at first hand, as his visits to the Tyumen oil-fields and the major cities of the Soviet Far East during his first 18 months in office have demonstrated — though his speeches there did not contain any obvious hints at any dramatic change of direction.[50] Whatever the ambiguities and imponderables of the immediate future, however, there can at any rate be little doubt that the next chapter in the history of Siberia will prove to be equally as fascinating and problematical as its distant and more recent past.

NOTES AND REFERENCES

1. The standard work is the five-volume work A. P. Okladnikov *et al.* (eds), *Istoriya Sibiri s drevneishikh vremen do nashikh dnei* (Nauka, Leningrad, 1968–9). The Siberian Branch of the Soviet Academy of Sciences publishes a valuable bi-monthly index of current publications in the field, viz., *Istoriya Sibiri: tekushchii ukazatel literatury* (Novosibirsk, 1966- in progress).

2. Stuart Kirby, 'Siberia: heartland and framework', *Asian Perspective*, vol. 9, no. 2 (1985), p. 274.

3. A. P. Okladnikov, *Otkrytie Sibiri* (Molodaya gvardiya, Moscow, 1979), pp. 18–22.

4. For a discussion, see Terence Armstrong (ed.), *Yermak's campaign in Siberia* (The Hakluyt Society, London, 1975), pp. 6–9.

5. R. G. Skrynnikov, 'Podgotovka i nachalo sibirskoi ekspeditsii Yermaka', *Voprosy istorii*, no. 8 (1979), pp. 44–56; idem, *Sibirskaya ekspeditsiya Yermaka* (Nauka, Novosibirsk, 1982).

6. Okladnikov, *Istoriya Sibiri*, vol. 2, pp. 25–60; R. J. Kerner, *The urge to the sea. The course of Russian history: the role of rivers, portages,*

ostrogs, monasteries and furs, 2nd edn (New York, 1971), pp. 66–88; Basil Dmytryshyn, E. A. P. Crownheart-Vaughan and Thomas Vaughan (eds), *Russia's conquest of Siberia: a documentary record 1558–1700* (Western Imprints/Oregon Historical Society, Portland, Oregon, 1985).

7. George Vernadsky, *The Mongols and Russia* (Yale University Press, 1953), p. 389.

8. Raymond H. Fisher, *The Russian fur trade, 1550-1700*(University of California, 1943), p. 29.

9. Ibid., pp. 118–22.

10. P. P. Yepifanov, 'K istorii osvoeniya Sibiri i Dalnego Vostoka v XVII veke', *Istoriya SSSR*, no. 4 (1981), pp. 71–2; F. G. Safronov, 'Solevarennie promysly Okhotska v XVIII-pervoi polovine XIX v.' in O. N. Vilkov (ed.), *Sibirskie goroda XVII-nachala XX veka* (Nauka, Novosibirsk, 1981), pp. 144–54.

11. Yepifanov, 'K istorii osvoeniya Sibiri . . .', pp. 74–5.

12. N. I. Nikitin, 'Voennosluzhilye lyudi i osvoenie Sibiri v XVII veke', *Istoriya SSSR*, no. 2 (1980), pp. 161–73.

13. *Aziatskaya Rossiya* (3 vols., St Petersburg, 1914), vol. 1, p. 81.

14. Terence Armstrong, *Russian settlement in the North*(Cambridge University Press, 1965); F.-X. Coquin, *La Sibérie: peuplement et immigration paysanne au XIX siècle*(Paris, 1969); Donald Treadgold, *The great Siberian migration* (Princeton, 1957). For a discussion of the Soviet historiography, see David Collins, 'Russia's conquest of Siberia: evolving Russian and Soviet interpretations', *European Studies Review*, vol. 12, no. 1 (1982), pp. 17–43.

15. V. G. Mirzoev, *Istoriografiya Sibiri: (domarksistskii period)* (Mysl, Moscow, 1970), p. 308.

16. Collins, 'Russia's conquest of Siberia', pp. 27–37.

17. N. V. Ustyugov, 'Osnovnye cherty russkoi kolonizatsii Yuzhnogo Zauralya v XVIII v.' in *Voprosy istorii Sibiri i Dalnego Vostoka* (Novosibirsk, 1961), pp. 67–8.

18. N. M. Yadrintsev, *Sibir kak koloniya: Sovremennoe polozhenie Sibiri: eya nuzhdy i potrebnosti; eya proshloe i budushchee* (St Petersburg, 1882), pp. 86–105; idem, *Sibirskie inorodtsy: ikh byu i sovremennoe polozhenie* (St Petersburg, 1891).

19. Yepifanov, 'K istorii osveoniya Sibiri . . .', p. 70.

20. For a case study of the fate of the Yukagirs, see Boris Chichlo, 'Yukagiry. Proshloe, nastoyashchee; a budushchee?', *SIBIRICA* (Lancaster, 1983), pp. 18–25.

21. Armstrong, *Russian settlement*, Appendix I, p. 184.

22. Marc Raeff, *Siberia and the Reforms of 1822* (University of Washington Press, Seattle, 1956), p. 112.

23. 'Sibir: Naselenie' in *Bolshaya sovetskaya entsiklopediya*, 3rd edn, vol. 23, p. 339.

24. Caroline Humphrey, *Karl Marx collective: economy, society and religion in a Siberian collective farm* (Cambridge University Press, 1983), pp. 373–432.

25. S. S. Savoskul, 'Urbanizatsiya i malye narodnosti severa SSSR', paper prepared for conference on 'The Development of Siberia:

Peoples and Human Resources', University of London, 7–10 April 1986, p. 34.

26. This section is an abridged version of the present author's article, 'Siberian exile in tsarist Russia', *History Today*, vol. 30 (1980), pp. 19–24.

27. Alexander Solzhenitsyn, *Arkhipelag GULag*, vol. 3 (Paris, 1975), pp. 351–6; for a critical comment on this view, see Alan Wood, 'Solzhenitsyn and the tsarist exile system: a historical comment', *Journal of Russian Studies*, no. 42 (1981), pp. 39–42.

28. Most of the literature on the Soviet period is in the prison-memoire genre, written by ex-victims of the system. It is of varied quality and reliability, much of it — for obvious reasons — impossible to authenticate in documentary form. Probably the best-known work, which blends personal experience and recollection with an attempt at historical reconstruction in Solzhenitsyn's *Arkhipelag GULag*.

29. A. D. Margolis, 'O chislennosti i razmeshchenii ssylnykh v Sibir v kontse XIX v.' in *Ssylka i katorga v Sibiri (XVIII-nachalo XX v.)* (Nauka, Novosibirsk, 1975) pp. 232–6.

30. Alan Wood, 'The use and abuse of administrative exile to Siberia', *Irish Slavonic Studies*, no. 6 (1965), pp. 65–81.

31. Alan Wood, 'Sex and violence in Siberia: Aspects of the tsarist exile system', in John Massey Stewart and Alan Wood, *Siberia: two historical perspectives* (Great Britain-USSR Association and School of Slavonic and Est European Studies, London, 1984), pp. 23–42.

32. 'Ssylka', in *Bolshaya sovetskaya entsiklopediya*, vol. 24(I), p. 387; see also Ivo Lapenna, *Soviet penal policy* (The Bodley Head, London, 1968), pp. 88, 94.

33. For the background, see Mark Bassin, 'The Russian Geographical Society, the "Amur Epoch" and the Great Siberian Expedition 1855–1863', *Annals of the Association of American Geographers*, vol. 73, no. 2 (1983), pp. 240–56.

34. Violet Conolly, *Beyond the Urals* (Oxford University Press, 1967), pp. 16–20.

35. Treadgold, *The great Siberian migration*.

36. A. A. Kallantar, 'Molochnoe khozyaistvo', in *Aziatskaya Rossiya*, vol. 2, pp. 331–8.

37. Okladnikov, *Istoriya Sibiri*, vol, 3, p. 312.

38. Ibid., pp. 212–45, 340–65; N. N. Shcherbakov, *Vliyanie ssylnykh proletarskykh revolyutsionerov na kulturnuyu zhizn Sibiri* (Irkutsk, 1984); see also the many articles contained in the journal of the Society of Ex-Political Prisoners and Exiles, *Katorga i ssylka*, nos. 1–73 (Moscow, 1921–30).

39. E. N. Khaziakhmetov, *Sibirskaya politicheskaya ssylka 1905–1917gg. (Oblik, organizatsii i revolyutsionnye svyazi)* (Tomsk, 1978); for further details see the numerous articles and references in the series *Ssylnye revolyutsionery v Sibiri (XIX v.- fevral 1917g.)*, issues 1–8 (Irkutsk, 1973–83).

40. Mirzoev, *Istoriografiya Sibiri*, p. 298.

41. On Siberian regionalism in the nineteenth century, see Wolfgang Faust, *Russlands goldener Boden: Der sibirische Regionalismus in der*

zweiten Hälfte des 19. Jahrhunderts (Cologne, 1980); Dmitri von Mohrenschildt, *Towards a United States of Russia: plans and projects of federal reconstruction of Russia in the nineteenth century* (London and Toronto, 1982), pp. 85–130; Steven D. Watrous, 'Russia's "land of the future": regionalism and the awakening of Siberia, 1819–94' (unpublished PhD thesis, University of Washington, 1970).

42. Alan Wood, 'Chernyshevskii, Siberian Exile and *oblastnichestvo*' in Roger Bartlett (ed.), *Russian thought and society, 1800–1917: Essays in honour of Eugene Lampert* (Keele, 1983), pp. 42–66.

43. M. G. Sesyunina, *G. N. Potanin i N. M. Yadrintsev — ideologi sibirskogo oblastnichestva (k voprosu o klassovoi sushchnosti sibirskogo oblastnichestva vtoroi poloviny XIX v.* (Tomsk, 1974).

44. S. F. Koval, 'Kharakter obshchestvennogo dvizheniya 60-kh godov v Sibiri' in *Obshchestvenno-politicheskoe dvizhenie v Sibiri v 1861–1917gg.: Materialy po istorii Sibiri: Sibir perioda kapitalizma,* vypusk 3 (Novosibirsk, 1967), pp. 35–54.

45. For example Okladnikov, *Otkrytie*, pp. 211–22.

46. T. I Zaslavskaya, V. A. Kalmyk and L. A. Khakhulina, 'Problemy sotsialnogo razvitiya Sibiri i puti ikh resheniya', *Izvestiya SO AN SSSR, seriya Ekonomika i prikladnaya sotsiologiya*, no. 1 (1986), pp. 36–45. This paper forms part of the proceedings of the All-Union Conference on 'Developing Siberian Productive Forces and Speeding up Technological Progress', Novosibirsk, 16–19 July 1985. The importance attached to the conference at government and party level is marked by the active participation of Politburo member V. I. Vorotnikov, President of the Council of Ministers of the RSFSR, ibid., pp. 10–22.

47. Ibid., pp. 41–2.

48. For a recent case study of these and other planning difficulties in East Siberia and the Far East, see Jonathan Schiffer, 'Post-war Soviet regional economic development policy in Pacific Siberia' (unpublished PhD thesis, University of Birmingham, 1986); see also Richard Bridge, 'The northern economy in the 1970s and 1980s: some factors, some results', *SIBIRICA II* (Lancaster, 1986), pp. 17–29, especially pp. 18–22.

49. Shabad's argument is further elaborated in his 'The Gorbachev economic policy: is the Soviet Union turning away from Siberian development?', paper read at the conference on 'The Development of Siberia: Peoples and Human Resources', University of London, 7–10 April 1986.

50. *Pravda*, 7 Sept. 1985; 29 July 1986; 2 Aug. 1986.

3

Economic Resources

Theodore Shabad

One of the economic realities of the Soviet Union has been a dichotomy between the location of population and economic activities, on the one hand, and resource endowment on the other. The European USSR, west of the Ural mountains, by virtue of being Russia's historical heartland, has been the focus of population growth and of development in agriculture and industry. Siberia, as the eastern pioneering fringe of Russia, has been traditionally underpopulated, but because of its vast size and diversified physical environment and geology, has been a potential storehouse of mineral resources, hydroelectric potential and other resources such as timber and furs. In the early stages of economic development, the industrial and population centres of the European part of the country were able to rely on local mineral resources. However, as the economy grew and became more complex and the resource potential of the European USSR became depleted, the region had to look increasingly eastwards for fuels, energy, raw materials and other supplies. Accordingly, the strategy of Siberian development has passed through several stages during the Soviet period, depending on the needs of the national economy, labour policies and the changing setting of international relations.[1]

During the Stalinist period, beginning with the programme of forced industrialisation under the five-year plans and continuing until the 1950s, the basic aim was to foster an integrated development of the Siberian economy. This strategy was based both on a desire to achieve a more uniform distribution of productive forces through development of Siberian resource-based industries and on strategic considerations calling for the construction of backup plants in key industries that would be in safer interior locations than the establishments in the European USSR closer to the exposed western frontiers. This early eastward movement was fostered by the availability of a pool of forced labour, estimated in the millions, that could be used at will in development projects under Siberia's harsh environmental conditions.

A new phase began after Stalin's death in 1953, as the large-scale use of forced labour in construction projects ended and the shortage of free labour in Siberia became a serious constraint. In addition, the gradual depletion of fuel and energy reserves in the economically developed western regions focused attention increasingly on the Siberian potential in these essential resources. Soviet planners came to the realisation that, under the new conditions, it was easier to move fuels, energy and raw materials from Siberia to the European USSR than to induce people to move eastwards to foster the rounded economic development of Siberia. Under the resulting geographical division of labour, manufacturing activities with large labour requirements were located in the European part of the Soviet Union, where population and markets were concentrated, while power-intensive industries with large fuel and energy require-ments were to be located to a greater extent in Siberia.

This policy, with additional refinements, has been affirmed under the new administration of Mikhail Gorbachev beginning in 1985. A programme of intensification calls for achieving further economic growth through more efficient use, modernisation or expansion of existing productive capacity rather than through the continuing construction of ever more industrial plants on green-field sites in undeveloped parts of the country. Such a programme, by its very nature, will further enhance the manufacturing potential of the Soviet Union's western regions rather than foster new industrial construction in Siberia. However, Siberia's fuel and energy resources are to be used not only to supply the economic centres of the European USSR, but also to attract power-intensive (but non-labour-intensive) indus-tries to Siberia. Furthermore, Gorbachev's economic strategy calls for greater preliminary processing of Siberian raw materials before shipment westwards, with a view to reducing bulk and thus easing the heavy transport burden on the railways.

Within the changing grand strategy of economic resource development, we can distinguish over the years a sequence of regional development programmes that focused on particular sections of Siberia. The first of these regional programmes was the so-called Urals-Kuznetsk Combine of the 1930s which combined Urals iron ore and Kuznetsk Basin coking coal in a 1,400-mile shuttle operation aimed at building up new iron and steel centres at each end of the line. The second regional programme, beginning in the early 1950s involved the development of East Siberia's vast hydroelectric power potential on the Angara and Yenisei rivers, attracting power-intensive industries such as aluminium. The third development programme, which started in the mid-1960s, was the use of the newly discovered oil and natural gas reserves of West Siberia, both for pipeline transportation to the fuel-short manufacturing centres of the western Soviet Union and to export markets, and for building up a petrochemical industry in Siberia itself. Beginning in the mid-1970s, the effort to develop Siberia's economic resources involved two additional regional programmes, one focused on the Baikal-Amur Mainline project, the other on the large reserves of lignite in East Siberia's Kansk-Achinsk Basin, to be used in large pithead power generating stations for extra-high-voltage transmission westwards. By the mid-1980s the East Siberian hydroelectric development and the exploitation of West Siberian oil and gas were still continuing. On the Baikal-Amur Mainline, despite a provisional linking-up of rails along its entire length in 1984, actual resource development has been postponed until the 1990s as the Gorbachev administration appears to be giving more immediate priority to the lignite-mining and power-generating project of the Kansk-Achinsk Basin.

Against this historical background, the present chapter reviews progress in the development of particular economic resources, problems encountered under the harsh Siberian environment, and prospects for the future to the extent that they can be assessed from published Soviet economic plans.

As the review will suggest, Siberia's economic resources have been making uneven contributions to the Soviet economy as a whole, with a strong role in the provision of energy resources, of some non-ferrous and rare metals and other minerals, but not in the iron and steel industry or in such ferroalloy ores as manganese and chrome, which tend to be concentrated in the western regions. In general, resource development west of Lake Baikal has been oriented westwards toward the industrial and population centres of the European part of the USSR, while resource exploitation east of Lake Baikal, a great overland distance away from the European zone, would be oriented more economically eastwards towards export markets of the Pacific Basin. One of the hallmarks of the Gorbachev administration, at least in its early stages, appears to be a turning away from export-oriented development of East Siberia and the Soviet Far East, and greater focus on western orientation and fulfilment of domestic needs. Such a hypothesis would account for the apparent shift in priorities during the twelfth five-year plan (1986–90) from development of the BAM zone to such domestically oriented projects as the lignite and electric power industry of the Kansk-Achinsk Basin.[2]

FUEL RESOURCES

All three major fossil fuels — oil, natural gas and coal — have been making increasing contributions to the Soviet economy as the depletion of reserves in the European zone has forced Soviet economic planners to look more and more to the resources of Siberia. Although coal resource maps of Siberia tend to be dominated by the seemingly huge deposits of the Tunguska Basin in central Siberia, and of the Lena Basin to the east, these deposits remain largely hypothetical, inaccessible and unexploited. The main producing basins such as the Kuznetsk Basin and the Kansk-Achinsk Basin lie in southern Siberia within the populated and economically developed settlement zone along the Trans-Siberian Railway. Even the South Yakutian Basin, though considered a bold northward advance in resource development, has a southerly location in Siberian terms, a little more than 200 miles from the Chinese border. The oil and natural gas region of West Siberia, by contrast, lies far to the north of the traditional zone of settlement, with the principal oilfields in the middle reaches of the river Ob, corresponding to the latitude of Hudson Bay in Canada, and the natural gasfields even further north, astride the Arctic Circle.

One of the main problems with the development of fuel resources in Siberia has been their transportation over long overland distances to consuming areas in the European USSR. The problem is probably least serious in the case of the oil transport system since oil, being a liquid, contains a high amount of heating value per unit volume and can therefore be moved fairly efficiently by pipeline. Gas pipelines, by contrast, deliver less than one-fifth of the heating value carried by crude oil pipelines of the same diameter, and steel pipe for gas lines is subject to more stringent quality requirements than that used to transport oil. Many more gas pipelines are therefore needed to transport natural gas from Siberia than are needed for oil. Another transport bottleneck has developed in the movement of coal, which must be shipped by railroads pending the projected development of more advanced transport systems such as coal-slurry pipelines. With increasing amounts of coal moving from Siberia to the European USSR, east-west rail traffic along some mainlines, such as the Trans-Siberian Railway, reaches some of the highest intensities in the world. (Siberian transport issues are discussed in greater detail in Chapter 5.)

Coal

By far the most important coal producer in Siberia is the Kuznetsk Basin, which yields high-grade coals such as coking coal for the iron and steel industry and high-calorific steam coals for electric power generation. It has long been the second largest producer of coal in the Soviet Union, after the Donets Basin of the Ukraine. Although the mining geology of Kuznetsk coal, some of which can be strip-mined, is generally more favourable than that of the Donets Basin, Soviet policy in the coal industry since the 1970s has been to support production in the increasingly deep mines of the Donets Basin because of its proximity to the markets of the European USSR. As a result, Kuznetsk production has been stagnating since the late 1970s when it reached a peak production of 148 million metric tons, or 20 per cent of the Soviet total. The 1980 target of 162 tons, set in the tenth five-year plan (1976–80), was thus missed by a substantial margin. There are indications that the policy of favouring Donets development is changing under the Gorbachev administration, and more investment will go into expansion of the Kuznetsk mines. Soviet planners now hope to achieve a 160m-ton output there by the end of the twelfth five-year plan (1986–90).[3] About one-third of Kuznetsk coal has been of the valuable coking variety, and it represents one-third of all Soviet coking coal production. The Kuznetsk Basin is also unusual among the Soviet producers of high-grade coal in having a substantial share

66

of its deposits close enough to the surface for strip-mining operation; about 38 per cent of Kuznetsk coal is strip-mined.

The second largest coal producer in Siberia is the Kansk-Achinsk Basin, which is situated just to the south of the Trans-Siberian Railway, and to the east of the Kuznetsk Basin. In contrast to the high-grade Kuznetsk coal, however, the product of the Kansk-Achinsk Basin is lignite, a fuel of low calorific value. Because of its low heating power, Kansk-Achinsk lignite cannot be economically transported over long distances; moreover it is technologically unsuitable for long-distance hauls because it is subject to spontaneous self-ignition and disintegrates when exposed to air. The lignite is therefore best used in electric power generating stations in the immediate vicinity of the mines or within a relatively limited transport radius. Efficient long-distance transport would require preliminary beneficiation to a briquette or carbon-like char, but such a process is still in the research and development stage. For the time being, therefore, the strategy will be to use Kansk-Achinsk lignite in very large mineside electric power generating stations, which would then attract power-intensive industries, as Siberia's hydroelectric stations have in the past, or transmit electricity westwards to consumers in industrial and population centres. Pending the lignite-based large-scale electric power development, the Kansk-Achinsk Basin, which is entirely accessible through strip-mining, has been gradually expanding its capacity to 40 million tons of lignite a year, with 25 coming from the Borodino pit and 15 from the Nazarovo pit. Despite the inefficiency of moving the lignite over long distances, it has been supplying power stations as far west as Novosibirsk and as far east as Bratsk, or a radius of 300 to 400 miles. Poor planning has resulted in even longer hauls of up to 2,000 miles. Near Tashkent, in Central Asia, for example, a new lignite-burning power station started up in 1985, but the local Angren lignite mine had not been expanded in time to provide the additional fuel. It had to be obtained from as far away as the Moscow Basin in central European Russia and the Kansk-Achinsk Basin, despite the uneconomic nature of such transport and the technological problems posed by the poor quality of the lignite.

Although the lignite-based electric power development in the Kansk-Achinsk Basin seems to have had low priority in the past, it is being given new impetus during the twelfth five-year plan. The plan calls for the start-up of the first of a series of gigantic power stations, the long-delayed Berezovskoe no. 1 station near Chernenko (the former Sharypovo), with a designed generating capacity of 6,400 mw (megawatts) (eight units of 800 mw each). The first of these generating units was tentatively scheduled to produce electricity in 1987, with others following at an initial rate of one a year and later, two a year. Lignite is to be supplied over a ten-mile-long conveyor belt from the new Berezovskoe no. 1 open-pit mine, which, with an ultimate mining capacity of 55m tons a year, will be one of the world's largest surface coal mines. Its output, at full capacity, will be sufficient to supply not only the Berezovskoe no. 1 power station, but also the second in the series, the Berezovskoe no. 2 station, on which construction is scheduled to begin by 1990.[4] As many as eight such power stations, and additional open-pit mines to supply them, are projected under the Kansk-Achinsk development programme, extending well into the twenty-first century. The management centre of at least the initial stages of the project is the new city of Chernenko, named in 1985 after the deceased Soviet leader, Konstantin Chernenko. This new town is ultimately planned to reach a population of 200,000, but its growth has been lagging because of the low priority accorded the Kansk-Achinsk project in the past. Although its population was initially planned to reach 70,000 by 1985, it was still short of the 50,000 level.[5]

The huge amounts of electricity that by the 1990s are expected to be generated by the Kansk-Achinsk power stations are to be transmitted westwards over ultra-high-voltage lines of 1,150 kv (kilovolts) AC (alternating current). Such an electricity transmission system has already been constructed from the Ekibastuz coal-burning power-generating complex in north-east Kazakhstan westwards to Chelyabinsk in the Urals. Work is under way on an eastward extension of the system from Ekibastuz through Barnaul to the Kuznetsk Basin and on to the Kansk-Achinsk district. The Soviet Union has been experimenting for years with two types of ultra-high-voltage transmission, the 1,150 kv AC system and a 1,500 kv DC (direct current) system. However, the DC system, though apparently more effective in reducing power loss along the line, has posed greater technical problems, and Soviet planners have gone ahead with the 1,150 kv AC system. These powerful transmission systems create very strong electrical fields, requiring wide rights-of-way in which no human activity is permitted, and are therefore most suitable for the wide open spaces of the Asian regions of the USSR.

East of the Kansk-Achinsk Basin exist a number of smaller coal-mining districts serving local needs along the Trans-Siberian Railway zone, and most of them yield lignite from open-pit mines. They include the Azei strip-mine near Tulun, first opened up in 1969 and now producing 15m tons of lignite a year, and the Gusinoozersk area south of Ulan-Ude. At Gusinoozersk, a small local strip-mine known as Khoboldzha has been supplying three million tons of lignite a year to the Gusinoozersk thermal power station, with a generating capacity of 840 mw. The local mine is inadequate to support a planned expansion of the power station, and the twelfth five-year plan therefore envisages the development of an additional coal source, the Tugnui deposit, 80 miles east of Gusinoozersk, on the boundary between the Buryat ASSR and Chita *oblast*. The Tugnui deposit is large enough to support an annual production of twelve million tons of coal when fully developed.[6] Another local lignite and power project that has long been planned is the Kharanor project, which may now finally be getting under way in the twelfth five-year plan. The Kharanor open-pit mine, which is in Chita *oblast*, north of Borzya, has been worked since 1957, and now has a capacity of seven million tons a year. But the development of a second stage, the so-called Kharanor no. 2 mine, has been needed to fuel a projected thermal power station at nearby Yasnogorsk, with a generating capacity of 1,260 mw. The expansion of the Kharanor mine was not listed in the twelfth five-year plan, but Soviet press reports said that development had started.[7]

A major new development in the Siberian coal industry has been the opening-up of the South Yakutian coal basin, with its centre in the new town of Neryungri. Unlike many of the local Siberian mines, the South Yakutian Basin yields a high-grade bituminous coal, suitable for coking and steam-raising uses. Development began in the mid-1970s under an arrangement with Japan that provided Japanese loans and technical assistance in exchange for deliveries of coking coal to Japan. Coal shipments from Neryungri began in late 1978 when the large open-pit mine was reached by the 'Little BAM', a south-north transverse railway intersecting the BAM east-west mainline at Tynda. The initial shipments from Neryungri were steam coal for power generation in the Soviet Far East. The deeper coking coal in the pit was reached only in 1984, and shipments to Japan began in

1985 after start-up of a coal washery that can convert nine million tons of raw coking coal into five million tons of export-grade coking coal concentrate. Washery residue is being used to fuel a local thermal power station, where a first stage of 600 megawatts was placed into operation by late 1985, and a second stage is to be built under the twelfth five-year plan. With the Neryungri pit having reached its projected mining capacity of 13m tons of raw coal a year, Soviet plans originally envisaged further development of the high-grade coal of the South Yakutian Basin, starting with the Denisovskaya deep shaft mine, ten miles north-east of Neryungri.[8] However, this project has been shelved by the Gorbachev administration in light of the shift of priorities away from East Siberia.

Since 1973, the Soviet Union has ceased to publish the Siberian share of a number of key production figures, including the output of coal. However, based on scattered information, Siberia can be estimated to produce close to 40 per cent of the Soviet Union's coal. Much of the Siberian production consists of low-grade lignite mined in open-pit operations and used in nearby electric generating stations. However, the valuable high-grade coal of the Kuznetsk Basin and of the South Yakutian Basin makes a significant contribution to the Soviet economy. Because of the slow decline of the Donets Basin, the main producer of high-grade coal in the European USSR, increasing amounts of Kuznetsk coal have been moving westwards, imposing a growing strain on the rail transport system. In 1980, the latest year for which such data are available, as much as 30 per cent of Kuznetsk coking coal moved to iron and steel mills west of the Urals, and 38 per cent of the high-grade Kuznetsk steam coals were used to fuel electric power stations in the European USSR.[9] With the Donets Basin no longer able to satisfy demand within its traditional marketing areas, Kuznetsk coal has even begun to move into the Ukraine, both for coking use and for power generation. As for the South Yakutian Basin, its steam coals are being used for power generation in the Soviet Far East, and its coking coal for export to Japan. A domestic demand for coking coal would also be opening up in the Soviet Far East if the long-planned new iron and steel centre in the region ever materialises.

Oil

The economic geography of the Siberian oil industry, together with that of natural gas, is discussed in detail in Chapter 3, and will therefore be only summarised here. The development of Siberia's oil resources contrasts with the exploitation of the coal resources in several important respects. The oil industry is distinguished by far greater spatial concentration, being found almost entirely in the West Siberian Plain, astride the Ob river, except for the small contribution of the Sakhalin oilfields in the Soviet Far East. Compared with coal mining, whose beginnings date from the opening up of the Trans-Siberian Railway at the turn of the twentieth century, the West Siberian oil industry is a modern development, having had its genesis in the mid-1960s.

Within the short span of two decades, West Siberian oil production soared to 392m metric tons in 1986 (7.8 million barrels a day), or 64 per cent of Soviet national output. The development is all the more remarkable because it occurred in once virtually unpopulated swampy woodlands where winter temperatures habitually drop to −40°C or lower. The early development of the West Siberian oil industry, centred on the new towns of Surgut and Nizhnevartovsk, was particularly rapid because a large share of the reserves was concentrated in a single supergiant field, Samotlor, north of Nizhnevartovsk. By 1980, this field alone accounted for one-quarter of Soviet oil production. Subsequent expansion of West Siberian oil production has been slowed by the need to develop many scattered smaller fields in the trackless terrain, each requiring road access, power transmission lines, oil-collection pipelines and other infrastructure. The effect of Samotlor development was to double West Siberian oil output during the tenth five-year planning period (1976–80), from 148m (1975) to 313m tons. In the eleventh five-year plan, the increase was only 20 per cent. The slowdown of West Siberian expansion had a crucial effect on the Soviet oil industry as a whole. As long as West Siberian output grew rapidly, it compensated for declines in older producing areas, notably the Volga-Urals province, and national oil production continued to increase. The slowdown that set in during the early 1980s was no longer adequately counter-balanced, and Soviet national output peaked in 1983 at 616m tons, stagnating thereafter.

In view of the importance of a sufficient oil supply, both for domestic consumption and for export in a world of high oil prices, Soviet economic planners hope to reverse the national decline by accelerating West Siberian development. The twelfth five-year plan projects a national output level of 630m tons by

71

1990, an increment of six per cent over the 1985 level of 595m tons. In view of the continuing decline of the Volga-Urals fields, such a projected increase in national production would require another 20 per cent increase of West Siberian output, from 372m tons in 1985 to perhaps 450m in 1990. This would necessitate an extraordinary effort, making continued expansion of oil production in West Siberia a matter of the highest national priority.[10] (See Chapter 4, Table 4.1)

The only other Siberian oil-producing region, the island of Sakhalin off the Pacific coast, has played a negligible role since the development of the West Siberian resources, with an annual production of about three million tons. This represents only one-fifth of the needs of the Soviet Far East, with the rest being brought in by tank cars along the Trans-Siberian Railway from the west. There have been expectations of more significant Sakhalin oil development since 1977, when drill ships first struck oil offshore, but exploration (with Japanese technical assistance) continues with no major discoveries leading to development.

The prospects of another potential oil-producing province, the so-called Siberian Platform, between the Yenisei river and the Lena, have become a matter of dispute, with some Soviet geologists and economic geographers predicting major discoveries and ultimate development.[11] However, published plans do not go beyond calling for continued geological exploration and, with an all-out development effort focused on West Siberia, do not appear to convey a sense of urgency regarding East Siberia's prospects.

Natural gas

While the long-term future of Soviet oil production seems problematical, this cannot be said about the natural gas industry, the priority fuel-producing industry of the 1980s. The opening-up of gas deposits in Siberia has been an even later development than the exploitation of the oilfields. Although the initial discoveries were made in the 1960s between the river Ob and the Urals, major production followed only after geologists identified a series of supergiant gas fields further to the north-east, near the coast of the Arctic Ocean. Since the early 1970s Soviet planners have proceeded to develop these supergiant fields, devoting approximately a five-year-plan period to each one. The first of the fields, Medvezhe, north-east of the new gas-development town of Nadym, yielded its first gas in 1972, reaching its designed capacity of 65 billion to 70 billion cubic metres in 1977–78 (one billion = one thousand million). This was followed by the development further east of the Urengoi field, where the new town of Novyi Urengoi arose. The Urengoi field yielded its first gas in 1978 and approached its designed capacity of 250 billion cubic metres in 1985. During the twelfth five-year plan the focus of development is on the Yamburg field, on the Taz Peninsula, north of Urengoi, with a production level of 200 billion cubic metres to be achieved around 1990. The twelfth five-year plan calls for starting work leading ultimately to the development of gas deposits on the Yamal Peninsula, thus suggesting the future direction of gas development in the region.[12]

Natural gas development in West Siberia has been remarkably close to schedule, or even ahead of plan, despite the sub-arctic location of the gas resources (further north than the oilfields) and despite the need for laying many thousands of miles of large-diameter pipelines to provide an outlet for West Siberian gas to the European USSR and for export to Europe. A major factor in the rapid development of the gas resources has undoubtedly been the concentration of reserves in a few supergiant fields, making it possible to focus work on a relatively limited area, in contrast to the many scattered, smaller oilfields to the south. During the eleventh five-year plan, West Siberian gas output rose from 156 billion cubic metres in 1980 to 374 billion in 1985, and its share in national production increased from 36 per cent to 58 per cent. This remarkable rate of growth is to be maintained for the foreseeable future, according to Soviet plans. During the current five-year planning period from 1986 to 1990, the production of natural gas in West Siberia is scheduled to rise to at least 550 billion cubic metres a year, representing two-thirds of Soviet national output. Longer-range projections, to the year 2000, envisage a national production level of 1,000 billion to 1,100 billion cubic metres; by that time, the West Siberian share may be up to 75 per cent of the Soviet total, suggesting a West Siberian output level of about 750 billion cubic metres.

By far the biggest problem relating to the exploitation of the vast West Siberian gas reserves is transportation of the gas to consuming areas in the European USSR and for export to Eastern and Western Europe. The largest diameter gas pipelines now in operation (1,420 mm diameter) can transmit 33 billion cubic metres of gas a year, and about a dozen such pipelines have been required to transmit the gas now being extracted in West Siberia. Alone during the five-year period 1981 to 1985, six lines, totalling 20,000 km, had to be laid to handle the incremental production from the Urengoi field. Although improvements in gas-transmission technology, through the use of thicker-walled pipe and larger-capacity compressors, may result in higher operating pressures and thus in larger annual throughput of gas, about ten more pipelines are likely to be required to move the projected additional gas production from West Siberia by the middle to late 1990s. Although most of the gas will continue to flow to the European USSR and to export destinations, Soviet plans also call for additional transmission to the southern, economically developed zone of Siberia, both as a raw material for the chemical industry (nitrogen fertilizer, for example) and as a cleaner-burning fuel for heat and power stations in urban centres, replacing the dirtier coal.

Because of the northerly location of the West Siberia gas industry, it is unlikely to generate any significant local economic activity, except gas-fuelled electric power generation. Like the projected lignite-burning power stations of the Kansk-Achinsk Basin, a power-generating complex based on West Siberian natural gas is envisaged as a major source for the long-distance transmission of electricity westwards. The beginnings of such a gas-burning power complex have already arisen at Surgut, the oil centre of the river Ob. The Surgut no. 1 central electric station, equipped mainly with 200 mw generating units, has become the principal source of power for the West Siberian oilfields since it started up in 1972, reaching a generating capacity of 3,345 mw in 1983. The Surgut no. 2 station, with much larger unit capacities of 800 mw each, is expected to produce a surplus of electricity for transmission to the energy-deficient Urals industrial region. The first 800 mw unit at the Surgut no. 2 station started up in 1985, and the twelfth five-year plan calls for installation of all six units, for a total capacity of 4,800 mw, by 1990. The plan also calls for the start-up of the first generating units at two additional West Siberian gas-burning power stations, in the oil town of Nizhnevartovsk and the gasfield of Urengoi.[13] The transmission lines within the West Siberian oil and gas region and the interconnection between it and the Urals are now at 500 kv; the future long-distance transmission of gas-generated electricity to the Urals will require the construction of ultra-high-voltage lines, at

1,150 kv, similar to those projected for the Kansk-Achinsk power complex.

In contrast with the transcontinental scope of the West Siberian gas industry, other Siberian gasfields serve local or limited regional needs. The northern Siberian metals centre of Norilsk has been supplied by natural gas since 1970 from the Messoyakha and Solenaya river gasfields, 250 km to the west. Three pipelines, each with a throughput of 1.8 billion cubic metres, now provide more than five billion cubic metres of gas a year to Norilsk smelters and to heat and power stations; and a fourth line has been reported under construction. In Yakutia the Mastakh gasfield centred on the settlement of Kysyl-Syr on the Vilyui river supplies less than one billion cubic metres to a Yakutsk heat and power station and to a cement plant at Mokhsogollokh, in the Bestyakh-Pokrovsk industrial area south of Yakutsk. The Vilyui river gasfields of Yakutia have large reserves, offering a potential for much wider distribution, and an export-oriented development involving Japan and the United States was under active discussion in the 1970s; it has been dormant since the Soviet military intervention in Afghanistan in 1979. A third local gas source in Siberia, Sakhalin, achieved a wider market in 1987 with the completion of a pipeline to the Siberian mainland. The pipeline, with an initial transmission capacity of 1.5 billion cubic metres, will supply heat and power stations, steel furnaces and residential housing in the city of Komsomolsk.[14] Ultimately Sakhalin gas will provide the basis for a nitrogen fertilizer industry projected for a new city in the area of Nizhnetambovskoe on the Amur river north-east of Komsomolsk.[15]

HYDROELECTRIC RESOURCES

Although hydroelectric development in the USSR began in the economically developed European portion of the country, it is Siberia that offers by far the largest potential. Most of this potential is concentrated in the Yenisei-Angara Basin of central Siberia, which became the focus of a major regional development programme starting in the early 1950s. The hydroelectric programme has involved the construction of a sequence of power stations, including some of the world's largest, and the development of associated power-consuming industries such as aluminium reduction and wood-pulp manufacture. As a result of this hydroelectric programme, the Siberian inter-connected electricity grid is the only power system in the Soviet Union in which installed hydroelectric generating capacity exceeds thermal electric capacity. At the end of the tenth five-year plan in 1980, the last year for which regional power system data are available, 18,700 mw (or 53 per cent) of Siberia's installed electrical generating capacity was in hydroelectric stations, with the remaining 16,400 mw in thermal power stations. The Siberian grid, extending from Omsk in the west to Chita in the east, was the third largest regional power system of the USSR, after the South (mainly the Ukraine) and Central Russia (centred on Moscow).[16] Also in 1980, 36 per cent of the Soviet Union's installed hydroelectric capacity was in the Siberian grid. While this Siberian grid was already part of the overall interconnected power system of the Soviet Union extending through northern Kazakhstan and across the Ural mountains into the European USSR, the Far Eastern grid was still isolated, with a total generating capacity of 4,000 mw, including 1,300 mw (or one-third) hydroelectric.[17]

The hydroelectric development programme in the Yenisei-Angara Basin began with a relatively small station of 660 mw on the Angara at Irkutsk; it went into construction in 1950, produced its first electric power in 1956, and reached its designed capacity in 1958. Subsequent dam projects in this development programme, which is now in its fourth decade, were all in the multi-million mw range. The Bratsk station on the Angara reached its designed capacity of 4,100 mw in 1966; it has since been upgraded to 4,500 mw. It was followed by the first big Yenisei project, the Krasnoyarsk station at Divnogorsk, which reached its designed capacity of 6,000 mw in 1971. Back on the Angara, the Ust-Ilimsk plant reached a capacity of 3,840 mw in 1979; it had originally been planned for 18 generating units of 240 mw each, but the last two have not been installed. The latest Siberian hydro-project to be completed is the Sayan-Shushenskoe dam on the Yenisei river at Sayanogorsk, which reached its designed capacity of 6,400 mw in late 1985, making it the largest hydroelectric producer in the USSR.[18]

During the current (twelfth) five-year plan the construction focus is on the Boguchany hydroelectric project on the Angara river at Kodinskii. Work on the project, whose designed capacity has been variously given as 3,000 and 4,000 mw, began in 1975 and is not expected to be completed until the early 1990s, a decade behind the original schedule. One reason for the delay has been the lack of railway access to the construction site. A rail spur running northwards from the Trans-Siberian mainline at Nizhnyaya Poima towards the village of Boguchany was designed as a logging railway rather than as an access route to the power station. The rail spur reached the logging settlement of Karabula, south of Boguchany, in 1977, but Soviet government agencies appear to have been unable thus far to co-ordinate continued construction of the access spur to the hydroelectric site. The twelfth five-year plan also calls for the start of preliminary work on the next big hydro-project, the Middle Yenisei station, for which a site has been selected at Abalakovo, just below the Yenisei-Angara confluence. The preliminary capacity of the Middle Yenisei power project, which will have its construction base in the lumber milling town of Lesosibirsk, has been planned at 6,000 mw, with possible later expansion to 7,500 mw. Considering the long lead times of construction of the large Siberian hydroelectric stations, the Middle Yenisei project is not likely to yield its first electric power before the year 2000.[19]

Hydroelectric construction has also been an important aspect of Siberian economic development in a number of isolated sites outside the Yenisei-Angara system. The slow-moving river Ob, with its gentle gradient, is generally less suitable for hydroelectric development and has only one station, of medium size, just south of Novosibirsk, with a capacity of 400 mw, built in the 1950s. However, the upper reaches of the river Ob, in the Altai mountains, offer favourable sites, and construction was getting under way in the mid-1980s on a dam at Yelanda, on the Katun river, with a projected capacity of 1,500 mw.[20] But some power projects like the Katun dam have come under review on environmental grounds and its future is in doubt.

Smaller isolated clusters of hydroelectric stations have also been built in four other regions: the Norilsk district of northern Siberia, the Vilyui Basin in Yakutia, the Amur Basin, and the Kolyma river in north-east Siberia. In northern Siberia, two hydroelectric sites on tributaries of the Yenisei river have been developed as part of the power supply for the all-important Norilsk metals centre, producing nickel, cobalt and platinum-group metals. One hydro-station, at Snezhnogorsk on the Khantaika river, reached its designed capacity of 441 mw in 1972 after nine years of construction and is feeding electricity to

Norilsk over a 100-mile, 220-kv line. A second station, with a designed capacity of 600 mw, has been under construction since 1975 at Svetlogorsk on the Kureika river, a hundred miles further south, and may yield its first power during the twelfth five-year plan of the late 1980s.

In Yakutia hydroelectric development has been associated with the diamond industry of the Vilyui river basin. Construction of the first station, at Chernyshevskii, began in 1960, and it reached its designed capacity of 308 mw in 1969. Its expansion, known as the no. 2 project, added 340 mw during the 1970s, so that by 1976, 648 mw of power-generation capacity was installed at Chernyshevskii. Work on the Vilyui 3 project began in 1979 at Svetlyi, further downstream, at the mouth of the Ochchugui (Malaya or Little) Botuobuya river, a right tributary of the Vilyui. It is planned for a capacity of 360 mw, with the first generating units of 90 mw each scheduled to start up by 1990 under the twelfth five-year plan.[21]

In the Amur river basin, the hydroelectric potential of two major left tributaries, the Zeya and Bureya, has been tapped for use in the electric power grid of the Soviet Far East. On the Zeya river, the 1,290-mw Zeya station at the town of Zeya reached its designed capacity in 1980 after 16 years of construction and has become the source of electric power for a 500 kv transmission line extending south-east along the Trans-Siberian Railway to Khabarovsk and Komsomolsk. During the twelfth five-year plan, this 500-kv grid is to be extended southward to join up with the Maritime *krai* power system between the coal-fired Luchegorsk power plant and Vladivostok. The Far Eastern power grid is to be further reinforced by the construction of the Bureya hydroelectric station at Talakan, 120 miles east of Blagoveshchensk. Construction on the Bureya station began in 1976, and the first of six projected 335-mw generating units is scheduled to start up by 1990, for an ultimate total power capacity of 2,000 mw.[22]

Finally, a hydroelectric system has been slowly taking shape in north-east Siberia, on the Kolyma river, to supply the important gold-mining industry of Magadan *oblast*. Construction on the first Kolyma station, at Sinegore south of Debin, began in 1970, with a designed capacity of 900 mw. The first 180-mw unit was reported to have started up in early 1981, but it was later revealed that the report was premature and that the generating unit was not operating properly; several high officials were dismissed in the ensuing scandal. By 1984, three generating units were in place, completing the first stage. The twelfth five-year plan calls for the start of construction on the next station in the Kolyma river series, the Ust-Srednekan station, at the mouth of the Srednekan river downstream from Debin.[23]

The large hydroelectric stations of the Angara-Yenisei system, by providing cheap power after the initial heavy investment in dam construction, have attracted industries that are distinguished by large consumption of electricity, notably the reduction of alumina to aluminium metal. It takes about 17,000 kilowatt-hours of electricity to produce one metric ton of aluminium. The pattern for a close association between hydroelectric power generation and aluminium production was set in the early 1960s when Irkutsk hydro-station gave rise to a medium-sized aluminium plant (240,000-ton capacity a year) at nearby Shelekhov. Larger aluminium plants (with capacities of up to 500,000 tons) arose at Bratsk and at Krasnoyarsk, and a third large aluminium plant began production in 1985 at Sayanogorsk. Preliminary plans also call for the construction of an aluminium plant next to the Boguchany hydroelectric station at some time in the 1990s. Some of the new industrial centres that have arisen at large Siberian hydroelectric stations· have also become the sites of major cellulose mills based on the surrounding timber resources and the abundant supplies of water; such large pulp mills have arisen at Bratsk and Ust-Ilimsk.

The predominance of hydroelectric power in the Siberian grid and the dependence of major industries on their continuous output of electric power have endowed the hydro-stations with the function of base-load stations, meaning the provision of a constant, basic supply of electricity. Normally hydro-stations serve as so-called peak-load stations, providing the additional supply of electricity needed during peak consumption periods. Hydro-stations are suited to meeting peak demand needs because the generation of power can be easily shut down and started up again merely by controlling the flow of water. Base-load requirements are normally met by fuel-burning steam electric stations (and nuclear stations), which cannot be quickly shut down and started up again, and run most efficiently on a steady, continuous basis. The reliance on hydro-stations for base-load requirements, as in Siberia, has a serious disadvantage in making industries dependent on fluctuations in the natural flow of water. In dry years, when the flow of water in streams is reduced, hydroelectric stations produce far below their designed capacity, affecting the performance of user industries. Soviet planners hope that the unreliability of much of the Siberian electric power supply will be improved with the development of the projected lignite-fired base-load power stations of the Kansk-Achinsk Basin.

MINERAL RESOURCES

Siberia's role as a purveyor of non-fuel minerals to the Soviet economy varies widely, from a minor contribution of ores for the iron and steel industry to a virtual monopoly in the production of tin, platinum-group metals, nickel, cobalt, diamonds and, until recently, gold. Many of these resources are in remote areas of northern Siberia, under harsh environmental conditions, and it is largely the acute need of the Soviet economy for these materials that has led to exploitation in the face of locational handicaps.

Iron ore resources

With its vast and diversified mineral base, Siberia is remarkable in not being particularly well endowed with iron ore resources. With the building-up of a substantial iron and steel industry during the Soviet period, notably in the Kuznetsk Basin, the inadequate ore base has led to an imbalance between ore supply and steel-making capacity. Siberia produces only six per cent of the Soviet Union's marketable iron ore (16m out of a national output of 250m metric tons) compared with about ten per cent of the nation's pig iron (eleven million out of 110m). This means that about eight million tons of ore must be shipped from the west into Siberia to help maintain the region's iron and steel industry.[24]

Siberia has been more or less dependent on iron-ore shipments from the west ever since the industry first arose in the Kuznetsk Basin in the 1930s. The initial plan was to exchange Kuznetsk coking coal for Urals iron ore, and on that basis to build up two new eastern iron and steel plants, one at Magnitogorsk in the Urals, the other at the town of Kuznetsk (known from 1932 to 1961 as Stalinsk, then Novokuznetsk). The ore and coal exchange gave rise to the railroad shuttle arrangement known as the Urals-Kuznetsk Combine. However, from the very beginning, a local ore supply was also beginning to be developed in the southern part of the Kuznetsk Basin, and by the mid-1960s when the Kuznetsk plant was producing about 3.5m tons of pig iron a year, three-quarters of the ore came from local deposits.

In 1964, a second major iron and steel plant, the so-called West Siberian Plant, began operations in the Kuznetsk Basin, also in the Novokuznetsk area, and this required the development of a distant Siberian ore deposit, at Zheleznogorsk in Irkutsk *oblast*. However even the additional ore supply was inadequate to meet needs. At its peak production level, from 1973 to 1981, the Zheleznogorsk mine supplied a little more than six million tons of concentrate; this was the equivalent of four million tons of metal, two-thirds of the requirements of the six-million-ton West Siberian plant. As Zheleznogorsk production declined in the 1980s to five million tons of concentrate a year, the nearby ore deposit of Rudnogorsk was developed to compensate. Despite these projects, Siberian iron-ore production remains short of needs and must be supplemented by shipments from as far west as the Kursk Magnetic Anomaly of Central European Russia.

Despite the unfavourable ore situation, there has long been discussion of developing yet another Siberian iron and steel centre, in the Soviet Far East. The current (twelfth) five-year plan in fact calls for preliminary work on such a project, which would be based on local coking coal (from Neryungri) and on local iron ore (from the Aldan area). The Neryungri coal deposit, reached by railroad in 1978, has already been developed, for export of coking coal to Japan. The Aldan iron deposit, which would be made accessible by the railroad now under construction northward to Tommot and Yakutsk, is yet to be developed.[25] Although several possible sites have been under study for a Far Eastern iron and steel plant, no decision has been announced.

Non-ferrous ore resources

Nickel, cobalt, platinum-group metals

These metals are all combined in an unusually rich concentration of deposits in the Norilsk area of northern Siberia that have given rise to one of the world's largest cities within the Arctic Circle and have stimulated the development of an unusual icebreaker-

81

supported year-round transport route through the Arctic Ocean.[26] The ore deposit of Norilsk was first identified in the 1920s but was not immediately developed because of remote location and difficulty of access. Serious development began on an emergency basis in World War II after a similar deposit in the Kola Penninsula near Murmansk fell into the military theatre of operations. Nickel and cobalt consumption increases in wartime because of the need for high-strength steel in armour plate and high-temperature materials in jet-engine components. Norilsk became a crucial industrial support centre of the Soviet war effort. Since 1960, the importance of Norilsk has become further enhanced by the discovery of the additional Talnakh deposits, 20 miles north-east of the older mines of Norilsk proper. A series of increasingly deep and large underground mines have been built to tap the rich ores. The city of Norilsk, with its satellite towns, now exceeds 200,000 in population, and a growing fleet of nuclear and conventional icebreakers has been ensuring a year-round cargo route between the Yenisei river port of Dudinka since 1978, serving Norilsk, and the northern European ports of Murmansk, Kandalaksha and Arkhangelsk. (For details on the Arctic sea route, see Chapter 5.)

The development of Norilsk, which has occurred in the face of a harsh Arctic environment, has propelled the USSR to the front rank of world producers of platinum-group metals (ahead of South Africa), nickel (surpassing Canada since the late 1960s) and cobalt (second only to Zaire). Platinum-group metals, particularly palladium and platinum proper, and more recently nickel have become major Soviet mineral exports to the West. Production figures for non-ferrous metals are kept secret in the Soviet Union, but the growing significance of Norilsk is evident from continuing reports of mine expansion. After the start of operations at the relatively smaller and shallow mines of Mayak (Lighthouse) in 1965 and Komsomol (Young Communist League) in 1971, the much larger and deeper Oktyabr (October) mine yielded its first ore in 1974. By early 1986, when it inaugurated its ninth and last stage, the Oktyabr mine workings covered an area of ten square kilometres.[27] In the meantime, the even deeper Taimyr mine, extending to 1,600 metres, began operations in early 1983 after nine years of construction, and a second stage opened in 1985; and the construction of yet another mine, the Skalistyi (Rocky), started in 1983, for probable initial production in the early 1990s. Geological exploration is still under way on a mineral body to be tapped by the projected Glubokii (Deep) mine.

The huge Norilsk operation, in which nickel and cobalt are extracted from sulfide ores, overshadows a much smaller mining enterprise, in the Tuva Autonomous Republic of southern Siberia, where cobalt, in association with nickel, is derived from arsenide ores. The mine opened in 1970 at Khovu-Aksy, a settlement that had been given urban status in 1956. The cobalt is recovered there in a hydrometallurgical factory by a leaching process.

Lead, zinc, copper

Although Siberia is currently making no significant contribution to the production of these base metals, the twelfth five-year plan augurs the start of substantial mineral developments in this area. Existing facilities include the old lead-zinc mine and lead smelter of Dalnegorsk (the former Tetyukhe) in the Soviet Far East, which was once operated by a British company under Selection Trust, the London-based mining finance house. The company gained a concession in 1925 under the Soviet government's New Economic Policy, which permitted a partial return to private enterprise, but handed back the property in 1931 after the New Economic Policy had given way to total government control of the economy. There is also an old zinc refinery at Belovo, in the Kuznetsk Basin, dating from 1930. It was originally opened to refine ores from the nearby Salair mine, but reserves have become depleted, and the refinery now processes zinc concentrates obtained as byproducts from a variety of small Siberian mines. Copper has also been derived as a byproduct from Siberian mines, notably from the Norilsk operation and from the tin mine of Solnechnyi, near Komsomolsk (see below).

However, Siberia has not been a match for the strong position of the lead-zinc and copper industries in Kazakhstan, Central Asia, the Urals and the Caucasus. This may change if plans for the development of Siberian resources materialise, as portended by the current five-year plan. It calls for the start of development, after many years of tentative discussion, of two major lead-zinc sites — the Gorevka deposit on the lower Angara river, and the Ozernyi deposit in the Lake Yeravnoe district of the Buryat Autonomous Republic. Soviet mining capacity in these metals has traditionally lagged behind smelter capacity, and the decision in the twelfth five-year plan to develop the Siberian resources appears intended to ensure a more reliable raw-material supply. Plans for the development of a promising third Siberian lead-zinc source, the Kholodnaya deposit, near the Baikal-Amur Mainline, north of Lake Baikal, have yet to be announced. The development of Ozernyi will require the construction of a 134-km rail spur from Mogzon on the Trans-Siberian Railway, on which work was reported to have begun in 1980.[28] The development of the Gorevka deposit is likely to be more complex because the deposit lies partly under the river bed of the Angara, which moreover will be widened by the construction of the Middle Yenisei hydroelectric station a short distance downstream. The development of the open-pit mine will require the construction of a succession of dikes holding back the water of the Angara River. The small mining settlement of Novoangarsk has arisen on the site, and a pilot plant to test the ore-processing technology is under construction, with completion scheduled for 1987.[29]

Technological complications also appear to have delayed development of the long-heralded Udokan copper deposit, now made accessible by the construction of the Baikal-Amur Mainline in northern Chita *oblast*. Although a large research literature on Udokan development has been accumulated and several conferences on the subject have been held, there still appears to be indecision on when and how to proceed, the processing technology for the ore, whether to build a substantial new town on the site, with a projected population of 60,000 to 100,000, or limit local settlement and bring in workers from afar for limited work-duty tours. Pending a resolution of these issues, the Udokan project remains in abeyance and has not been included in the twelfth five-year plan.[30]

Tin, tungsten, molybdenum

Tin is not a common resource in the Soviet Union, and its economy was long dependent on imports, notably from China, until relations between these two countries deteriorated after 1960. In a high-priority programme to develop domestic resources at any cost, the USSR tripled tin production in the 1960s and 1970s, from about 10,000 metric tons in 1960 to more than 30,000 in the early 1980s[31] Virtually all the tin deposits available for development were in Siberia, whose resources appear to have raised the Soviet Union to second rank among world producers after Malaysia. The USSR still imports some tin from Malaysia and Bolivia, but its position as a tin producer has been greatly strengthened as a result of the Siberian development. Most of the mines are in the Soviet Far East, some in remote northern locations with a harsh Arctic environment; however, the main Soviet producers are in more readily accessible southern areas of the Far East. They are the Solnechnyi district, 25 miles north-west of Komsomolsk, and the Kavalerovo district, in Maritime *krai*. Solnechnyi, which has been in production since 1963, is of particular interest because it yields a wide range of byproduct metals, including tungsten, copper, lead and zinc.[32] Kavalerovo is an older producing-area, dating from World War II. The Khrustalnyi concentrator at Kavalerovo now processes ores from a wide range of mines.[33] A smaller operation in the southern part of the Soviet Far East is at Khingansk, near Obluche, also developed in World War II. The oldest Soviet tin mines are in Chita *oblast*, where small operations still appear to be under way in Sherlovaya Gora and Khapcheranga.

However, in an effort to develop scarce tin resources, the Russians have also been forced to penetrate far to the north, to Magadan *oblast* and the Yakut Autonomous Republic. Magadan *oblast* was the leading tin-producing region before the rise of the Solnechnyi complex in the south. The principal mines are the Valkumei lode mine and the Krasnoarmeiskii placer mine near Pevek, on the northern, Arctic Ocean coast, and Iultin, which is accessible by road from the port of Egvekinot, on the southern, Bering Sea coast. The Iultin ore reserves have been running down since mining operations began in 1959, and a new deposit, Svetlyi, is under development. Tin mining in the Iultin district also yields tungsten as a co-product. An older Magadan *oblast* tin mine, Galimyi, near Omsukchan, became depleted in the 1970s after more than 30 years of exploitation.

In the Yakut Autonomous Republic, early tin mining was focused on Ege-Khaya (Ese-Khaya), near Batagai on the Yana river, where a deposit first worked in 1941 became virtually depleted by the 1970s. The focus then shifted to the more isolated Deputatskii deposit, where tin placer operations had begun in 1951. Deputatskii offered prospects for a major tin-lode mine, but development of a deep shaft and concentrator, starting in the late 1970s, was slowed by difficulty of access. Deputatskii can be reached overland only seven months a year by a seasonal winter road, 150 miles long, from the Yana river landing of Ust-Kuiga. Light planes can use an airfield at Deputatskii, but heavy equipment for the project must be flown to the Tenkeli airport, 70 miles to the north. The lode mine and concentrator project started experimental test runs in 1986, although full-fledged production in the first stage of the project is likely to begin only later in the twelfth five-year plan.[34]

Compared with the virtual monopoly in tin production, Siberia makes a more marginal contribution to Soviet output of tungsten and molybdenum. The USSR is the world's leading producer of tungsten, and most of the production stems from mines in association with molybdenum in the Caucasus, in Kazakhstan and in Central Asia. In Siberia, tungsten is associated both with tin, as at Iultin in Magadan *oblast*, and with molybdenum, as at Zakamensk in the Buryat Autonomous Republic. A major tungsten mine was also developed in the late 1970s and early 1980s at Vostok, in north-west Maritime *krai*, where the mining settlement of Vostok received urban status in 1980. Molybdenum, in which the USSR ranks third (after the United States and Chile), is also obtained mainly outside Siberia, either in association with tungsten, as at Tyrny-Auz in the Caucasus, or in association with copper, as in the Kadzharan district of Armenia and the Balkhash area of Kazakhstan. In Siberia, the main molybdenum mine is at Sorsk, in southern Krasnoyarsk *krai*.

Gold

As in the case of tin, Siberia long had a virtual monopoly in gold mining, with the focus shifting gradually from the Transbaikal region (at Balei and Darasun) to the Aldan district in the 1920s, the Kolyma district in the 1930s and the Chukchi Peninsula of north-easternmost Siberia in the 1960s.[35] Since that time, major gold-mining operations have also been started outside Siberia, notably the lode mines at Zarafshan (opened in 1969) and Mardzhanbulak (1980) in Uzbekistan, and the Zod mine of Armenia, opened in 1976.

In Siberia, the general trend has been from readily accessible stream-gravel deposits in placer mines to the development of large, deep lode mines from which gold can be recovered only through complex milling and treatment. In Magadan *oblast*, for example, the gold resources of the Kolyma district were long exploited by simple manual panning of stream gravels, especially during the forced-labour period from the mid-1930s to the mid-1950s. Since then, large placer mines have been increasingly worked by mechanical dredges and production has shifted to the exploitation of deep lode deposits. The Polyarnyi lode mine and concentrator opened in 1969 on the Arctic Ocean coast, 60 miles to the west of the settlement of Mys Shmidta (Cape Schmidt). In Magadan *oblast* proper, the Karamken complex began production in 1978[36] and the Dukat complex, near Omsukchan, in 1980.[37] Gold is, of course, used for its monetary value rather than as a metallic commodity, and the USSR, as the world's second largest gold producer (after South Africa), relies on its gold reserves mainly for adjusting its balance of payments, selling gold in the West when additional convertible currency is required.

Non-metallic minerals

Siberia also makes significant contributions to the Soviet economy in some non-metallic minerals, again with a virtual monopoly position in diamonds (from Yakutia), boron (from Dalnegorsk in Maritime *krai*) and lithium (from Chita *oblast*). Significant shares of national output are also provided by Siberia in fluorspar as well as mica and asbestos.

The most significant of these developments from the point of view of exports has probably been the discovery of diamonds in western Yakutia, placing the Soviet Union in the front rank of the world's diamond producers and exporters.[38] Although precise figures are not available, diamonds appear to represent the Soviet Union's third largest earner of foreign exchange, after crude oil and refined products, and natural gas. Both gem diamonds and industrial stones are marketed through the London-based DeBeers organisation, so that an estimated 70 to 80 per cent of the diamonds figure in trade with Britain. The discovery of diamonds in western Yakutia in the mid-1950s first gave rise to the development of the Mir (Peace) kimberlite pipe, as diamond-bearing deposits are known, with the associated new town of Mirnyi receiving the urban status of city in 1959. In the 1960s two additional diamond centres were developed 250 miles further north, astride the Arctic Circle, Aikhal and the more important Udachnyi. The Udachnyi open pit, by then excavated to a depth of around 200 metres, was in the news in December 1985 when the Soviet Union's largest cargo plane, the An-124, flew in a giant Canadian-made Euclid mining truck for testing under the winter temperatures of 40° below zero that are common in that area. Udachnyi has no year-round overland access, and much of the heavy equipment used in the diamond operation must be flown in.[39]

Siberia is a major source of exotic materials with modern nuclear and aerospace applications such as boron, lithium and the associated beryllium. The world's principal source of boron minerals is the open-pit mine of Boron and the underground brines of Seales Lake, both in the Mojave Desert of southern California. In the 1960s, however, the Soviet Union was able to develop its own major source near Dalnegorsk. In contrast to borax (sodium borate), which is the major mineral in California, the Soviet Union derives its boron from datolite, a calcium borosilicate, which is not commercially used elsewhere in the world. By 1980, a work-force of 6,400 was employed in the Soviet boron operation.[40]

Little is known about lithium and beryllium production in Siberia, except that development began in the 1950s in connection with the growing interest in lithium and beryllium for use in nuclear energy and aerospace applications. Chita *oblast* was then described as the leading Soviet source of lithium, which is often associated with beryllium. Among the probable production centres are the mining settlements of Klichka, founded in 1952, and Kadaya, founded in 1958.[41]

Even more secrecy surrounds the mining of uranium, in which Siberia also makes a significant contribution. Uranium mines are not publicly identified by the Soviet Union, but indirect indications suggest the existence of at least two producing centres — Vikhorevka, west of Bratsk, and the new town of Krasnokamensk, in Chita *oblast*. Krasnokamensk appears to be particularly important; it was officially given city status in 1969, and had a population of 65,000 in early 1985.[42]

Asbestos is a traditional export of the Soviet Union, and Siberia has had a stake in the industry since the development of the Ak-Dovurak deposit in the Tuva Autonomous Republic in 1964. Tuva asbestos is considered particularly valuable because of its long, spinning-grade fibres, although its output of more than 100,000 tons is only a fraction of the Soviet Union's total asbestos production, estimated at more than 2.5m metric tons. However, prospects for the development of a second major Siberian asbestos deposit have been delayed because of the postponement of resource development along the Baikal-Amur Mainline. The construction of the BAM provides access to the

Molodezhnyi asbestos deposit in the northern Buryat Autonomous Republic. Molodezhnyi asbestos is also attractive because of its long textile-grade fibres, but its development will have to await the construction of a 20-mile rail spur from Taksimo station on the BAM.[43]

A belated start is to be made during the twelfth five-year plan to develop Siberia's chemical fertilizer potential. Although several possible sources of phosphatic fertilizer have long been known in Siberia, none had been developed and the region was entirely dependent on long hauls from other parts of the Soviet Union. Similarly, in the case of nitrogenous fertilizers, which use natural gas as a raw material, Siberian production was far below needs despite the abundant availability of natural gas. The twelfth five-year plan apparently intends to improve the situation, both by initiating the development of the first phosphate deposit in Siberia and by expanding nitrogen fertilizer capacity. The proposed source of phosphatic fertilizer is the Seligdar apatite deposit in the Aldan-Timpton interfluve south-west of the town of Aldan.[44] Although the Seligdar apatite is of low grade, containing six per cent of the nutrient P_2O_5 compared with 15 per cent in the apatite mines of the Kola Peninsula, it appears to be amenable to beneficiation to a 35 per cent concentrate, with potential byproduct recovery of fluorine and rare earths of the cerium group. The development of Seligdar is to be made possible by the construction of the railway running north of Yakutsk, which will pass close to the deposit. The decision to proceed with Seligdar development suggests that plans to develop another phosphatic deposit, the apatite of Oshurkovo, have been shelved. The Oshurkovo site, on the northern outskirts of Ulan-Ude, the Buryat capital on the Trans-Siberian Railway, had been better studied and is more accessible; but it is situated on the Selenga river, which flows into Lake Baikal, and there had been concern over water pollution.

The twelfth five-year plan has also announced the construction of two nitrogenous fertilizer plants, to be known as the West Siberian and the Altai plants. The Altai plant is expected to be associated with the coal-chemical centre of Zarinsk, deriving its hydrogen requirements from coke gases. (Hydrogen and nitrogen, recovered from the air, are the two basic ingredients of nitrogenous fertilizer.) The West Siberian plant, for which no location has been identified, is expected to use natural gas as a source of hydrogen.[45]

A third nitrogen fertilizer project, though not officially listed in the current five-year plan, has been started in the Soviet Far East. Ground for a new town associated with the project was broken in early 1986, north-east of Komsomolsk on the right bank of the Amur river, just downstream from the village of Nizhnetambovskoe. The nitrogen fertilizer factory in the new town, as yet unnamed, will be using natural gas brought in by the new Sakhalin-Komsomolsk pipeline, which came into operation in 1987.[46]

The three new plants are expected to enhance Siberia's position in nitrogen fertilizer production, which has been limited to factories in Kemerovo (Kuznetsk Basin) and Angarsk (Irkutsk *oblast*), accounting for only six or seven per cent of Soviet output of this type of chemical fertilizer.

TIMBER AND FURS

It remains to discuss two traditional Siberian resources other than minerals, namely timber and furs. Siberia has accounted for a growing share of Soviet timber production as logging activity has shifted from the older forest-industry areas of northern European Russia to the virgin woodlands of Siberia. However, the utilisation of the cut timber, or roundwood, has long been unsophisticated and at a rather primitive level, with too great a share of roundwood being consumed in unprocessed form or by industries using simple mechanical processes (sawmilling, railway sleepers). In recent years, Soviet planners have indicated increasing interest in emulating the advanced industrial nations of Western Europe and North America in making more intensive use of available roundwood for conversion into processed wood products such as pulp, paper, paperboard, plywood, fibreboard and particleboard. In 1975, the last year for which detailed regional statistics on logging operations were made public by the Soviet Union, Siberia accounted for 34 per cent of the national timber cut, or 135m out of 395m cubic metres. Of the Siberian cut, 81 per cent was commercial roundwood (usable as sawtimber, pulpwood, pitprops, etc.) and 19 per cent was fuelwood. Also in that year, the Siberian share of Soviet sawnwood was only 28 per cent, suggesting that a substantial share of the round timber was used locally, or even shipped to destinations outside Siberia, without any processing. A more detailed regional analysis shows that shipments of unprocessed roundwood were particularly large in the westernmost and easternmost parts of the Siberian timber lands, close to the domestic markets of European Russia or to the export markets of the Pacific Basin. Roundwood shipments were less significant for some of the major logging areas of central Siberia, in Irkutsk *oblast* and Krasnoyarsk *krai* far from markets. In these interior logging regions, the volume of sawnwood represented 27 per cent (Krasnoyarsk *krai*) and 23.7 per cent (Irkutsk *oblast*) of the timber cut, compared with a Soviet national average of 29.4 per cent. However, the yield of sawnwood was much lower in the extreme eastern and western logging regions of Siberia: 16.4 per cent in Khabarovsk *krai* and only 14.9 per cent in Tyumen *oblast*.

The suppression of regional logging statistics since 1975 makes it difficult to assess the extent to which the Soviet wood industry has been successful in making more effective use of Siberian timber by increasing the yield of processed wood products and reducing the heavy transport cost of hauling unprocessed roundwood over long distances to markets. On the one hand, total logging volume in the USSR has declined since the 1975 peak of 395m cubic metres, and was down to 368m in 1984. On the other hand, the Siberian share of Soviet sawnwood was up to 32 per cent in 1984 (from 28 per cent in 1975), suggesting that shipments of unprocessed roundwood have decreased.

Logging operations in Siberia have been spearheaded by the construction of special logging rail lines running north from the Trans-Siberian Railway. In Tyumen *oblast*, new commercial timberlands were opened up in the late 1950s and in the 1960s by the construction of railways running from Ivdel in the northern Urals to Sergino on the lower Ob, and from Tavda north to Mezhdurechenskii on the Konda river. In Tomsk *oblast* in the 1960s, a rail spur was driven northwards form Asino to Belyi Yar to provide access to timberlands in the interfluve between the Chulym and Ket rivers. In Krasnoyarsk *krai* the Achinsk-Lesosibirsk railway provided access to the area of the Yenisei-Angara confluence, and the spur running northward from Nizhnyaya Poima (Reshoty station), on the Trans-Siberian, toward Boguchany, on the Angara, opened up timberlands along the boundary between Krasnoyarsk *krai* and Irkutsk *oblast*. Within Irkutsk *oblast* itself, the largest timber producer, the key rail project was the line from Taishet through Bratsk to Ust-Kut on the river Lena, eventually forming the initial segment of the

Baikal-Amur Mainline. Finally, in Khabarovsk *krai*, a logging railway running north from Komsomolsk to the Amgun river eventually became the easternmost segment of the BAM.

With regard to processed wood products, Siberia's contribution depends largely on the determining locational factors. Large pulp mills require extensive resources of timber and abundant water and electric power, and some of the largest Soviet enterprises of this type have been located in Siberia, notably the Bratsk and Ust-Ilimsk mills. As a result, Siberia accounts for about one-quarter of Soviet pulp production. Paper, on the other hand, tends to be more market-oriented, and Siberian paper mills, mainly in Sakhalin and Krasnoyarsk, contribute only four per cent of national output. Paperboard, on the other hand, tends to gravitate more towards raw material sources, and the Siberian share is about 18 per cent.

Furs, a traditional product of Siberia, continue to be obtained by professional hunters and trappers, although the significance of furs in Soviet exports has become negligible, and fur-farming has assumed an increasingly important role, as has recreational hunting. The administrative structure of the hunting economy tends to be fairly complex, with state enterprises under the jurisdiction of the Main Hunting Administration of the RSFSR, and co-operative enterprises under the Russian Republic's Consumer Union. Of the 97 state enterprises (as of 1979, the last year of detailed regional data), 80 were in Siberia, and of the 122 co-operatives, 97 were in Siberia, indicating the dominant role played by that region. Characteristic fur animals of Siberia's forests are the sable, squirrel, muskrat, with the Arctic fox a typical object of hunting in the northern tundra. The most common problem hindering efficient management of fur resources is the uneven distribution of hunting activity. Fur-bearing animals near accessible transport corridors such as rivers and railways tend to be overhunted, while in more remote back-country a number of species may exceed the carrying capacity of the land.

CONCLUSION

There is no doubt that in view of Siberia's vast resource potential, it will continue to play a key role as a purveyor of raw materials to the Soviet economy, particularly in fuels and electric power as well as in a number of strategic metals, diamonds, gold and so forth. However, there is an indication that the relative weight of the Siberian contribution to Soviet economic power may be declining since Mikhail Gorbachev took office in 1985.

In keeping with a worldwide trend, the use of energy and industrial raw materials is expected to play a decreasing role in relation to the output of finished goods as a result of modernisation, growing productivity of existing plant and equipment, and a variety of energy- and resource-saving techniques such as recycling and byproduct use. As the Kremlin focuses its economic development effort on the manufacturing potential of the developed western (European) regions of the Soviet Union under what has been labelled a policy of 'intensification', there is likely to be less investment in the 'extensive' approach to economic development in the eastern regions. Fewer large new regional development projects may be started in the environmentally hostile Siberian realm as the Soviet planners count on more rapid recoupment of outlays from modernisation and expansion of the existing industrial potential, largely concentrated west of the Urals.

Siberia may thus be entering yet another stage in the changing grand strategy of Soviet economic development as prestige shifts from ever more development of natural resources to the refinements that have been increasingly shaping the modern world economy — synthetic materials, nuclear energy, electronics and computers.

NOTES AND REFERENCES

1. Theodore Shabad, 'Siberian resource development in the Soviet period' in Theodore Shabad and Victor L. Mote, *Gateway to Siberian resources (the BAM)* (Wiley, New York, 1977), pp. 1–61.
2. 'Basic guidelines for the economic and social development of the USSR in 1986–1990 and in the period to the year 2000', *Ekonomicheskaya gazeta*, no. 46, 1985, pp. 3–15.
3. *Pravda*, 17 Dec. 1985.
4. Theodore Shabad, 'Geographic aspects of the new Soviet five-year plan, 1986-90', *Soviet Geography*, vol. 27, no. 1 (1986), p. 3.
5. 'News notes', *Soviet Geography*, vol. 26, no. 6 (1985), pp. 496–8.
6. Shabad, 'Geographic aspects', p. 8.
7. *Gudok*, 31 Dec. 1985.
8. Shabad, 'Geographic aspects', pp. 8, 12–13.
9. *Ugolnye Basseiny Sibiri* (Nedra, Moscow, 1985), p. 65.

10. Shabad, 'Geographic aspects', p. 5.
11. B. V. Robinson, 'Economic-geographic assessment of oil resources in East Siberia and the Yakut ASSR', *Soviet Geography*, vol. 26, no. 2 (1985), pp. 91–7.
12. Shabad, 'Geographic aspects', pp. 6–7.
13. Shabad, 'Geographic aspects', p. 3.
14. *Gudok*, 23 Oct. 1985; *Stroitelnaya gazeta*, 15 Feb. 1984.
15. 'News notes', *Soviet Geography*, vol. 26, no. 10 (1985), pp. 771–2.
16. 'News notes', *Soviet Geography*, vol. 23, no. 7 (1982), pp. 538–9.
17. Ibid.
18. 'News notes', *Soviet Geography*, vol. 27, no. 2 (1986), pp. 137–8
19. Shabad, 'Geographic aspects', p. 4; 'News notes', *Soviet Geography*, vol. 25, no. 4 (1984), pp. 289–90.
20. Shabad, 'Geographic aspects', p. 4; 'News Notes', *Soviet Geography*, vol. 24, no. 10 (1983), pp. 779–80.
21. Shabad, 'Geographic aspects', p. 4.
22. Ibid.
23. Ibid.
24. 'News notes', *Soviet Geography*, vol. 26, no. 10 (1985), pp. 762–7.
25. 'News notes', *Soviet Geography*, vol. 26, no. 1 (1985), pp. 62–4.
26. Andrew R. Bond, 'Economic development at Norilsk', *Soviet Geography*, vol. 25, no. 5 (1984), pp. 354–68.
27. *Ekonomicheskaya gazeta*, no. 4, 1986, p. 4; *Sotsialisticheskaya industriya*, 5 Jan. 1986.
28. 'News notes', *Soviet Geography*, vol. 21, no. 6 (1980), pp. 397–9.
29. Shabad, 'Geographic aspects', p. 12.
30. *Ekonomicheskaya gazeta*, no. 3, 1986, p. 7.
31. Central Intelligence Agency, *Handbook of Economic Statistics, 1985* (Washington, 1985), p. 158.
32. Central Intelligence Agency, *Soviet tin industry: recent developments and prospects through 1980* (Washington, 1977), pp. 7 and 14; 'News notes', *Soviet Geography*, vol. 18, no. 2 (1977), p. 134.
33. Raymond S. Mathieson, 'Kavalerovo tin-mining district', *Soviet Geography*, vol. 21, no. 2 (1980), pp. 107–10.
34. 'News notes', *Soviet Geography*, vol. 27, no. 10 (1986), p. 758; Shabad, 'Geographic aspects', pp. 14–15.
35. Michael Kaser, 'The Soviet gold-mining industry' in Robert G. Jensen, Theodore Shabad and Arthur W. Wright (eds), *Soviet natural resources in the world economy* University of Chicago Press, 1983), pp. 556–77.
36. 'News notes', *Soviet Geography*, vol. 21, no. 3 (1980), p. 185.
37. 'News notes', *Soviet Geography*, vol. 21, no. 5 (1980), pp. 323–4.
38. Theodore Shabad, 'The Soviet potential in natural resources: an overview' in Robert G. Jensen, Theodore Shabad and Arthur W. Wright (eds), *Soviet natural resources in the world economy* (University of Chicago Press, 1983), pp. 269–70.
39. *The New York Times* 13 Jan. 1986.

40. *Khimicheskaya promyshlennost*, no. 7, 1981; *Gornyi zhurnal*, no. 4, 1985.

41. Theodore Shabad, *Basic industrial resources of the USSR* (Columbia University Press, New York, 1969), pp. 265–6.

42. Leslie Dienes and Theodore Shabad, *The Soviet energy system* (Wiley, New York, 1979), p. 174.

43. Shabad 'The Soviet potential in natural resources' in Jensen, Shabad and Wright (eds), *Soviet natural resources*, pp. 268–9

44. Shabad, 'Geographic aspects', p. 13.

45. Ibid., p. 11.

46. 'News notes', *Soviet Geography*, vol. 26, no. 10 (1985), pp. 771–2.

4

The Siberian Oil and Gas Industry

David Wilson

The USSR is the world's largest producer of oil, gas and coal, and Siberia is the largest source within the USSR of these fuels. In 1984, the Soviet Union produced 612.6 million (m) tons of oil, of which 380m (62 per cent) came from Siberia and 587 billion cubic metres of gas, with Siberia yielding 329 billion or 56 per cent (one billion = one thousand million).

In fact, as a potential source of fuel and energy, Siberia is even more important than these figures suggest. It accounts for over 80 per cent of the country's potential oil reserves, 90 per cent of its gas and at least 90 per cent of its coal. There are known to be vast oil, gas and coal fields in East Siberia and the northern areas of the Far East so remote and inaccessible that their exploitation is unlikely to occur this century, but may nonetheless be feasible should the USSR ever face the energy crunch that some in the West have been predicting for many years.

Siberia now accounts for all the growth in Soviet primary fuel output, as well as making up for the declines experienced by other producing regions. Between 1975 and 1984, oil production has grown by 122m tons while output from Siberia has risen by 229m tons and that from the rest of the country has dropped by 107m tons. Similarly the rise in gas production of 298 billion cubic metres over the same period has been accompanied by an increase of 289 billion by Siberia.

The climate and geography of Siberia has made its development a truly daunting task. During the early 1960s, there were many in the USSR as well as in the West who doubted that large-scale exploitation of the West Siberian oil- and gasfields was possible. The climate is atrocious, with temperatures dropping to −60°C in the middle of the seventh-month winter, rising to 40°C in summer, transforming the frozen forest-tundra into an impassable swamp. Few people lived there from choice and the economic infrastructure had to be built virtually from scratch. Transport links had to be created with the outside world, power stations built and a huge programme to build housing and amenities implemented. It was conceivable that however much effort and expense the Soviets put into the region, it could turn out to be a gigantic disaster — a 'desperate gamble' as one US pundit called it. However, the development of the West Siberian oil and gas region, which accounts for almost all hydrocarbon production in Siberia, has been accomplished very rapidly since 1970 (Tables 4.1 and 4.2), and despite problems with oil production since September 1983, the output of both oil and gas is planned to continue growing until well into the twenty-first century.

The West Siberian Basin covers an area of 3.35m sq km, mostly in Tyumen *oblast*, but extending south-eastwards into Tomsk and Novosibirsk *oblasts*, eastwards into Krasnoyarsk *krai* and northwards into the Kara Sea. About 55 per cent of the region is potentially oil- and gas-bearing and a further 17 per cent marginally promising. Most of the oil is found in the Khanty-Mansiiskii Autonomous *okrug* of Tyumen *oblast*, while practically all of the gas is located 600 km to the north in the Yamalo-Nenetskii Autonomous *okrug*.

OUTPUT AND RESOURCES IN WEST SIBERIA

The West Siberian Basin is the world's largest known storehouse of hydrocarbons, with proved plus probable reserves of oil, gas and gas condensate amounting to an estimated 53 billion tce (tons of coal equivalent) in 1984. Oil was discovered in the Shaim field in 1960, but the deposits were small and a furious debate began over whether the region was worth exploiting, or, indeed, exploring further. Even when much larger fields were found 400–500 km to the east on the river Ob during the following eight years, the debate continued to rage; only after the discovery of the supergiant Samotlor field in 1968 did it subside. Samotlor was initially believed to have 2,000m tons of proved plus probable recoverable reserves, but the discovery of deeper payzones and outlying pools has since raised this figure to 3,500m tons. The USSR has not published data on oil reserves since 1938, but West

Table 4.1: Oil production in the USSR, 1970–1990 (millions of tons)

	1970	1975	1980	1983	1984	1985[a]	1990[b]
USSR	353	491	603	616	613	595	630–640
of which: SIBERIA	34	151	317	372	380	376	458–468
Tyumen *oblast*	28	143	303	357	365	360	440–450
Tomsk *oblast*	3	5	11	12	12	13	15
Sakhalin	3	3	3	3	3	3	3
Rest of USSR	319	340	286	244	233	219	172

Table 4.2: Gas production in the USSR, 1970–1990 (billions of cubic metres)

	1970	1975	1980	1983	1984	1985[a]	1990[b]
USSR	194	289	436	536	587	640	830–850
of which: SIBERIA	11	40	158	284	329	373	
Tyumen *oblast*[c]	10	38	156	281	326	369	
Yakutsk ASSR	0	1	1	1	1	1	
Sakhalin	1	1	1	2	2	3	
Rest of USSR	187	249	277	252	258	267	

Notes: a. Anticipated.
b. Five-year plan target.
c. Includes 4 bn cu m/yr produced in Krasnoyarsk *krai*.

Figure 4.1: Western Siberia oil- and gasfields

Siberian reserves can be estimated at about 9,000m tons, slowly rising from year to year despite annual output rates approaching 400m tons.

Reporting to the Communist Party's Central Committee in June 1985, the head of the Ministry of Geology's local organisation in Tyumen *oblast*, *Glavtyumengeologiya*, confirmed that (contrary to some Western assertions) oil reserves were rising when he said that 'so as to maintain the rates of increase of oil and gas reserves and provide for the continuous growth in the level of extraction, a sharp increase in the volume of drilling is required'. Nevertheless, despite the growth in reserves, rapidly rising output has caused the reserve-to-production ratio to fall steadily to less than 24 in 1984. This is little more than the 23 for the USSR as a whole, which is estimated to have 14 billion tons of oil, and means that Tyumen *oblast* is fast losing one of its most important advantages over the USSR's other oilfields, a factor noted by Mikhail Gorbachev during his September 1985 visit to the region.

The big gasfields of Tyumen *oblast* were discovered during the period 1965 to 1970. They included the world's largest deposit, Urengoi, with reserves now thought to exceed 10,000 billion cubic metres as well as other giant deposits, such as those at Medvezhe, Yamburg and Zapolyarnoe. During the early 1970s, more giant deposits were found on the Yamal Peninsula, including Bovanenkovsk, Arkticheskoe and Kharasavei. Data on gas reserves are published sporadically in the Soviet Union and the most recent indications are that Tyumen *oblast* has 34,000 billion cubic metres from a Soviet total of 42,000 billion.

For exploration purposes, the basin is divided into 31 zones. Work has been concentrated in twelve zones and hydrocarbons have been found in eleven of them. By far the most important are the Middle Ob zone, containing most of the major oil deposits, the Nadym-Pur zone, which includes the two biggest producing gas deposits of Urengoi and Medvezhe as well as Yamburg, and the South Yamal zone on the Yamal Peninsula, where some very large gas deposits and one major oil deposit, Novoportovsk, have been found. By 1980, 273 oil and gas deposits had been found in the West Siberian Basin.

Exploration work is undertaken by *Glavtyumengeologiya*, which administers 28 oil and gas exploration expeditions grouped into six associations. Two of these are responsible for searching the Yamalo-Nenetskii region and the other four are charged with exploring the oilfields of the Khanty-Mansiiskii region. Exploratory drilling for oil and gas rose rapidly from 533,000 metres in 1977 (9.7 per cent of the national total) to 1,037,000 in 1980 (17.5 per cent) and 1.6m metres (24.7 per cent) in 1983. The five-year plan target for 1981–5 of 10m metres (with 7m in the Khanty-Mansiiskii region and 3m in Yamalo-Nenetskii region) has been badly underfulfilled with only 7.4m likely to have been drilled. However the Ministry of Geology, which is responsible for practically all exploration work in West Siberia (although only 55 per cent nationally), has defended its policy to continue drilling nearly 2m metres a year in the rest of the USSR on two grounds. Firstly, much of its non-Tyumen effort is concentrated on highly promising areas in Kazakhstan and the Komi republic where large oil and gas finds are anticipated; and secondly, it claims to have confirmed sufficient reserves in Tyumen *oblast* to justify earlier hopes for eventual production levels of 500m tons per year. Despite the poor drilling record, its main association on the oilfields, *Obneftegazgeologiya*, passed its 1981–5 five-year-plan target for new oil reserves in May 1985, implying an overfulfilment of perhaps 14 per cent, and found 30 new oil deposits.[1] Many of these deposits, located on the burgeoning new Noyabrsk oilfield, are large and it is from this field, straddling the Khanty-Mansiiskii border with the Yamalo-Nenetskii region, that most of the increase in oil production planned for 1986 to 1990 will come.

The Tyumen oil workers are not as sanguine about the reserve position as the explorationists. Of the 200 significant oil deposits, a quarter are now being worked;[2] they contain over 70 per cent of the region's proved plus probable reserves and for production to continue rising, large numbers of small deposits, often at great distances from the existing infrastructure, must be worked. Gorbachev took the opportunity afforded by his much-publicised visit in September 1985 to criticise the Ministry of Geology. While accepting the complaints of the explorationists about poor quality equipment, particularly in the field of large capacity computers, and a grave housing shortage, he called on the Ministry to accelerate the rate of wildcat drilling. Too much effort has been put into appraisal drilling at established deposits at the expense of wildcatting in the more remote areas. In particular, work on the Krasnoleninsk Arch has been going slowly, and the exploration of the deep-lying Palaeozoic strata where large accumulations of oil are anticipated has hardly begun. While the USSR is expected to accomplish a 40 per cent increase in exploratory footage from 1986 to 1990 compared with 1981 to 1985 (implying the drilling of 25m metres), West Siberia is planned to achieve an increase of 90 per cent to 14m metres over the period.

Oil

The production of oil is administered by the *Tomskneft* Association in Tomsk *oblast* (producing nearly 13m tons in 1985) and *Glavtyumenneftegaz* Association in Tyumen *oblast* (360m tons). The five-year plan target for 1985 was 399m tons, of which Tomsk was expected to produce 14m tons and Tyumen 385m tons, but output is likely to have fallen 26m tons short. *Glavtyumenneftegaz* consists of six associations, based on the Nizhnevartovsk, Surgut, Yugansk, Noyabrsk, Krasnoleninsk and Varyegansk oilfields. The most important of these is *Nizhnevartovskneftegaz* which, after reaching 213m tons per year in 1982, declined to 203m tons in 1984 as a result of production problems at the supergiant Samotlor. Samotlor reached its projected peak output of 155m tons per year in 1980 and surpassed a cumulative output of 1,000m tons in July 1981 when it was claimed that the next 1,000m tons would take only six years to produce.[3] It was thus anticipated that production by the deposit would rise to as much as 170m tons per year but in the event it has declined to 145m in 1984 and possibly 135m tons in 1985. One problem has been the large size of *Nizhnevartovskneftegaz* and the attendant administrative difficulties. Consequently, the Varyegansk deposits were detached in 1985 and henceforth administered by a new association, *Varyeganskneft*.[4] Another group of deposits, centred on Pokachevo and Urevsk, has also been detached and placed under the direct jurisdiction of the *Tatneft* Association of the Tatar republic, which sends in crews of oilmen on tours of duty to work it.

The Surgut field produced 49m tons in 1980,[5] and output probably passed 70m tons in 1984. The largest deposit, Fedorovsk, was said to have peaked in 1982 at 36.5m tons,[6] but production is still increasing because of the timely conversion of 1,000 wells to gaslift and because of the use of new techniques for extracting oil beneath substantial gas caps. A string of smaller deposits stretching away into the swamps north and west of Surgut is being developed, including significant producers such as Yaunlorsk, Lyantor and Bystrinsk, and it is likely that the Surgut field will eventually be producing over 100m tons per year.

The Yugansk field, administered from the town of Nefteyugansk, produced 45.8m tons in 1980 and nearly 71m tons in 1985. Output rose partly because of the transfer of some deposits from the old *Shaimneft* Association, dismembered in 1983, but also because of continuing growth at the giant Mamontovo deposit which was previously thought to have peaked at 26.4m tons per year in 1981.[7] Between 1981 and 1985, the planned output by the field of 285m tons was exceeded by 11.8m, most of it coming from Mamontovo.[8] Between 1986 and 1990, the Yugansk field plans to produce 337m tons, an increase of 40m over 1981 to 1985.

The Noyabrsk field was detached from the *Surgutneftegaz* Association in 1981 and the *Noyabrskneftegaz* Association was set up to administer it. It initially consisted of the Kholmogorsk deposit, but with the commissioning of Karamovsk, Muravlen-kovsk, Sutorminsk and several other deposits, output has grown to 19m tons in 1984 although the 1985 target of 36 to 40m tons was missed by a wide margin. Muravlenkovsk was expected to produce 10m tons in 1985, even though its 1984 plan of 5m tons was badly underfulfilled. The Kogalymsk group of deposits has also been lagging badly despite the mass influx of tour-of-duty workers from the Bashkir republic and its 1985 target of 13m tons[9] will have been missed by a wide margin.

When the Shaim field was split up, its western part was incor-porated into a new association, *Krasnoleninskneft*, based at Nyagan and charged with developing new deposits on the Krasnoleninsk Arch. There have been considerable difficulties due to underfunding, and only 9m tons were produced in 1984.

In September 1983, West Siberia began producing below target, and this situation continued to the time of writing (January 1986). Of the likely 26m tons shortfall in 1985, about half will be claimed by Samotlor and the other half by new deposits which should have been commissioned at regular intervals between 1981 and 1985. More than half of these, 15 out of 27, came on-stream during 1985, and then from only a handful of wells at each deposit. The problems at Samotlor and at the new deposits are very different, but both stem from the same cause —

the failure to allot sufficient capital investment to the region. In 1983, the Soviet oil extraction sector received 9.1 billion rubles of capital investment while producing oil worth 98.8 billion rubles at world market prices. In 1984, investment in the West Siberian oilfields actually declined when a steep rise was required, and the substantial increase in 1985 was barely sufficient to get output moving upwards again in October of that year. Consequently, the 1986 Annual Plan anticipated a huge increase of 31 per cent in the Soviet oil extraction sector while industrial investment as a whole grows by only 8.2 per cent to 164 billion rubles.

Between 1981 and 1985, it was planned to drill 77m metres of development wells in West Siberia[10] from a national total of 130m metres, with 25,000 wells to be drilled from a planned national total of 56,000.[11] A further 3m metres of appraisal drilling was to be carried out, making an overall task for the drilling directorates of *Glavtyumenneftegaz* of 80m metres. During the first four years of the period, however, only 52.6m metres of development footage was achieved, including 15.7m in 1984[12] and the five-year plan target was clearly out of reach. Nonetheless, an average annual increase of 18.7 per cent was obtained during the period 1981 to 1984.

During his September 1985 visit to the Tyumen oilfields, Mikhail Gorbachev accused *Glavtyumenneftegaz* of attempting to meet its drilling targets by concentrating its effort at the long-established deposits where conditions were easiest. *Nizhnevar-tovskneftegaz*, for example, has fulfilled its drilling target at Samotlor ahead of schedule at the expense of drilling at the Varyegansk, Pokachevo and Urevsk deposits. It has been suggested that the most prolific reservoirs of Samotlor have been overworked,[13] and this assertion has been repeated by a number of Western observers. Overworking a deposit means drilling more than the optimal number of wells (i.e. creating a denser well-network) so as to achieve a faster oil output in the short term while suffering a lower output-to-investment ratio and (possibly) a lower recovery rate in the long term. There is no evidence that this has happened at Samotlor with the planned 64-hectare well density maintained at the biggest reservoirs. The well-drilling programme has been speeded up with the planned number of wells achieved ahead of schedule, leading to the premature ageing of the deposit. This is not necessarily a bad thing if the conversion of wells to pumping and gaslift is also achieved ahead of schedule, and the provision of well-servicing and repair increases at the same rate as the stock of wells. But they have not, and consequently the development programme at Samotlor has been seriously violated.[14] The head of a local oil industry research institute claims that as long ago as 1978 he warned a deputy minister that the installation of secondary recovery equipment at Samotlor was falling behind schedule, but was ignored. By May 1985, the installation of gaslift and waterflood systems was said to be four years behind schedule with little more than one-third the planned number of wells converted to gaslift and 2,000 wells idle awaiting repair, the installation of pumping equipment or handover from drillers to production directorates.

Samotlor's gaslift project was particularly urgent because of the high salt content of some reservoirs, with salt corrosion reducing the inter-repair period of electric submersible pumps to 60 days compared with the 400 days achieved at the low-salt Yugansk field and 310 in West Siberia as a whole. The first stage of the project involving the conversion of 1,500 wells with 14 compressor stations and 1,000 km of gas pipeline was to have been completed by 1983,[15] and it was planned that with the completion of the second stage in 1985, Samotlor would have 3,804 gaslift wells, yielding 50m tons per year. The first compressor station became operational two years behind schedule in 1983,[16] and by May 1985 only 1,376 wells had been converted.[17] By contrast, the creation of a gaslift system at Fedorovsk deposit on the Surgut field has been accomplished on schedule with 1,000 wells converted by 1985. Their average daily yield subsequently increased by 50 per cent.

One advantage of gaslift is that it is a very reliable method, seldom breaking down and requiring little servicing. There is currently a severe shortage of well repair crews in West Siberia. At the beginning of 1984, the shortfall amounted to more than 100 crews, partly due to an underestimate of the breakdown-rate of wells in extremely cold conditions where cementing is more difficult to accomplish than in the temperate climes, and partly because of the large size of some associations and the resulting organisational difficulties. It is necessary to decentralise decision-making and to restructure production crews for all-round capability rather than narrow specialisation. An experiment was carried out at *Tsekh* no. 7 of *Belozerneft* NGDU (Oil and Gas Production Directorate) which works part of Samotlor in the summer of 1984 after the increasing number of idle wells awaiting repair caused output to plummet. All the necessary oilfield services were located directly in the area worked by *Tsekh* no. 7 including four well repair crews, which were previously ensconced in Nizhnevartovsk and had to be called in over a distance of 70 km to carry out repairs. The repair crews were placed under the direct jurisdiction of the NGDU whereas they had previously been answerable to their own department of *Nizhnevartovskneftegaz* Association, and this meant that unsatisfactory work could now be penalised immediately. Hitherto, the only recourse open to *Belozerneft* in the event of a bad repair job was to send a telegram of complaint (with foreseeable consequences) to *Nizhnevartovskneftegaz*. By the end of 1984, West Siberia had 2,000 wells idle awaiting repair from a total of 28,000. While the USSR has one repair crew per 54 wells, *Glavtyumenneftegaz* has one per 68, with one per 85 wells on the Surgut field. This compares with one per 27 wells on the Azerbaidzhan oilfield. If the organisational reform carried out at *Belozerneft Tsekh* no. 7 were repeated throughout the West Siberian oilfield, it is claimed that the productivity of the repair men would rise sufficiently to outweigh the perceived shortage of 100 crews.

Even the drillers, traditionally the most highly praised workers in the oil industry, have come under criticism in recent years. They are supposed to oversee the testing of a well and be responsible for it until it is handed over to the NGDU when it is ready for operation. The drillers are paid according to footage drilled (a scheme introduced in the Tatar republic in 1979 to relate pay to the volume of oil produced from newly drilled wells has not been implemented in Siberia because of the huge difference in well yields at different deposits) and once the well has been drilled, the drillers have no further interest in it. Consequently, testing is delayed and repairs to the defects revealed by the tests take weeks to carry out. By June 1984, 2,464 newly drilled wells were awaiting commissioning, i.e. eight per drilling crew. The Surgut field had nine wells per crew and Nizhnevartovsk eleven awaiting handover to the NGDUs. The Yugansk field, on the other hand, had only three per crew despite a doubling of the well stock between 1981 and 1985, a further testimony to the competent administration of the field by *Yuganskneftegaz* under R. Kuzovatkin. If all outstanding test and repair work were completed, West Siberia would have an additional 4,500 operational oil wells, an increase of about 15 per cent on the number functioning at the end of 1985.

Delays in the installation of pumping equipment have been sharply criticised by the Soviet leadership, despite the volume of oil obtained from pumped wells rising from 112m tons to 265m during the four years 1980 to 1984. The installation of pumps at the Varyegansk deposit, for example, has proceeded painfully slowly; although the deposit has been producing oil at its projected level, only 27 per cent of the planned assembly work was achieved in 1984. This means that existing pumps are overworked without the necessary stand-downs for routine servicing which makes them less reliable and more susceptible to breakdown. At the Yugansk field, on the other hand, the installation of pumps and the creation of water supply and cleaning networks was accomplished 'strategically' according to *Izvestiya*. During the five years 1981 to 1985, 4,200 wells were converted from free-flowing to pumping, mainly with electric submersible pumps,[18] which account for about half the field's output, and 77.5 per cent of all wells are now mechanised. The inter-repair period for wells with electric pumps rose from 244 to 400 days over the five years and is planned to reach 430 in 1986[19] and 450 in 1990.

Between 1981 and 1985, 27 new deposits were planned to commence production. By the beginning of 1985, only 14 had been commissioned and although oil began flowing at a further 15 during 1985 (thereby overfulfilling the plan by two deposits), the scale of development has been quite inadequate. This is partly because of the shortfall in drilling, with only 91 per cent of the footage target achieved, and partly because of the failure to accomplish the necessary infrastructural oilfield installation work at the new deposits.

The drilling target for the 1986 to 1990 period is 130m metres,[20] which compares with 123m drilled between 1964 (when oil production began in West Siberia) and the end of 1985. Part of the 85.5 per cent increase to be obtained between 1986 and 1990, compared with 1981 to 1985, will result from faster drilling speeds, particularly by those crews which are currently drilling less than the norm. While many crews drill over 100,000 metres a year (including all seven belonging to the Surgut no. 2 Directorate of Drilling Work led by G. Levin) compared with an average for West Siberia of 50,000,[21] 20 per cent of all crews drill less than 30,000 metres a year and a substantial improvement in annual footage is expected from these crews. The *Yugansknef-tegaz* Association, for example, aims to follow a 31 per cent improvement in drilling crew productivity from 1981 to 1985 by achieving a further 10,000–15,000 metres a year per crew by 1990.[22]

A big rise in the number of drill crews must be achieved by 1990. At the beginning of 1984, there were 308 crews in Tyumen *oblast* of which 175 consisted of workers permanently domiciled in the region and 133 were tour-of-duty crews flown in for two-week or ten-day shifts from other regions in the USSR, mainly in the Urals and Volga regions. Tour-of-duty crews are more likely to operate at the remoter deposits, and in 1983 managed an average 45,200 metres while the local Tyumen crews drilled an average 50,900 metres. It is likely that an average 70,000 metres a year can be achieved by 1990, suggesting that the total number of crews is planned to reach 460. Perhaps 260 of these will be local and 200 working tours-of-duty, and the responsibility of workers from the European oilfields for developing new deposits in West Siberia will become greater.

Drilling has not been the main problem at some of the more rapidly expanding oilfields, partly because many of the newly worked deposits are shallower and can therefore be drilled more rapidly. The Yugansk field, for example, slightly over-fulfilled its 1981–5 drilling target by completing 4,800 wells of total footage 13.2m metres.[23] This compares with 2,000 wells and 6.3m metres between 1976 and 1980. The drilling speed increased by 46 per cent, partly because the average well depth declined from 3,150 metres to only 2,750. The Noyabrsk field also overfulfilled its drilling target of 5m metres between 1981 and 1985,[24] although the average well-yield was much lower than planned because too much effort was put into existing low-yield deposits while insufficient drilling was accomplished at the more productive deposits at great distances from Noyabrsk.

The principal reason for the delays in the development of the newer fields is the slow progress in fitting them out. This involves the construction of oil treatment plants (which clean the oil of water and sand prior to transportation), oil-gathering pipelines (which collect the oil from the artificial islands on which the clusters of wellhead gear are located and despatch it to the deposit's storage tanks), storage-tank farms, oilfield pumping stations (which pump the oil along the gathering pipelines) and water-pumping stations for the waterflood systems. Delays in building infrastructural and auxiliary objects such as tour-of-duty settlements, roads, power lines, boilerhouses, water-cleaning plants for the waterflood system and so on are even more notorious.

During 1985, particular attention was paid to oilfield construction work. During the first nine months, six oil preparation plants each with a capacity of 3.5m tons per year, were built at the Severo-Varyegan, Talinsk, Kholmogorsk, Trekhozernoe, Sutorminsk and Fedorovsk deposits. Some 28 oil-pumping stations, of total capacity 63.6m tons per year of mixed oil and water, 28 water-pumping stations of total capacity 77.7m tons per year of water, 430,000 cubic metres of storage tanks, 2,750 km of oil-gathering pipeline and 730 km of electricity transmission line were built, and the plan for construction work was considerably overfulfilled.[25] Twelve new deposits were commissioned: Vostochnyi Surgut, Lor Yegansk, Pogrannichnyi, Permyakovsk, Novogodnoe, Yershonoe, Khokhryakovsk, Novo-Purpeisk, Barsukovsk, Zapadno-Solkinsk, Tarasovsk and Novoportovsk. At Novoportovsk, on the Yamal Peninsula, test production began in October 1985.[26] Located 15 km inland of Novyi Port, it will be developed by 400 workers living in the Yamalsk tour-of-duty settlement, and belongs to the Ministry of Gas's *Nadymgazprom* Association. The oil will be shipped out by tanker, although its high paraffin content is raising problems requiring further study.

In 1986, it was hoped that an increase of 38 per cent in the construction of new oil-pumping stations and 60 per cent for new water-pumping stations could be achieved. A further 16 new deposits are to be brought on-stream, including the large Orekhovo-Yermakovsk on the south bank of the river Ob, opposite Nizhnevartovsk, and they are expected to have provided 9m tons of oil in 1986.[27] The Ministry of Construction of Oil and Gas Enterprises will spend 40 billion rubles between 1986 and 1990, half of it in West Siberia according to its deputy minister, V. Kuramin.

Condensate

Gas condensate was first discovered in West Siberia in 1964 at Novoportovsk on the Yamal Peninsula.[28] Now, dozens of deposits have been found, of which the biggest is Urengoi with more than 20 productive horizons. Only the highest horizon at Urengoi, in the Senomanian suite, has been exploited for gas; it contains very little condensate which is found mainly in the Valanginian suite at a depth of 2,500 to 3,000 metres and occurs as deep as 3,500 metres.[29] More than 85 per cent of Urengoi condensate is found in the Valanginian, and there is said to be enough to maintain a high level of output for many years.

Condensate production was supposed to begin in 1983 at Urengoi.[30] In May 1982 the drilling of the first well began, and it was planned that 4m tons should be produced in 1985. There have however been delays for a number of reasons. The drilling of wells is difficult, partly because of their comparatively great depth of 3,000 metres (gas wells are only 1,200 metres deep) and partly because a definite correlation must be maintained between temperature and pressure. With a small deviation, the condensate can change form and be irretrievably lost. Special equipment is needed to avoid this, and although by September 1983 ten wells had been drilled from the 40 needed to produce 4m tons per year, it was said that the drillers were having a hard enough time meeting targets for gas wells without having to drill wells to 3,000 metres.[31]

The construction of a wellhead stabilisation plant began only in the summer of 1983[32] and the commissioning date of 1985 was not met. Eventually, there will be four of these plants at Urengoi. The construction of a 755 km pipeline to Surgut began in March 1984, and it was built at breakneck speed for completion in November of the same year.[33] Its diameter of 720 mm suggests an eventual throughput of 20m tons per year.

At Surgut, the condensate is refined into petrol, diesel and kerosene at a 3.5m tons per year refinery. However it is planned to pump some of the products into the Surgut-Polotsk crude oil pipeline, and this decision has been sharply criticised at a time when Urengoi suffers from periodic shortages of diesel. There is a small condensate refinery at Urengoi which processes 12,000 tons per year and covers 20 per cent of local diesel requirements. The Surgut refinery will be gradually extended over the period to the year 2000 to perhaps 20m tons per year.

The first stage of the production facility at Urengoi officially started up in April 1985, with the condensate refined into motor fuel at the Urengoi refinery.[34] During the first week of 1986 the Surgut refinery began operating, transforming condensate into diesel. Other recent discoveries of condensate have occurred at Utrennyi on the western coast of the Gyda Peninsula,

Zapolyarnyi gasfield at a depth of 3,360 metres, Verkhne-Chaselsk and in the far north of the Yamal Peninsula.

Gas

The development of the gasfields is proceeding in stages. The first important stage involved the working of Medvezhe deposit from the nearby town of Nadym. This was completed in 1977 when Medvezhe reached its design capacity of 65 billion cubic metres, although output has been running at 74 billion per year since 1982. Medvezhe initially had 1,550 billion cubic metres of reserves and should be starting to decline during the late 1980s. The second stage began in 1978 when Vyngapur, which reached its design capacity of 20 billion cubic metres per year in 1980, and Urengoi began producing. Urengoi was initially planned to peak at 100 billion cubic metres a year, but this has been periodically raised to 250 billion in 1985, and output may even go higher to perhaps 300 billion by 1990. The Urengoi deposit covers an area of 167 km from north to south and 35 km from east to west,[35] and has as many as ten payzones[36] between 1,000 and 4,000 metres deep.[37] Its surveyed reserves were put at 7,500 billion cubic metres in 1980, although the General Director of the *Urengoigazodobycha* Directorate has claimed that they exceed 10,000 billion.[38] During the period 1981 to 1985, 955 wells were to be drilled at Urengoi, with a total meterage of 1.24m metres, out of 1,200 gas wells planned for West Siberia as a whole.[39]

In the past, development work has been plagued with problems, mainly infra-structural in nature, and plan targets were underfulfilled every year until 1982 when the 117 billion cubic metres target was met. In 1984, 204 billion were produced, and the 1985 target of 250 billion cubic metres will have been overfulfilled by at least 9 billion. However the over-fulfilment of plan targets has been achieved by concentrating on drilling the most productive reservoirs, and there have been complaints from some local officials that the optimal development strategy for Urengoi has been violated. Targets for the drilling of wells, laying of gasfield pipelines and gas treatment plants have been consistently underfulfilled. There were supposed to be 15 treatment plants by the end of 1985, but the eleventh was only completed in October 1985. The Russians have tried to compensate for the slow progress in building treatment plants by

111

raising their capacity. The plants at Medvezhe were designed to handle 7 billion cubic metres per year,[40] while the first seven at Urengoi were of 15 billion each and the last four are of 20 billion.

The third stage will be the development of Yamburg, 250 km to the north of Urengoi in a continuous permafrost zone on the Taz Peninsula. It is generally thought to be smaller than Urengoi with 7,500 billion cubic metres of reserves, although some reports suggest that it may turn out to be just as big.[41] Development of the deposit began in 1983 when the first production well was drilled,[42] and production began in 1984 when gas began flowing to a gas turbine power station. Commercial exploitation is to begin in 1986 with the completion of the first Yamburg-Yelets pipeline, scheduled for February 1986, although the capacity of Yamburg will not be sufficient to fill the pipeline and it will initially be fed with gas from the no. 11 treatment plant at Urengoi. A pipeline has been built from the plant, 70 km north of Novyi Urengoi, to Yamburg for this purpose. During the 1986–90 planning period, a further six intercontinental gas pipelines will be built to carry Yamburg gas westwards to the European USSR and Eastern Europe.[43] By 1990, Yamburg's output is planned to reach 200 billion cubic metres per year and the production of gas condensate is tentatively planned to begin in 1989.[44]

The large gas deposits on the Yamal Peninsula will not be worked until the early 1990s unless the oilfields found at Novoportovsk and in the Nurmin mega-arch prove to be the precursors of much bigger finds of oil anticipated in the Sredne-Yamal Arch. In this case, the development of the Yamal Peninsula could begin quite soon.

Small amounts (22 billion cubic metres in 1984 and slightly more in 1985) of casinghead gas are produced from the Middle Ob oilfields. It is stripped of valuable liquids in gas refineries at Nizhnevartovsk, Surgut, Lokosovo and Belozernyi. About 9 billion cubic metres of the dry gas was burned by the Surgut no. 1 and no. 2 power stations in 1985 while the rest flows down a pipeline to the Kuzbass. A much larger output is anticipated at oil deposits with very high gas factors, held in conservation until the capacity of Surgut no. 2 is extended beyond the 1,600 mw (megawatts) operational at the end of 1985.

DRILLING

Drilling wells into the swamps of West Siberia has required the creation of essentially new technology. Artificial islands must be created, usually by dredging sand from the bottom of lakes and rivers. This is comparatively cheap, costing an average of 44 rubles per square metre compared with the erection of platforms on tubular driven piles (107 rubles) and screwed piles (220), but sand often has to be brought over considerable distances; time rather than cost is the principal constraint. Experiments have been carried out using insulation materials which maintain the frozen state of the ground during the summer. The method is reliable and cheap and is to be widely introduced.

Rigs mounted on artificial islands must drill a number of inclined wells, usually 24 on the oilfields and six on the northern gasfields where the depth of the producing reservoir is not so great. At some of the very deep oilfields, such as Sutorminsk, up to 80 wells can be drilled from one island while maintaining a typical 64-hectare penetration density (i.e. wells 800 metres apart) in the reservoir. The most common rigs in West Siberia are those designed for cluster drilling, such as the Uralmash 3000-EUK from Sverdlovsk and the Barrikady BU-125 from Volgograd. The rigs are divided into two parts; a stationary part which includes pumps, mud tanks and the power source etc., and a mobile part which moves from one inclined well to another (the well heads are usually three metres apart) on rails, and which consists of the derrick, rotary table and drawworks.

POPULATION AND URBAN DEVELOPMENT

When the geologists first came to the West Siberian oil and gas basin, it was uninhabited apart from small numbers of forestry workers, fishermen and fur-trappers. For a number of years, a debate took place concerning the best way to develop the region. Comprehensive development, with all the required workers actually living on the oil- and gasfields together with the necessary services and facilities, would be immensely expensive with no guarantee that the workers would stay there. On the other hand a tour-of-duty system would by itself clearly be inadequate. Consequently, a strategy was drawn up, based on a hierarchical structure of settlements.

113

There are four levels of settlement. The first consists of the 'mainland', i.e. the rest of Tyumen *oblast*, including the cities of Tyumen and Tobolsk, and some cities and regions beyond the *oblast*'s borders. These are assigned the tasks of providing technical and engineering support, delivering agricultural produce to the oil- and gasfields and fulfilling the educational and scientific requirements. Although hydrocarbons are not produced within 550 km of Tyumen city, it has grown rapidly as a direct consequence of the oil and gas industry with a technical university educating oil workers, many administrative organisations having offices there, and more than 70,000 workers employed in hundreds of engineering factories making equipment for the sector. In 1959, it had only 150,000 people, but it expanded to 269,000 in 1970 and 411,000 in 1984. The ancient city of Tobolsk had 72,000 people in 1984 compared with 36,000 in 1959.

The second level consists of the leading cities on the oil- and gasfields — Surgut, Nizhnevartovsk, Nefteyugansk, Noyabrsk, Urai, Novyi Urengoi and Nadym, plus Strezhevoe in Tomsk *oblast*. They have been elaborately developed with a full range of services and amenities, and a balanced population of men and women. Their functions are both production-oriented and administrative, and contain the sub-divisional offices of the various ministries and organisations working in the region. The third level consists of permanent towns and settlements inhabited by workers involved directly in the exploration, production and transportation of oil and gas. Services and facilities are rather limited and most workers are single men who have come to West Siberia for a limited period to earn high wages and bonuses before returning to the 'mainland'. Finally, the fourth level consists of tour-of-duty settlements composed of hostels with a very limited range of facilities and a constantly changing population.

Between 1970 and 1982, the two major cities of Surgut and Nizhnevartovsk accounted for 40.6 per cent of the region's increase in population, but this share fell to only 25.8 per cent between 1982 and 1984, and although they will continue to grow, other towns such as Noyabrsk are expanding more rapidly. It is hoped, rather optimistically, that many of the problems which arose at Surgut and Nizhnevartovsk can be avoided when the *genplan* (general plan) for other cities is drawn up. Surgut, for example, was promoted to city status in 1965 and the construction of prefabricated blocks of five-storey flats began immediately. However the *genplan*, elaborated by the Moscow *Giprogor* institute, was not confirmed until 1970 and for its first five years of urban status, Surgut developed in an unplanned way. Perhaps because of this, the *Giprogor* plan became obsolete by the mid-1970s and in 1979 a new plan was presented by a Leningrad institute.[45] This foresaw the population rising to 175,000 by 1985, but it has been growing much more rapidly to over 200,000 by the beginning of 1985, leading to an unforeseen strain on housing and amenities. In some areas of the city, such as the neighbourhood of the Central Tank Farm, people are still living in *vagonchiki* (caravans) with no facilities, not even shops, and an unreliable heating system.[46] The Leningrad plan envisages 300,000 people living in 18 neighbourhoods of five- and nine-storey blocks by the end of the century with a range of amenities comparable to that of a very large city. The cost is enormous, amounting to well over the 450m rubles a year anticipated by the *genplan*, partly because construction costs are much higher with thick wall-insulation and triple glazing in the flats, and partly because the standard of construction needs to be much higher than in the rest of the country (the flats are ten per cent larger, for example) in order to attract and retain residents.

Because of the planning confusion, Surgut has grown up with some glaring deficiencies. All flats are provided with central heating from boilers, mostly local rather than centralised, burning fuel-oil imported from the Omsk refinery. This is expensive, polluting and unreliable, while the Surgut power station ejects great volumes of heat into the atmosphere through its cooling towers. This is an extraordinary situation for the country with the world's most advanced combined heat-and-power (CHP) sector, and only in 1982 was the first CHP set installed at the power station with hot water sent through pipes to the houses in the adjacent neighbourhood.

By contrast with Surgut, Nizhnevartovsk is growing slightly more slowly than expected. With a population of 178,000 at the beginning of 1984, the forecast of 200,000 by 1985[47] proved unfounded. The *genplan* makes provision for 350,000 people by the year 2000 because although Samotlor has reached its projected peak, Nizhnevartovsk will serve as a centre for a number of third-level towns such as Megion, Langepas and Raduzhnyi.

Nefteyugansk became a city in 1967 but its *genplan* was only completed in 1979. It envisages a population of 100,000 by the end of the century, but the city is growing faster than planned, having gained 21,000 between 1980 and 1984 to reach a population of 72,000.

Noyabrsk is a very new town, with construction starting in 1976 and urban status achieved in 1982.[48] It is unusual in that it has never experienced any transport problems because it is located less than 10 km from the Surgut-Urengoi railway, and was therefore able to grow extremely rapidly. Originally, there were to be two towns, Noyabrsk and Khanto, 14 km to the north, but these have been merged as the projected population of the region grows. As the centre of a new oilfield and an existing gasfield (based on the Vyngapur deposit which began producing in 1978), Noyabrsk has attracted a plethora of ministries and departments, all intent on building housing for their own workers. As the headquarters of the *Kholmogorneft* Directorate and the *Noyabrskneftegaz* Association, Noyabrsk is greatly influenced by the Ministry of Oil but also has sub-divisions of the Ministry of Gas, Geology, Transport Construction, Communications, Electricity, and Oil and Gas Construction. The result is several temporary settlements located at distances of up to 10 km from each other, and a mass of low-capacity facilities — for example, there are more than 40 small boilerhouses, 20 bakeries, ten communications centres and several small power stations. In addition, there are also sizeable settlements on the Vyngapur and Muravlenkovsk deposits, with the latter having more than 6,000 people. Consequently Noyabrsk is growing in a completely unco-ordinated, haphazard way, quite contrary to planners' intentions. The problem here is typical of Soviet urban planning: conflicts between urban planners and industrial ministries are generally resolved in favour of the latter, particularly when the town is still small and its administration is not very powerful. This is precisely the sort of problem that *Gosplan*'s Interdepartmental Commission for the West Siberian Oil and Gas Complex should be able to overcome, although it does not seem to have had much success at Noyabrsk.

Novyi Urengoi, the capital of the northern gasfields, consisted largely of temporary wooden housing and caravans until 1979 when the first permanent flats were completed. Although a *genplan* was created in good time by *Giprogor* in 1974 (the gasfield did not begin producing until 1978), numerous upward revisions of the size of gas reserves and projected peak output levels had led to successive *genplans* being scrapped. The first saw an eventual population of only 30,000, the second (1979) raised it to 70,000 and then to 100,000. In 1979, the LenNIIEP institute of Leningrad was given responsibility for planning, but complaints were made that 18 months later its presence still had not been felt.[49] The *genplan* finally arrived in early 1982 when the city had only 240,000 square metres of permanent housing, sufficient for only 15,000 people of a total population of over 30,000 and the number of people living in caravans was still growing rapidly. It is planned that Novyi Urengoi should have 100,000 inhabitants by the end of 1985[50] compared with 55,000 two years earlier and an eventual population of 160,000.[51]

At Strezhevoe, a *genplan* has been drawn up which foresees a population of 60,000 by the end of the century. Plans for several other towns have been completed, including Nyagan, Tikhii, Kogalym, Pyt Yakh (Mamontovo) and Khokhryakovsk. Nyagan, formerly known as Nyakh, is located on the Serov-Serginskii railway and became the capital of the Krasnoleninsk oilfield with the completion of a 100-km road to the Krasnoleninsk Central Tank Farm. It is designed to have an eventual population of 60,000. Tikhii is located near the old Urengoi settlement on the Surgut-Novyi Urengoi railway, where a large power station is being built, and will eventually house 150,000 people.[52] Kogalym, 130 km north-east of Surgut on the railway to Novyi Urengoi, is being built by Baltic construction workers and is likely to grow to a considerable size in view of the decision to create a combine manufacturing prefabricated housing and a factory making concrete sections. A town for 60,000 inhabitants is being built at Langepas for the workers of the giant Urevsk deposit and in all it was planned that twelve new settlements (some reports say 15) with eventual populations varying between 20,000 and 80,000 should be started on the oil- and gasfields between 1980 and 1985.[53] These will all be concerned with the production of fuel as the settlements arising at pumping and compressor stations on pipelines tend to be much smaller.

Although a great deal of criticism has been levelled at the provision of housing and facilities, the construction organisations have actually managed to cope with their plans. It is the plans which have fallen short of requirements, and it has been claimed that between 1981 and 1984 'hundreds of thousands of square metres' of housing had been under-supplied. During this period, more than 9m square metres of housing were built, together with schools for 74,000 children and kindergartens for 47,000, and the eleventh five-year-plan target of 11–12m square metres for 1981–85, compared with 6.5m actually built over the preceeding five years,[54] will certainly have been fulfilled. Of the total, 2m square metres was to be built on the northern gasfields, although the target at Yamburg is not being met. The construction of housing and amenities was expected to cost 4 billion rubles between 1981 and 1985 compared with 1.5 billion from 1975 to 1980, and the sheer size of the construction programme is encouraging planners to re-evaluate the advantages of the tour-of-duty method of developing remote regions.

Few new large towns will be built. One will be at the existing village of Krasnoselkupsk, 1,500 km from Tyumen, where a very large oil deposit has been discovered. Others will include Arkticheskii and Bovanenkovsk on the Yamal Peninsula, which will be built to complement the existing settlements of Yar Sale and Mys Kammenyi according to a complex scheme for habitation of the peninsula devised by the Leningrad Research Institute of Civil Engineering.[55] Otherwise many more tour-of-duty settlements will be built to serve remote deposits, and on the Nizhnevartovsk field alone there are now 42 such settlements with places for 17,000 workers. However some tour-of-duty settlements become unofficially promoted to permanent settlements. On the Surgut oilfield, for example, there are 15 of these which remain unregistered and therefore unable to claim funds for more facilities or even acquire regular bus service to the nearest big town.

The size of the construction materials sector on the oil and gas fields is inadequate. Although it produces 900,000 metres of pre-stressed concrete sections per year, 180,000 cubic metres of construction gravel and 960,000 square metres of insulation panels per year, it covers only 45 per cent of the need for concrete sections. Despite the large timber industry in Tyumen *oblast*, only 26 per cent of the necessary joinery products are made locally.[56]

However, rapid expansion is taking place. A second stage of the Kharp construction base was built in 1985 and plans for 1990 foresee the annual output from Kharp of one million cubic metres of concrete sections per year. The Surgut, Nadym, Urengoi and Tyumen housebuilding combines are to be extended with improved housing designs. Between 1986 and

1990 it is planned that the volume of new housing should amount to a 60 per cent increase over the previous five years, suggesting that 20m square metres are to be built. This implies an increase in the population of the oil and gas regions of at least one million on top of the 1.5m people resident at the end of 1985.

TRANSPORT AND SUPPLY

Until 1975, equipment for the oilfields was delivered by river, either down the Ob from Novosibirsk or down the Irtysh from Omsk. The gasfields were supplied by sea to Novoportovsk where freight was transhipped to riverboats for delivery to Nadym. From here it was sent by rail to Pangody and then hauled by crawler to Urengoi. The rivers in Tyumen *oblast* are ice-free for only five months of the year and freight has to be stored until the ground freezes in winter before it can be hauled to its destination.

Railways

The railway connecting the oil- and gasfields with the Trans-Siberian Railway at Tyumen reached Surgut in 1975 and 18 months later had arrived at Nizhnevartovsk. In November 1976, work began on extending the line northwards to Novyi Urengoi which was completed in 1982. Regular traffic to Novyi Urengoi began in November 1985[57] with most freight for the Urengoi gasfield unloaded at the Farafontevskaya station, and the 712-km line is making an immense contribution to the development of Urengoi and the Noyabrsk oilfield. It will permit other large accumulations of oil and gas (in the Tarko Sale area for example) to be opened up very quickly. Work is now progressing on the stretch between Novyi Urengoi and Salekhard, thereby closing the circle and permitting freight for the gasfields to be railed from two directions.

The railway is also being extended 234 km northwards from Novyi Urengoi to Yamburg. Construction began in October 1984,[58] and the completion date is February 1986. Eventually, this extension will carry 3m tons of freight per year to Yamburg, compared with the 1m tons originally envisaged when a debate raged over whether the line was necessary. Between 1986 and

119

1990, a 530-km line will be built from Labytnangi to Kharasavei on the Yamal Peninsula, with a branch line to the Novoportovsk oil deposit. The line will run through, and permit the development of, giant deposits such as Arkticheskoe, Bovanenkovsk and Kharasavei. The construction of a railway line in such difficult geographical conditions is unprecedented, even in the USSR, and the Minister of Transport Construction, V. I. Brezhnev, says that there are no normative documents from which to draw up blueprints. There is practically no suitable ground for building roadbeds, with the soil either too salty or full of ice. Sand must be shipped in from hundreds of kilometres to the south, or penoplast and polymer insulation materials must be used to insulate the ground, thereby preserving its permafrost state.

Roads

Roadbuilding is difficult in the West Siberian swamps and costs about one million rubles per kilometre.[59] In the past, the swamp has been cut away and replaced by a roadbed of sand which frequently had to be brought over considerable distances. Recently, tests have shown that it is possible to compact the peat and build the road directly on top. The 1981–5 five-year-plan target of 2,000 km of hard-surface roads was almost fulfilled. These roads have a mainly local significance, connecting artificial islands within oil and gas deposits and linking the deposits with railway stations. Recent examples are the road from Nefteyugansk to Ostrovnaya station and Kholmogorsk to Noyabrsk. They were built with products from the new asphalt-concrete factories now operating at Nefteyugansk and Noyabrsk.[60] Until 1984, all roads in West Siberia were made of concrete, but they have fallen rapidly into disrepair due to the climate and asphalt-concrete roads should last longer. In 1985, another asphalt plant opened at Urengoi.

The biggest single problem at the Urengoi gasfield is the shortage of roads, and the delayed commissioning of gas treatment plants is said to be due to transportation difficulties. Development work is extending ever further away from Novyi Urengoi (the eleventh treatment plant is located 70 km north of the city, 20 km above the Arctic Circle) and road construction now has the highest priority. However, while the north-south road traversing the deposit is being built on schedule, those connecting it with the artificial islands are lagging very badly. In winter, so called 'corduroy roads' made of compacted snow held together with tree trunks are of crucial importance. They carried 350,000 tons of freight during the winter of 1983–4. Between 1986 and 1990, it is planned to build 5,000 km of all-weather roads (an increase of 150 per cent over the previous five years) including the vitally important 250-km road from Novyi Urengoi to Yamburg, and the Yamal Peninsula has been mentioned as an important destination for the builders of intra-field roads.

Waterways

Despite the growth of the rail and road network, the waterways will remain the principal means of getting freight into the region for many years yet. They currently carry 25m tons per year,[61] or 60 per cent of all freight destined for the oil- and gasfields. Although they can operate for only 150 to 180 days a year, they are much cheaper than road and rail, and have the added advantage that dredging the rivers for navigation purposes is also the principal source of sand for artificial islands. Accordingly, the Ministry of Inland Waterways has far greater importance in West Siberia than in most other parts of the USSR, and there is an extensive programme to build new ports and more wharves at existing ports. At Urengoi river port, for example a second stage was opened towards the end of 1984, and in 1985 it became an important transhipment centre with freight being sent on down small rivers to remote settlements.[62] The ports at Nadym and Nizhnevartovsk are also being expanded. The twelfth five-year plan calls for the construction of 3,270 metres of new river wharves (some reports say 4,000) from 1986 to 1990.

Paradoxically, fuel shortages are sometimes cited as a reason for the poor work of transport organisations. This is because petrol and diesel must be shipped in from Omsk during the summer months and distributed overland during the winter to fuel bases at the oil and gas deposits. Shortfalls in deliveries can result in fuel bases running dry without any immediate prospect of replenishment. Academician V. Koptyug, Vice-President of the Academy of Sciences, has called for the widespread introduction of plants able to convert gas condensate into motor fuel at the wellhead.[63]

Electricity

The western Siberian oil and gas complex has been dogged by electricity shortages since its inception. The 3,360 mw Surgut no. 1 power station is one of the largest in the USSR, but each of its 16 sets has been introduced behind, rather than ahead of, the growth in the demand for power, so the region has had to be assisted with electricity delivered from Refta power station in the Urals and from stations in the Kuzbass. Nevertheless, many settlements are still served only by small, unreliable and expensive diesel stations, and the power shortage continues.

Gosplan's Interdepartmental Commission has concluded that, until recently, the provision of electricity was five years behind schedule,[64] and its chairman has subsequently reiterated that if power stations had been built in good time, 'the oilfields would not be on starvation rations now'.[65] The Ministry of Electricity blames mistaken forecasts by its customers in Tyumen *oblast* for its failure to acquire sufficient generating capacity. Initially a demand for 28 twh (terawatt hours) was foreseen for 1985, although the actual requirement is likely to be nearer 40 twh,[66] while output by Surgut no. 1 power station was planned to grow from 17 twh in 1980 to 25.5 twh in 1985.[67] Samotlor tends to bear the brunt of the power cuts because it is one of the most distant deposits from Surgut power station and the Urals-Surgut power line, and the 500-kv (kilovolt) transmission line from Surgut only reached Samotlor in 1982.[68]

Throughout the West Siberian oilfield, 1,000 power cuts are said to have caused the loss of one million tons of oil in 1984.[69] However it is believed that the shortages of generating capacity will be overcome in the near future, and that the flow along the Refta-Surgut power line will be reversed as capacity at Surgut no.2 power station builds up. Destined to have six sets of 800 mw each, it will be the USSR's largest thermal power station when completed, and the construction of identical stations has begun at Nizhnevartovsk[70] and Tikhii (near Urengoi).[71] Another such station will be built at Nyagan for the Krasnoleninsk field.[72] Surgut no. 2, expected to cost 1,000m rubles was planned to start up in 1984, but was slightly delayed with the first set operational in March 1985[73] and the second the following November.[74]

Between 1986 and 1990, about 7,000 mw of capacity will be commissioned in Tyumen *oblast*, implying the completion of Surgut no. 2 station (four more sets of 800 mw each during 1986 and 1987), two sets of 800 mw each at the Nizhnevartovsk station and two more at Urengoi, plus a further 600 mw at other stations. The reliability of the power supply will be enhanced by the construction of a 500-kv line running for 950 km from the Itat sub-station via Tomsk to Nizhnevartovsk. More 500-kv lines are to be built in the region, including another alongside the existing line from Surgut via Noyabrsk and Tarko Sale to Novyi Urengoi, and 12,000 km of 110- and 220-kv lines are to be built to new oil and gas deposits. The volume of construction and assembly work is to rise by 120 per cent between 1986 and 1990 (over 1981–85) with work continuing at the above-mentioned power stations and construction work beginning at Nyagan. The oil- and gas fields will have a total electricity generating capacity of 24,600 mw when Nyagan is completed in 1996, and will be producing perhaps 150 twh per year or about seven per cent of total Soviet electricity output. The stations will burn casinghead or natural gas at an average rate of about 40 billion cubic metres per year.[75]

Pipelines

To transport the oil and gas from West Siberia to its customers, systems of large-diameter pipelines have been built, mostly in a westerly direction to the European USSR, with only one oil pipeline and one line carrying casinghead gas running towards the east. About 40m tons of Siberian oil a year is piped southwards to the Omsk and Pavlodar refineries, and on through a pipeline completed in 1983 to Chimkent where a new refinery started up in late 1984. An extension to Chardzhou is now under construction. The pipeline to Anzhero-Sudzhensk on the Trans-Siberian Pipeline also carries 40m tons per year, destined for the Achinsk and Angarsk refineries, and 3m tons of this is transhipped to the railways at Angarsk bound for the Khabarovsk refinery. During the 1970s, two major pipelines each of 90m tons capacity per year were built to the Volga region. The first was completed in 1973 and mostly supplies the refineries of the Volga region, and the second (completed in 1976) runs to Kuibyshev. From here, oil is distributed throughout the western USSR as far as Odessa and Novorossiisk on the Black Sea and Baku on the Caspian Sea. The next pipeline to be built was from Surgut to Polotsk in Belorussia, serving the Perm, Gorkii, Yaroslavl, Moscow, Ryazan, Novopolotsk and Mazheikyai refineries as well as supplying crude for export from Ventspils. Another pipeline has now been built, following the Surgut-Polotsk corridor as far as Klin, north of Moscow. It brings the total capacity of oil pipelines running out of West Siberia to nearly 450m tons per year, enough to handle the volume of output planned for 1990, and it is certain that work on another 90m tons per year pipeline will begin during the 1986 to 1990 period.

The gas pipeline construction programme has been much more extensive, as a gas line carries only 20 per cent as much fuel (in comparable calorific values) as an oil pipeline of the same diameter. Consequently, a large share of the Soviet pipeline effort now goes into building 1,420 mm diameter gas pipelines from West Siberia to the western USSR. There are currently 14 such lines in five corridors. A further 13 or so will be built during the rest of this century before West Siberian gas production peaks at about 800 billion cubic metres per year (from total national output of 1,000 billion per year). One of these, the first from Yamburg to Yelets, was scheduled to be completed by early 1986, and five more lines will be built from Yamburg to the western regions of the USSR between 1986 and 1990. In 1986, the construction begins of the 'Progress' pipeline, planned to run for 4,600 km from Yamburg to Uzhgorod along the Urengoi-Uzhgorod corridor. It will deliver 22 billion cubic metres per year to those East European countries which participate in its construction.

Building large diameter pipelines through swamps at extremely rapid rates (the Urengoi-Uzhgorod Export Pipeline, known in the West as the 'Yamal' or 'Siberian' pipeline, was built over a distance of 4,500 km in less than a year) has been possible only by the creation of some very effective Soviet technology. The *Styk* and *Sever* automatic welding machines, the TG-502 pipelayer, the ETR-254 trench excavator and the *Tyumen* swamp vehicle are just some examples of the sort of equipment which has enabled the USSR to lead the world in pipeline construction technology.

EAST SIBERIA AND THE FAR EAST

By comparison, the other oil- and gasfields in Siberia and the Far East are of little importance. The Yakutsk gasfields yield a little over one billion cubic metres per year, for the local needs of Yakutsk city and Mirnyi and the diamond and the precious metals mines of the region. However, in spite of interest shown by the USA and Japan during the period 1974 to 1978 in a long-term deal to develop the fields for the import of liquified natural gas via Vanino, it is unlikely that the reserves of 12,000 billion cubic metres will be exploited to any great extent this century.

Sakhalin island delivers 3m tons of oil per year through two pipelines which run across the Strait of Nevelskoi to Komsomolsk refinery on the mainland. It also yields a small amount of gas for local use, but gas output will rise substantially when a 600-km pipeline to Komsomolsk is completed. The line was started in 1984 for completion in 1986 and will carry 3 billion cubic metres per year. In 1971, a large offshore oilfield was discovered in the Odoptu structure, 40 km south-east of Okha. An agreement was signed with Japan to set up a joint company, *Sodeco*, to carry out exploration with Japanese technology and a rig was sent for this purpose. However, the results have been only mildly encouraging, and the project suffers periodically from Japanese participation in various US sanctions campaigns. Meanwhile, the Russians are steadily adding to the capacity of their Far Eastern Marine Oil Exploration Expedition, suggesting that they may be thinking of continuing exploratory work on their own. The expedition now has twelve ships and a semi-submersible rig, the *Okha*, and in 1984 obtained its first dynamically self-positioning exploration ship, the *Mikhail Mirchink*. Some of the *Neftegaz* class of rig supply ships made by Poland have been sent to Sakhalin. Numbers 6 and 28 have specially strengthened hulls designed for the iceberg-ridden seas off Sakhalin.

In the Krasnoyarsk and Irkutsk regions, large volumes of oil, gas, condensate and bitumen are thought to exist, and sporadic drilling has revealed significant reserves of all fuels. There are plans to begin the commercial exploitation of small oilfields on the Nepa Arch, and the area has been designated a Territorial Production Complex for this purpose, but the larger oilfields such as those in the Vanavara area are too remote to be developed while there are still huge reserves of oil awaiting development in the more accessible West Siberian Basin. One of the problems is that the geology of the eastern Siberian fields is quite different to that of western Siberia, and Academician Koptyug has called for the timely creation of the necessary

DAVID WILSON

equipment for the exploration and development of the eastern Siberian fields.[76]

CONCLUSION

There has been much confusion in the West concerning the intentions of Soviet planners for the long-term development of their oil industry. A leading American pundit, Robert Campbell, has claimed that 'the guidelines for the Soviet long-range energy plan make clear that the energy planners expect oil output to fall by the end of the 1980s', and also that 'an earlier study [also by Campbell — D. W.] concluded that energy consumption in 2000 would be more like 2,500m tce and the guidelines suggest a similar figure.'[77] In fact, however, the official long-range energy plan makes it quite clear that during its first stage, to 1990, 'the reliable energy supply for the economy will be provided by the maintenance of high levels of extraction of oil', and that 'the energy programme of the USSR foresees an *increase* in the extraction and production of liquid fuel over the extent of the entire period embraced by the programme.' Moreover, during the 1980s, 'there is planned the rapid increase of extraction of gas and oil in West Siberia'.[78] Nowhere does the programme suggest that oil production is planned to decline, and the twelfth five-year plan calls for a modest increase in output to 630–640m tons in 1990.[79] It can be estimated that Tyumen *oblast* must account for 440–450m tons of this, a significant increase over the 360m anticipated for 1985, and it is known that Tomsk *oblast* is planned to yield 15m tons per year by 1990.

Nowhere does the programme mention energy consumption in the year 2000 and it most certainly does not suggest that consumption will amount to a mere 2,500m tce as claimed by Campbell. On the contrary, energy consumption is planned to rise by 60 per cent over 1985 to as much as 3,500m tce,[80] with natural gas production planned to increase by 60 per cent to 1,000 billion cubic metres and the generation of nuclear power expected to rise by between five and seven times to as much as 1,200 twh compared with 170 twh in 1985. The implication is that oil production is expected to rise to perhaps 700m tons per year by the end of the century, as predicted by the present author in 1982.[81] West Siberia should be accounting for 500m tons of this total and numerous high-ranking Soviet officials have confirmed that oil production is planned to go on rising until well into the twenty-first century. As recently as November 1985, for example, the First Deputy Chairman of the Siberian division of the Academy of Sciences and Director of the Comprehensive Programme 'Siberia', Academician Trofimuk, stated that 'it can be claimed without reservation that not only in the twentieth century but also at the beginning of the twenty-first century, extraction will increase thanks to what lies beneath the West Siberian Plain'.

By the year 2000, the Middle Ob oilfields will be in decline, and production should be growing from the more northerly fields including Tarko-Sale, the Yamal Peninsula and the Kara Sea, particularly from the Palaeozoic strata. Work may well have started on exploiting the East Siberian fields, notably in the Lena-Anabar Trough on the northern coast, and the Nepa Arch 900 km north of Irkutsk. The vast Silgiri bitumen field is unlikely to merit attention unless a world-wide oil shortage raises prices sufficiently to justify the cost of overcoming the immense logistical problems. The twelfth five-year plan makes little reference to East Siberia, and it can be safely assumed that the 9 billion tons of proved plus probable reserves of oil in West Siberia will be sufficient to keep the USSR comfortably supplied with oil, both for its domestic market and for the export of perhaps 160m tons per year, for the foreseeable future.

POSTSCRIPT

In 1986, the decline in oil production of 1984 and 1985 was reversed, with output amounting to 614.8 mn tons. In November 1986, oil was pumped at a new Soviet (and world) record of over 12.48 mn b/d. The 1987 plan foresees another small increase to 617 mn t and the five year plan for 1990 has been finalised at 635 mn t. The problems experienced by the Tyumen oilfield between September 1983 and the end of 1985 have been largely overcome with an enormous increase in the installation of oilfield production facilities, an overfulfilled drilling programme and the commissioning of 19 new deposits. Output by the field rose by 23 mn t in 1986.

Gas production has surged ahead with 686 bn m^3 produced in 1986, 14 bn ahead of target. Western Siberia accounted for about 420 bn, and delays in the completion of the first 20 bn m^3/yr treatment plant at Yamburg meant that Urengoi had to be pushed to almost 300 bn m³ in 1986. Yamburg began pumping gas westwards in October 1986, and it will account for all the planned increase in Soviet output to 850 bn m³ in 1990. Despite much talk in the West of 'energy crises', Western Siberia looks set for a long period of stable growth in the production of oil and gas.

NOTES AND REFERENCES

1. *Pravda*, 21 May 1985.
2. *Izvestiya*, 27 June 1985.
3. *Pravda*, 28 July 1981.
4. *Izvestiya*, 1 Sept. 1985.
5. *Izvestiya*, 15 Oct. 1980.
6. *Pravda*, 11 Nov. 1982.
7. *Pravda*, 2 Nov. 1981.
8. *Ekonomicheskaya gazeta*, no. 46, 1985.
9. *Pravda*, 11 Feb. 1985.
10. *Neftyannoe khozyaistvo*, no. 3, 1982, p. 3.
11. *Ekonomicheskaya gazeta*, no. 14, 1981.
12. *Neftyannoe khozyaistvo*, no. 2, 1985, p. 11.
13. *Izvestiya*, 17 May 1985.
14. *Izvestiya*, 28 May 1984.
15. *Izvestiya*, 26 Aug. 1981.
16. *Izvestiya*, 23 Oct. 1983.
17. *Izvestiya*, 28 May 1985.
18. *Ekonomicheskaya gazeta*, no. 46, 1985.
19. *Ekonomicheskaya gazeta*, no. 38, 1985.
20. *Pravda*, 4 Nov. 1985
21. *Pravda*, 22 Sept. 1985.
22. *Ekonomicheskaya gazeta*, no. 46, 1985.
23. Ibid.
24. *Izvestiya*, 18 Sept. 1981.
25. *Ekonomicheskaya gazeta*, nos. 39 and 42, 1985.
26. *Izvestiya*, 21 Oct. 1985.
27. *Izvestiya*, 22 Nov. 1985.
28. *Izvestiya*, 9 Sept. 1983.
29. TASS, 4 Dec. 1981.
30. *Pravda*, 3 March 1982.
31. *Izvestiya*, 9 Sept. 1983.
32. *Pravda*, 25 Aug. 1985.
33. *Pravda*, 5 Nov. 1984.
34. *Pravda*, 29 Apr. 1985.
35. *Izvestiya*, 11 Dec. 1980.
36. TASS, 4 Dec. 1981.
37. Moscow Radio, 19 May 1982.
38. Moscow Radio, 9 Dec. 1980.

39. *Izvestiya*, 9 Feb. 1982.
40. *Izvestiya*, 3 Nov. 1982.
41. *Izvestiya*, 26 Aug. 1984.
42. *Izvestiya*, 14 Oct. 1983.
43. *Stroitelstvo truboprovodov*, no. 1, 1985.
44. *Izvestiya*, 26 Aug. 1984.
45. *Izvestiya*, 15 Jan. 1981.
46. *Izvestiya*, 3 Dec. 1984.
47. *Pravda*, 26 March 1982.
48. *Izvestiya*, 14 May 1982.
49. *Izvestiya*, 18 July 1981.
50. *Izvestiya*, 1 Feb. 1984.
51. *Ekonomicheskaya gazeta*, no. 9, 1984.
52. *Pravda*, 27 Nov. 1980.
53. *Izvestiya*, 28 April 1981.
54. *Izvestiya*, 18 July 1981.
55. *Izvestiya*, 14 June 1984.
56. *Stroitelstvo truboprovodov*, no. 10, 1984.
57. *Pravda*, 20 Nov. 1985.
58. *Pravda*, 15 Oct. 1984.
59. TASS, 28 July 1981.
60. *Izvestiya*, 31 July 1984.
61. TASS, 18 Oct. 1984.
62. Moscow Radio, 17 Oct. 1984.
63. *Izvestiya*, 20 Nov. 1985.
64. *Pravda*, 3 March 1982.
65. *Izvestiya*, 24 Feb. 1984.
66. *Pravda*, 21 Jan. 1983.
67. *Izvestiya*, 15 Oct. 1980.
68. *Pravda*, 15 April 1982.
69. *Izvestiya*, 7 Dec. 1984.
70. *Izvestiya*, 21 June 1983.
71. *Izvestiya*, 16 May 1982.
72. *Ekonomicheskaya gazeta*, no. 10, 1985.
73. *Pravda*, 11 March 1985.
74. *Izvestiya*, 20 Nov. 1985.
75. *Ekonomicheskaya gazeta*, no. 10, 1985.
76. *Izvestiya*, 20 Nov. 1985; a fuller account of the localities and characteristics of the East Siberian fields can be found in *Soviet energy to 2000* (Economist Intelligence Unit, 1986); see also David Wilson, 'Exploration for oil and gas in eastern Siberia', paper read at the conference on 'The Development of Siberia: Peoples and Human Resources', University of London, 7–10 April 1986.
77. *Soviet Geography*, September 1984.
78. *Ekonomicheskaya gazeta*, no. 12, 1984.
79. *Izvestiya*, 9 Nov. 1985.
80. Ibid.
81. David Wilson, *The demand for energy in the USSR* (Croom Helm, London, 1983).

5

Transport and Communications

Robert North

From the fur-trading era to the present, Siberian development has faced formidable transport problems. Many of these problems stem from the size and emptiness of the region. It is nearly 30 per cent larger in area than Canada, the world's second-biggest country, but has a population smaller than that of France. To cross Siberia from west to east takes five days by passenger train, and freight moving northwards from the railway by river may still need more than one navigation season to reach its destination.

The problems of size are compounded by those of severe natural conditions. North-western Siberia has thousands of square miles of swamp; the north-east has continuous permafrost and the coldest winters in the northern hemisphere; and the south-east, the site of the newly-built Baikal-Amur Railway (BAM) experiences frequent seismic activity. All of these problems raise construction and operating costs for all modes of transport: for example, permafrost, through alternate freezing and thawing, buckles roads, railways and airport runways if they are not built to demanding specifications. It also promotes quick runoff in hilly regions, so that rivers like the Lena experience rapid fluctuations in depth during the navigation season. Extreme cold in the north-east has disastrous effects on the metal, tyres and glass of ordinary vehicles; and construction costs in the BAM zone are three to four times the national average for a single-track railway and two to three times for an all-weather highway.[1]

In several respects the transport problems of Siberia are like those of Canada, but worse. The density of population is about one-third greater in Siberia, but the distribution is similar: most people live in large towns scattered along the southern border, leaving huge areas almost empty except for mines and forest-products operations. In both regions, therefore, transport links have to be maintained across vast stretches of territory which generate little or no traffic. In Siberia, however, the distances are greater and the climate is more severe. That is not to say that all is disadvantageous: both regions have large areas with gentle gradients and are fortunate, from the point of view of transport costs, in the linear distribution of the bulk of the population.

The comparison with Canada is of interest because the two countries have often chosen different ways to cope with similar situations. In one respect Siberia is better off: the rivers are much more useful than those of Canada for access to northern regions. For example; whereas Canada has a far greater length of railway, Siberian railways are more heavily used. In addition national policies differ in one particularly important respect: Canadian natural resources are exploited primarily in response to world market conditions, while Siberian resources are exploited in response to a national policy of maximum feasible self-sufficiency in strategic raw materials.

This chapter will discuss influences in the evolution of Siberian transport; attempt a regionalisation of the network; identify the main tasks of transportation; and examine some problem areas. The final section will discuss long-term prospects for transport in Siberia, returning for the purpose to the comparison with Canada.

FORMATIVE INFLUENCES

Throughout its history the Siberian transport system has been moulded by initiatives from outside the region. The present network strongly reflects the interests of successive national governments in St Petersburg and Moscow. National goals of recurring importance include:

(1) the utilisation of Siberian natural resources. This has usually involved their removal from the region, either raw or processed;
(2) the provision of a transit route to the Far East; and
(3) the ensuring of effective occupation, control and defence of the national territory.

Two further goals are important in Soviet times:

(4) The distribution of manufacturing industry, especially heavy industry, as widely as possible through the country, in order to promote a more rounded regional development, create 'proletarian bastions' in outlying regions, and ensure the dispersal of potential military targets; and

(5) The minimisation of investment in transport. The concept of using transport as a development leader has always been foreign to Soviet regional policy.

The requirements for resource extraction have been influential since long before the Bolshevik revolution. The needs of the fur trade, non-ferrous mining in the Altai mountains, and wheat and dairy farming all helped mould the transport systems of their day. In recent years, with coal, oil and natural gas the principal resources and their scale of production exceeding by orders of magnitude anything envisaged even three or four decades ago,[2] the requirements of resource extraction have dominated transport investment decisions.

During much of the pre-revolutionary era the desire for a route to the Far East ranked with or above that for access to Siberia itself. Even the Trans-Siberian Railway was originally conceived of as primarily a transit line. Elements in this concern included Russian imperial expansion around the Pacific Basin and, eventually, into the crumbling Chinese empire; the China tea trade; and most traumatically, the defeat by Japan in 1905, which was due in part to the slowness of the railway in moving military reinforcements eastwards. The railway was indeed designed as a transit line, but one suited to carry tea and silk rather than troops and their equipment. However, it was also located to serve the best agricultural land of western Siberia, the most attractive natural resource of the time. The first two objectives listed above, therefore, together produced the east-west axis across southern Siberia which has formed the backbone for all subsequent development. In Soviet times the Trans-Siberian Railway has functioned as a transit route in that it has provided an economic lifeline for the Soviet Far East. But foreign trade through Pacific ports has been and remains of minimal importance except for one development, to be discussed later: the container land-bridge.

Strategic considerations have always played a role in the development of the east-west transport axis, and recently in the duplication of the axis where it is most vulnerable, through the building of the BAM. However, they have also been an element in northern and maritime transport including the Northern Sea Route, which at least in its eastern section has never appeared to be commercially viable.

The goals of dispersing industry and economising on transport have together moulded the settlement pattern of southern Siberia. Until the era of pipeline building, most traffic moved along the east-west railways, and industry has been located mainly in large nodes along them. Like the transit theme, the idea of regionally polarised development has re-emerged in modern guise, in the form of the Territorial Production Complex (TPC).[3] A characteristic of widely-spaced nodal development is that it helps to preserve the advantages of rail over road transport. Those advantages are likely to be perpetuated as long as the TPC remains the preferred approach to planning.

A REGIONALISATION OF THE SIBERIAN TRANSPORT SYSTEM

As the preceding account suggests, the Siberian transport system can be divided into two major regions. A southern east-west belt of relatively continuous settlement (though as yet much less continuous in the east than in the west) is based on the east-west railways. The railways are paralleled in part by roads and pipelines, but they have been the principal form of transport throughout this century. Indeed, expansion of the belt to north and south has taken place and continues to take place primarily through the building of more railways parallel to the original Trans-Siberian: the South Siberian line west of the Kuzbass by 1959 and much of the Central Siberian by 1963[4], the Abakan-Taishet-River Lena line by 1965, and now the BAM. Other transport modes have also expanded, first in western Siberia, then further east, but neither roads nor pipelines yet offer a continuous east-west route east of Lake Baikal.

The southern belt extends westwards out of the region, widening as it crosses the Urals, though the railways through Chelyabinsk and Sverdlovsk take most traffic. In the east the main termini are the ports of Vladivostok, Nakhodka, Vostochnyi and Vanino. They handle three-quarters of the exports from the Soviet Far East, though nearly half their loadings are for domestic destinations along the Pacific and

Figure 5.1: Siberia and the Far East; major communications and transport routes

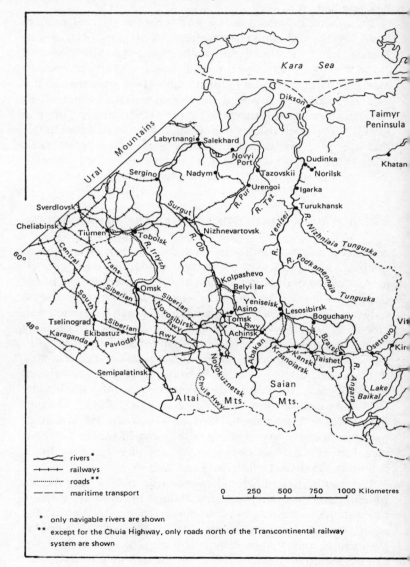

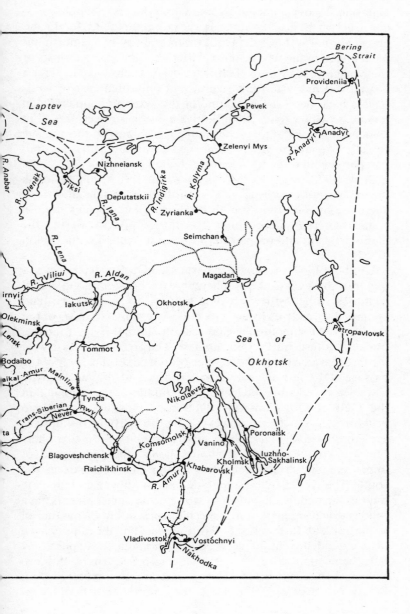

Arctic coasts.[5]

North of the east-west axis the transport network has evolved to facilitate resource exploitation. Raw or semi-processed materials move outwards, and producers' supplies — construction materials, machinery and equipment, food, and above all fuel — inwards. Until recently, most of the north has been linked in the first instance with either the east-west axis or the Northern Sea Route. Traffic for destinations outside Siberia has moved firstly north or south and only then east or west. Rivers have been the backbone of the system,[6] supplemented mainly by winter roads. So primitive a system subjects freight to frequent, costly and time-consuming transhipment: the average for all Siberian freight is about eight transhipments per ton, compared with three for the Soviet Union as a whole.[7]

Since 1970 this pattern of movements has begun to break down, but not everywhere. The northern zone falls into three subdivisions, differing in both the history and current state of transport. They approximate to the Ob-Irtysh Basin; the Yenisei Basin; and the northern Far East, including the Yakut ASSR.

Until the 1960s the northern part of the Ob-Irtysh Basin was a region to be bypassed. Its inherent attraction had disappeared centuries earlier with the exhaustion of the fur resource, and swampiness made its forest a secondary resource to those of the Urals, the Altai mountains and eastern Siberia. Even its attractions for transit traffic were limited. The rivers took east-west traffic so far north that the ice-free season could close before the passage of the current year's grain exports, and links north to the Kara Sea were hampered by poor conditions for transhipment in the Gulf of Ob. Consequently transport facilities remained primitive. In the 1960s, however, the discovery of oil and gas brought massive investment. Apart from one or two short railways built eastwards from the Urals, the first round of improvements strengthened ties to the east-west axis in the south. The river fleet was upgraded and a railway and pipeline built to the middle Ob oilfields. More recent developments have followed a different pattern, especially since attention has turned to the gasfields further north. River services and the railway have been extended from the south, but for bringing in supplies they have been supplemented by the Northern Sea Route. A more radical change is that natural resources are now exported from Siberia directly by pipeline across the central or northern Urals, rather than by either the east-west railway axis or the Northern Sea Route.[8]

Improvements to transport stimulated by oil and gas discoveries have made the forests more accessible. Wood comprises over half of river traffic, mostly brought to Tomsk, Novosibirsk and Omsk for transhipment to the railway. Mineral building materials account for one-quarter of traffic. Supplies for the north are transhipped from the railway at the same ports, plus Tobolsk and Labytnangi.[9]

The Yenisei offers much better access to ocean-going vessels. It has been closely linked to the Northern Sea Route since the 1930s, with lumber and mineral shipments from Igarka and Dudinka respectively. The former accounts for 14 per cent of Soviet lumber exports,[10] the latter sends copper-nickel ores and concentrates to the Kola Peninsula for smelting.[11] Shipments from Dudinka have increased greatly since about 1969, and the sea route is now kept open almost year-round. In the south, railways push northwards from the east-west axis to provide better access to commercial forests and hydroelectric dams than river transport can offer.

The northern Far East is more complex and can be further subdivided into an interior and a Pacific zone, overlapping in Magadan *oblast*. In the former the principal resources currently of interest to the outside world are gold, diamonds and tin. All generate only small volumes of export traffic after initial processing. By contrast with the rest of the northern zone, therefore, supplies moving in outweigh resources moving out by about six to one. Surface access is by the Northern Sea Route to the Arctic and Bering Strait coasts, linking with river transport inland; by sea to Magadan on the Sea of Okhotsk, linking with road transport inland; and from the east-west rail axis, either by river transport down the Lena or road from Never. Until the 1950s the first two routes were the most important, but since 1951, when the railway from Taishet, on the Trans-Siberian Railway, to Osetrovo on the Lena was completed, the Lena route has taken the great bulk of traffic. In 1980 it handled about 85 per cent of regional imports, or 3.2m tons.[12] Some goes all the way down the Lena and then by coastal or river-sea vessel to other northern rivers, including virtually all cargo for rivers between the Khatanga and Yana and 35-40 per cent of that for the Indigirka and Kolyma. (The remainder is delivered by sea from the Far East.[13]) Only 20 per cent of freight for the Yakut ASSR goes by non-seasonal routes: 17.5 per cent by road from Never and 2.5 per cent from Magadan.[14]

The Pacific zone, engaged more in fishing and forestry, is served by sea from ports in the southern Far East: Vladivostok, Nakhodka and Nikolaevsk. However, river-sea vessels operating from the river Amur have been increasing their share of traffic around the Sea of Okhotsk.[15]

South of the east-west axis is a smaller zone where transport is also oriented primarily to resource extraction. Most of it is in Kazakhstan, but in the Altai and Sayan mountains of southern Siberia are mineral workings, including iron ore and asbestos, served by rail and road. There are also transit routes to Mongolia: the railway south of Lake Baikal, and the Chuya highway through the Altai mountains. The latter has operated since the 1930s and carried 54,200 tons, mainly petroleum products, in 1982.[16]

THE TASKS OF SIBERIAN TRANSPORT

The tasks facing Siberian transport can be summarised as follows. In the north they are to move natural resources out and supplies in. In the south they are in part the same, since several exportable resources (coal and wood, for example) originate there, and the south is still far from self-sufficient in manufactures,[17] many foods and even some industrial raw materials, especially those for aluminium production. Transport in the south has additional functions, however: to provide for considerable traffic within the southern belt, both industrial and agricultural; and to facilitate transit traffic between the Pacific and European USSR. Each task presents current and prospective difficulties, on which the rest of this chapter will focus.

PROBLEMS IN THE SOUTH

The east-west capacity problem

During the past decade there have been numerous complaints in the Soviet press about congestion and delays on the Trans-

Siberian Railway and its companion east-west lines. They mainly reflect failure to meet traffic demands west of the Kuzbass and especially across the Urals, but there are evident problems in eastern Siberia as well. They almost entirely reflect an inability to cope with westbound traffic, which far outweighs eastbound. The main components of westbound traffic are coal and forest products.[18]

Though immediately evident as a railway problem, the situation is part of the broader problem of utilising Siberian natural resources. That problem might be solved by improving the railways, using other forms of transport, relocating resource-using activities, or even postponing the use of some Siberian resources. We shall firstly examine the difficulties faced by the railways, then turn to the wider context.

Capacity problems for east-west transport are nothing new in Siberia. In the first decade of this century the dairy industry quickly rose to prominence, producing such high value-to-weight ratio products as butter and cheese, and eventually non-dairy items like bacon and honey, for the west European market. It emerged partly because the capacity of the new Trans-Siberian Railway was inadequate to move out the quantities of grain offered. Later, in the 1930s, the most notorious transport bottlenecks of the Stalin era were those which arose on the same railway as it tried to cope with the traffic of the Urals-Kuznetsk Combine (UKK).

Each successive crisis engendered innovations to raise capacity. The Trans-Siberian was first built with a capacity of only seven trains a day each way, and simply required passing loops. The UKK crisis was solved partly by double-tracking, partly by military-style organisation and intensive shift-working. Since World War II, when traffic has grown enormously, capacity has kept ahead partly through major technical innovations. The principal change has been the replacement of steam traction with electrification for the most part and diesel in parts of the east. Electric and diesel traction enable the railways to run bigger, faster and more frequent trains; they improve efficiency in winter; and they relieve the railways from carrying coal for their own use, which might comprise one-quarter of all traffic.[19] Electrification and dieselisation have usually been accompanied by a move to more advanced traffic control systems, which again raise capacity. The results in Siberia have been impressive: the Omsk-Novosibirsk stretch of the Trans-Siberian Railway has for

139

many years had the most heavily used tracks in the world.

Now once more traffic has caught up with capacity. This time, unfortunately, no big new technical advance is in sight. The problem could be solved by putting in new east-west lines. Extra-high capacity and even extra-wide-gauge lines have been suggested, but so far the government has evidently preferred two approaches, the first being to upgrade the Central and South Siberian railways. Compared with the Trans-Siberian they have been neglected hitherto: in the late 1970s the South Siberian had only one-tenth as much traffic as the older line.[20] The second approach has been to implement a mass of small improvements: for example, freight cars can be filled closer to capacity; longer, heavier trains can be run; and more powerful, reliable and versatile locomotives can be introduced. The US Central Intelligence Agency believes that measures currently being undertaken could enable another 40 to 50m tons of coal per annum to move westwards.[21] However, even the small measures are not always as simple to introduce as might be expected. Heavier loading increases the failure rate of wheel bearings, which means that the plain bearings used on much Soviet rolling stock should be replaced by roller bearings — no minor expense. Longer trains need longer passing loops and sidings, but in many places along the main east-west lines, no more lengthening is possible without major reconstruction. To make the best use of long trains, by using them as unit trains which are not broken up and re-assembled in freight yards, requires special equipment for loading and unloading. Finally, Soviet locomotives have a poor reputation for reliability, and as yet few can be remotely controlled and spaced along a very long train in the north American fashion. In fact, although the Soviet railways have increased train lengths substantially, using ingenuity to overcome technical problems — by, for example, assembling trains in sections in short freight yards — they have scarcely progressed to the unit-train technology which could radically lower turnaround times.[22]

So far the railways' many small improvements have enabled them to cope, more or less, with increasing traffic. It is hard to tell how fully they are coping, because if capacity is lacking, freight moves in order of priority, and it is the less-publicised freight which gets left behind. However, serious delays have been affecting not only forest products and mineral building-materials, fairly low-priority items, but even coal.[23] How effective the current round of investments will prove to be is a matter of debate among Western analysts. In part it depends less on the railways themselves than on trends in traffic offered. So far the railways have been fortunate in the sense that traffic growth in the past few years has been much smaller than would have been the case if the traffic-generating industries had met their production targets. Thus, for example, national coal output has been slipping below target since the mid-1970s, and the timber cut has scarcely increased in the past quarter-century. (Admittedly national figures are not a perfect guide to the Siberian situation, since for several commodities declining production elsewhere has been offset by increases in Siberia.) The railways are facing an actual and a potential crisis. The former is low-key, but given the methods so far chosen to tackle it, semi-permanent; the latter will come into being if the resource industries start meeting their production targets. The Kuzbass alone, for example, has a target for the 1990s of an additional output of 50m tons per annum, and it has been suggested that it could ultimately supply the European USSR with 200–250m tons of energy coal per annum alone.[24] Such a crisis will be much more severe but perhaps shorter in duration. In the first place it will require a decisive response; in the second place such growth should mean growth in manufacturing industries, which in turn should make more resources available to the railways.

The wider context can be examined in two stages, by investigating, firstly, whether other means of transport could relieve the railways, and secondly, whether growth in the long-distance movement of Siberian resources westwards could be avoided altogether.

The railways have not had to cope with the growth of crude oil and natural gas movements out of Siberia, and it is possible that pipelines could offer further relief. Nationally, railways still carry 83 per cent of petroleum products (excluding those moving by road) and the figure for Siberia is probably no lower. That for the USA is 3.3 per cent.[25] Coal slurry pipelines are another possibility. There is no precedent for one of the length required to bring Siberian coal to the European USSR, but the Soviet government is experimenting with shorter slurry pipes, including one of 32 km at Norilsk and another of 250 km from the Kuzbass to Novosibirsk.[26] If Siberia-European USSR coal slurry pipelines proved feasible, they could not only relieve the east-west railways of their major burden but also enable Kansk-Achinsk coal to move westwards. Unlike Kuzbass coal, Kansk-Achinsk coal cannot be moved by train over long distances, because it tends to self-ignite (see Chapter 3).

There seem to be few other possibilities for moving the bulkier Siberian resources westwards. The improved Northern Sea Route offers some opportunities but not many. Kuzbass coal, for example, could move that way in summer, but it would be moving away from its main market area. In winter it could not move: the Northern Sea Route can keep open all year, but the rivers connecting with it cannot, now or in the foreseeable future. At present the average navigation season on the Yenisei ranges from four-and-a-half months at Igarka to six months at Lesosibirsk, the northernmost point served by a branch railway. The maximum feasible extension, as on most northern rivers, would be one to two months if the most powerful icebreakers could be used and cost were ignored, or ten to thirty days otherwise.[27]

The particular problem of Kansk-Achinsk coal has attracted suggestions ranging from briquetting (which would still involve rail transport) to gasification, a capsule pipeline, and 'coal by wire'. None seems to be economically feasible in the immediate future: for example, current experiments in long-distance electrical transmission are focusing on Ekibastuz, which is only half as far from the Urals as the Kansk-Achinsk coalfield.

The use, or at least continuing growth in the use, of Siberian resources west of the Urals can be avoided. One objective of the TPCs is to establish in Siberia industries which in the European USSR would require Siberian resources, mainly energy or wood. But reducing one set of costs can increase others. Firstly, most of those industries are linked to others, and if their linked industries remain in the European USSR, a different set of transport needs must be met. Secondly, infrastructure and labour costs can be very high in Siberia. Another approach is to use non-Siberian resources in the European USSR. Re-exploration of the East European Plain and improvements in technology have yielded resources which may be more expensive to exploit than those in Siberia but are much closer to market. Examples include north European forest resources, now more fully utilised than before, and Kursk Magnetic Anomaly iron ore. In addition nuclear energy can be substituted for coal-based energy, and the Soviet government intends this to occur. Foreign coal can be substituted for Kuzbass coal too, which raises fundamental questions about

Soviet foreign trade policy. At present Polish coal is used in the north-west European USSR, but none is imported from Western countries, despite substantial surplus production capacity, low prices, and the ability of even Pacific-rim producers to offer coal to Eastern Europe at competitive prices. A willingness to consider world prices as well as strategic self-sufficiency would of course affect Soviet policies on the exploitation of more Siberian resources than just coal. Tin, for example, might be a doubtful investment at present (see Chapter 3).

Perhaps the most effective way to reduce the need for Siberian resources west of the Urals would be to use them more efficiently. Judging from recent improvements in countries already much more efficient in resource utilisation, like Sweden and Japan, energy resources could be employed far more efficiently than is currently the case. A major thrust of the twelfth five-year plan, recognising this, is the technical reconstruction of much of the older industry in the European USSR.

So far this section has focused on resource movements out of Siberia as a source of pressure on the east-west railways. Pressure also arises, though less acutely, from movements to the Pacific coast, imports into Siberia and internal Siberian movements. They will be examined briefly.

Traffic to the Soviet Far East has caused pressure on railway capacity in the past. Before the revival of Soviet interest in maritime transport, the Trans-Siberian Railway was the region's only lifeline. It brought supplies from the European USSR and took back valuable minerals and canned fish. Eastward traffic greatly outweighed westward. The railway remained technically inferior east of Lake Baikal, even retaining main-line steam traction into the 1970s, and it was soon overloaded by the growth of activity which culminated in the building of the BAM.[28] It might be expected that completion of the BAM, including associated port facilities, should resolve that problem for some time to come. Two of the reasons for building BAM were to provide extra transit capacity[29] and to facilitate mineral and forest-product exports. Since foreign markets for most of the potential exports are extremely soft at present, and are not expected to improve for some years, capacity should not be a problem. There remains one area of strain, however. The BAM leads to the port of Vanino, but most railway traffic moves to or from the southern ports — Vladivostok, Nakhodka, and Vostochnyi — or local points also in the south. The line from Komsomolsk through

Khabarovsk to the south, therefore, remains overloaded. A parallel line has been suggested, to run from a point east of Komsomolsk, southwards to Nakhodka.[30]

Both imports and internal Siberian movements are increasing pressure on the east-west railways. The dependence of the region on the European USSR for manufactured goods is growing, because so high a proportion of new investment is allocated to resource extraction. In addition, both iron ore — probably about 7m tons per annum — and alumina come in from the west. Siberian internal movements include about 6m tons of iron ore moving to the Kuzbass from Zheleznogorsk in Irkutsk *oblast* (plus another 10 m tons from mines closer at hand), some 40m tons of petroleum products, and about 130m tons of coal distributed from the Kuzbass, Kansk-Achinsk, Chita, and other coalfields. Finally, supplies for the BAM and other construction projects impose 'temporary' strains which may in fact last several years.

It is evident that the future of transport along the east-west belt of southern Siberia depends on far more than the capabilities of transport itself: it is tied up with fundamental questions of Soviet domestic and foreign policy. At present the most likely scenario for the next five years seems to be that the measures to slow down the growth in demand for Siberian resources will have some effect; Siberian producers will continue to fall short of target; and relatively minor measures will enable the railways to cope with traffic, at some cost and inconvenience to their customers.

The container land-bridge

The land-bridge was set up in 1971, presumably with the primary aim of earning foreign currency, and by 1980 had captured about ten per cent of the container traffic between the Far East and Western Europe, including a quarter of that between Japan and Western Europe. The traffic in 1984 is estimated at 108,000 TEU, and it is hoped to handle 330,000 in 1990 and 600,000 in the year 2000.[31] If such expansion does take place, capacity and quality of service may both be problems. Capacity is limited by terminal and line capacities. The former is less likely to be a problem in so far as the expansion of the main eastern terminal, at Vostochnyi, seems to have kept ahead of demand. The latter does not seem to be a problem at first sight, since the land-bridge accounts for only a small proportion of total traffic on the railways across Siberia — an average of three trains a day at present. However, most full containers move east-west, which is the overloaded direction, and if they are to perform effectively, the container trains should be as demanding as passenger trains in terms of speed and punctuality.

Quality of service is important in a competitive world market. Container shipping lines have been fighting back after the initial Soviet success, and they have strong advantages. At its best, the land-bridge can offer very fast service, but delays are difficult to avoid on an overcrowded line. Shippers have also complained of damage from jostling and rough handling (normally worse for rail than for seaborne freight), and from winter cold. All these problems can be overcome, but clearly the future of the service will depend on the priority accorded to it by the Soviet government. As an earner of foreign currency, it can expect high priority.

Road transport

By Western standards the state of road transport is pitiful throughout the Soviet Union, but it is at its worst in Siberia and a continual source of complaint by Soviet writers.[32] Few roads have all-weather surfaces. By comparison with them, earth roads lower speeds by 50–70 per cent, raise fuel costs by 50–100 per cent, and halve the distance over which vehicles can operate between overhauls. They cannot be used by high-capacity highway trucks with high axle loadings, and in sum they raise transport costs between three- and five-fold.

From the local Siberian viewpoint the roads problem is serious everywhere, but from the national point of view it is especially a problem for the surplus-producing agricultural belt of south-western Siberia. The growing season is short, so it is even more important than in the rest of the main Soviet agricultural zone to start sowing immediately following the spring thaw, and to bring in the harvest as soon as it is ready. At the time of spring thaw, the writer has seen rural roads widened to nearly one hundred metres by successive vehicles trying to skirt the mudholes created by their predecessors, and fields being worked only because the farmers had been brought to them by fully-tracked personnel carriers. There is no cure but massive investment, though how the investment should be used — what types of road should be improved to what standards, in co-ordination with what rural resettlement policies — remains in debate.[33]

PROBLEMS IN THE NORTH

The Ob-Irtysh Basin

The two basic tasks, of moving resources out and supplies in, can conveniently be separated, since for the most part they use different transport modes: pipelines for the resources, and river, sea, road and air transport for supplies.

Some oil moves by river tanker from minor deposits, but the great bulk moves by pipeline. Production fell in 1985 but is supposed to increase by 20–24 per cent (73–88m tons) over the 1985 figure by 1990. Effort will have to be focused on exploiting several small fields to compensate for declining production from the supergiant Samotlor field. This means that pipeline-building will concentrate on feeder lines from the new fields rather than major additions to the trunk network: a new trunk line to the European USSR was completed in 1985, and even fulfilment of the most ambitious target for 1990 should not require more than one additional pipeline of similar size (1,220 mm). This situation is unlikely to change until production shifts from the middle Ob to new regions, which would probably be further north, where oil is found below the natural gas, or further east.

Natural gas production developed later. Major additions have been made to the trunk pipeline network to the European USSR in each recent five-year plan, and the twelfth plan will be no exception. With a dozen large-diameter pipelines already serving the supergiant Medvezhe and Urengoi fields, and capable of moving out over 360,000m cubic metres of gas a year (75 per cent more than in 1980), it is now planned to bring gas to the European USSR from the Yamburg deposit, located further north-east. This will require another six pipelines, to move some 200,000m cubic metres a year.[34] The problem facing natural gas transport is simply to build pipelines fast enough. Since natural gas is the only major fuel of which the Soviet Union has managed to increase production substantially and continuously during the past two decades, with no immediate barrier in sight, the industry will continue to receive top priority for supplies, to open up further fields in north-western Siberia, and to build further trunk pipelines. The demand for pipeline has strained domestic production facilities and required imports (which Western producers are happy to supply, since they have few other customers at present), but there are few alternatives. When Soviet-American relations were better, it was proposed to pipe natural gas across the northern Urals to a liquefied natural-gas terminal on the Pechora Sea, but the idea is no longer prominent.

Oil and gas exploitation on such a scale has presented the Soviet Union with the world's biggest northern-supply problem. In 1985 it was planned to move 70m tons by river in western Siberia including 20-22m tons directly for the oil and gas industry.[35] These are very high tonnages for seasonal transport. A railway from Tyumen via Tobolsk reached the middle-Ob oilfields at Surgut in 1975 and Nizhnevartovsk in 1976, and an extension to Urengoi was opened for temporary use in 1980 and for full use four years later. But the railway has not replaced river transport. Firstly, traffic volumes soon exceeded railway capacity. The line was carrying about 10m tons per annum in the early 1980s, when additional construction began in order to double the capacity of the Tyumen-Surgut stretch. As has been characteristic of Soviet railway-building, traffic potential had been grossly underestimated. Secondly, it would be enormously expensive to duplicate the area-coverage capability of river transport. In the flat, waterlogged terrain a multitude of small rivers can be used for short periods each summer. Some 4,000 km of new routes have been brought into use since oil and gas exploitation began.[36] Thirdly, the demand for transport is likely to fall after the main construction stage in each area, leaving an expensively built railway network underused, and finally, in the northern gas fields modular construction techniques are coming into favour in order to save labour. The modules, large in weight and volume, are much more suited to water than to rail transport. The same consideration has helped bring sea transport into prominence for the Yamburg development.[37] A rail extension to that field is due to open in 1986 but is expected to cover only one-third of its traffic needs. (The line to Urengoi covered about half of the local needs there.) Part of the rest will move by river and sea, either by transhipment or using river-sea vessels, and part will come in by the Northern Sea Route. Pipes as well as modules can conveniently use the sea route: pipes have been brought in

147

from both West Germany and Japan.[38]

Rail, river and sea transport are supplemented by road, all-terrain, air and air-cushion transport. Most roads are winter roads: the building of all-weather roads has fallen short of plans, which compels the use of all-terrain vehicles and should make hovercraft attractive. Their development, however, has been held back by interdepartmental squabbling. The river ministry clearly has jurisdiction over marine hovercraft: the dispute concerns amphibious vehicles, which have not so far entered serious production.

The Yenisei Basin

The northern Yenisei region faces a different situation in two respects. Firstly, both mineral and wood exports, and incoming supplies, are likely to use the same modes of transport. Secondly, traffic volumes generated by the Norilsk mines through Dudinka were already considered sufficient to justify building a railway from the European USSR in the late 1960s.[39] The route in mind could have been the one built eastwards from Salekhard in the 1940s and abandoned before completion. In any event, it proved impossible to build a railway in the late 1960s 'for various reasons' — presumably the allocation of resources elsewhere — and instead, efforts were made to extend the Northern Sea Route navigation season from the Yenisei westwards. The sea route was in fact the most direct route to the Kola Peninsula, where smelters with surplus capacity could use copper-nickel ores produced at Norilsk in excess of the capacity of its own smelters. Since 1978 it has been possible, using river, shallow-draft marine, and deep-draft nuclear icebreakers, to keep the route open for all but the spring break-up period in late May and early June, when the port of Dudinka has to be closed to avoid damage from high water and floating ice.[40] At present the sea route takes between three and four million tons of ore per annum. The expense is very high but is offset by the avoidance of stockpiling and the balancing of mine and smelter capacities.

Keeping the Northern Sea Route open has enabled other freight to use it, including petroleum products for Norilsk. Wood from Igarka only moves during the summer, since the river cannot be kept open all year. Despite its short season, the river carries over 30m tons of freight per annum, which probably includes from two to four million tons moving to Dudinka. Recently it has also moved sulphur south from Norilsk — about 200,000 tons in 1985.[41] It is perhaps because of the volume of freight moving by river that proposals for a railway continue to appear, since any railway would provide only a very roundabout route to the Kola Peninsula. Routes suggested include one along the bank of the Yenisei, and an extension of the line to Urengoi. It is of course possible that the expense of the all-year sea route outweighs its advantages more heavily than Soviet writers admit.

It was suggested above that Soviet planners have tended to underestimate the traffic potential of new railways. A similar problem affects rivers, particularly in the Yenisei Basin. To justify putting locks or boat lifts in hydroelectric dams, a traffic forecast of six to eight million tons is required.[42] Consequently no dam on the Angara, potentially the most useful tributary of the Yenisei for transport, has a lock. The forecasts must have been made on a very narrow basis, since even traffic moving north from Osetrovo on the river Lena, with all its problems of fluctuating depth, is planned to reach 5.5m tons by 1990, and the Yenisei carries far more.

North-eastern Siberia and the Far East

The situation in the north-east is again quite different from that in the other two sub-areas of the north. Firstly, regional imports and exports use the same transport facilities, but the former substantially outweigh the latter. Therefore the location of routes reflects the locations of export production, but capacities mainly reflect import requirements. Secondly, during the past few years access to the north-east has been in a state of flux, partly caused by the building of the BAM.

The transport network is characterised by very long links joining small nodes. Often the nodes are single-purpose and the traffic flow is extremely imbalanced.[43] There are some exceptionally long journeys to tin, gold and diamond-mining sites. A journey from Osetrovo down the Lena, along the Arctic coast and up the Anabar is longer than that from Moscow to Osetrovo and can take over a year, since it may need two navigation seasons. The same applies to the Indigirka.[44] When 80 per cent of freight is moving by such seasonal routes, the most careful planning of inventories and deliveries, and intermodal co-operation, are essential if remote projects are to function smoothly.[45] It is not surprising that in one part of the region, investigated in 1978, transport was found to account for 24 per cent of the labour force and 20–21 per cent of the payroll and general expenditures.[46]

Traffic with the north-east has been growing rapidly for the past 20 years — about three times as fast as the national rate for interregional traffic for much of the time. The growth is expected to continue, stimulated by mineral exploration and the expansion of existing projects, such as tin-mining at Deputatskii. Amounts are not comparable with those of the Ob-Irtysh Basin, but they are large compared with existing transport capacities. The river Lena, the region's main transport artery, has been able to cope with only 80 per cent of traffic offered in recent years.[47] The main point of strain has been the port of Osetrovo. Firstly, physical conditions are poor, with frequent low-water problems. Secondly, those problems have been exacerbated by dredging for gravel in the river bed below Osetrovo. And thirdly, poor organisation, including poor co-ordination and lack of trust between railway and river authorities, has caused serious delays in transhipment. One reason for lack of trust on the part of the railway has been the failure of the river authorities to return containers. They in turn have been unable to retrieve them from customers who use them for storage in the north.[48] Inadequate capacity continues to plague Osetrovo despite the fact that it is now the largest river port in the eastern USSR, following a three-stage expansion completed during the 1975–80 five-year plan.[49]

Construction of the BAM has affected the situation in several ways. On the one hand BAM construction supplies, moving along the Taishet-Lena line, have strained a facility of limited capacity. Furthermore, BAM as a priority project has received resources which might otherwise have been used to improve northern transport. On the other hand, that priority ranking meant that BAM construction had to begin simultaneously at as many points as possible. Tributaries of the Lena, especially the Kirenga, were used to bring in supplies.[50] While this brought more pressure on Osetrovo initially, the deepening carried out to facilitate the operation has created a potential alternative to Osetrovo for northern access.

A number of approaches have been taken to relieving the pressure on northern access. In 1981 freight was sent from Krasnoyarsk, down the Yenisei and eastwards along the

Northern Sea Route. This does not seem to have been success-ful.[51] Two or three transhipments could be needed and the stretch of the route north of the Taimyr Peninsula is particularly subject to ice delays. Another solution is to send more freight all the way from Murmansk or Vladivostok by the Northern Sea Route. This is feasible in so far as more suitable Arctic cargo vessels are entering service. They include icebreaking lighter-carriers (LASH vessels)[52] and ships with roll-on/roll-off capabilities,[53] able to offload onto ice. In addition, such ports as Tiksi and Pevek are being improved, but the eastern section of the Northern Sea Route has more severe ice conditions and lacks the icebreaking capabilities of the western section: the big nuclear icebreakers are allocated primarily to keeping the route open from the Yenisei westwards. Furthermore, ice conditions have in general deteriorated over the past 30 years.[54] The winter of 1983 was especially bad: one vessel was lost and several were damaged. As a result, vessels from the east and west will in future only put in at Pevek and Tiksi. This will presumably mean an extra transhipment to coastal vessels for some cargoes, at increased expense.

There are further problems in co-ordinating river transport with the Northern Sea Route. The ice-free season in the eastern section of the Northern Sea Route is 70–90 days, whereas the rivers are ice-free earlier and for longer (Lena 110–160 days, Yana 105–120, Kolyma 110–130). The opening of navigation on the sea route often coincides with low water on the rivers, which particularly affects those with deltas, like the Lena, or river-mouth bars. A further problem is shallow water near the coast, which hampers transhipment to and from ocean-going vessels. One advantage of the Lena route over the use of the Northern Sea Route is that movement along the coast, between the river mouths, is often possible when the Northern Sea Route proper is closed. It is even possible to avoid transhipments altogether by using river-sea vessels both on the rivers and along the coast. Their utility should be improved as a new generation of ice-strengthened dredgers enters service to maintain deep water at the river mouths.

Another route to the north-east is through Magadan. Its port has been kept open throughout the year since 1962, and the new icebreaking general cargo vessels and tankers normally manage without icebreaking assistance. Here the limitation is the capacity of road transport from Magadan, operating in the most severe conditions.[55] Road transport to Yakutsk, the main generator of traffic in the north-east, is easier from Never, on the Trans-Siberian Railway, and this route has become the main relief route for northern access. Early in 1985 it was employing 9,000 more drivers than before the crisis, and further heavy increases in traffic were anticipated.[56]

The problems of access to the north-east, or at least to central Yakutia, should ease during the 1990s. It is planned to extend the 'Little BAM' north to Yakutsk by 1995. Experience suggests, of course, that relief will be contingent on both the new railway and the connecting east-west lines having adequate capacity.

THE LONG-TERM FUTURE

It seems fairly clear how transport in Siberia will develop during the next decade, provided there is no startling leap forward in natural-resource extraction and immediate bottlenecks can be eradicated. But what of the longer term? Can we discern the outlines of future policies? Consider firstly northern transport, and then the east-west problem.

It is not easy to see how the Soviet government envisages the long-term role of the Northern Sea Route. On the one hand heavy investment is taking place in both ships and ports — more than seems necessary simply to update ageing facilities and keep open the route westwards from Dudinka the year-round. On the other hand, access to northern regions from the south has almost invariably been preferred to access from the Arctic, given a choice, and the effective southern boundary of the sea route's zone of influence has moved steadily northwards. Also, it seems clear that the route is heavily subsidised and will require more support as ice conditions deteriorate.

However, the Northern Sea Route does have certain advantages apart from its strategic importance, especially for a country prepared to subsidise a degree of self-sufficiency in natural resources. It allows much quicker access to new discoveries along the Arctic coast and for some way inland, compared with building railways or roads from the south; and it will be of vital importance if offshore deposits of oil, natural gas or other minerals are to be exploited. Indeed it is precisely these considerations which have revived interest in Canadian Arctic navigation. What seems least likely is that the investment reflects a major revival of interest in through-voyages, despite a recent increase in their occurrence. The type of equipment coming into service is designed primarily for servicing points along the Arctic coast.

What about those parts of the northern zone outside the sphere of influence of the Northern Sea Route? The traditional evolution of transport facilities has been from rivers and winter roads to all-weather roads and railways as tonnages increase.[57] Once the railway to Yakutsk is finished, what others are likely to be built? Apart from the one to Norilsk discussed above, a Yakutsk-Magadan line seems possible by the end of the century.[58] It might be uneconomic by Western, but perhaps not by Soviet standards. Good access to the north-east from an all-year Pacific port could relieve pressure on the east-west railways, if they become congested again when, eventually, resources along the BAM are exploited; and traffic volumes would probably be much more stable than in a comparable Canadian situation, where extreme northern mines tend to be marginal producers, vulnerable to world market fluctuations.

Several authors have suggested that the future of northern development lies with more exotic forms of transport than those discussed here: hovercraft (air-cushion vehicles), vertostats (a combination of balloon and helicopter), dirigibles and the like.[59] For the most part this seems unlikely, except for construction projects. For regular traffic, simple, robust, and well-tested technology has great advantages in severe conditions. Hovercraft might prove attractive if maintenance were simplified — track can be cleared very cheaply and used the year-round,[60] though the vehicles are expensive to operate — but they have not proved a success in the Canadian north. Dirigibles are cheap to operate, but aircraft technology has been developing rapidly for half a century while balloon technology has been static. What does seem likely is growth in conventional air transport, again for construction projects rather than regular freight flows. Soviet specialists have shown great interest in Canadian and Alaskan experience, using, for example, Hercules aircraft to supply the Trans-Alaska Pipeline and Schefferville-Sept Iles Railway construction projects.[61] Furthermore, the Soviet Union is now acquiring a new generation of heavy transport aircraft of its own.

The second major long-term problem is east-west rail capacity. Assuming that demand does continue to grow, three solutions seem most promising: a coal-slurry pipeline, long-distance electrical transmission, and a new east-west railway. The first two require technical advances, and the distances and capacities involved are very large to risk using untried technology. There have been several suggestions for a new railway between Tyumen and Ust-Kut (Osetrovo), joining the heads of the several lines which push northwards from the Trans-Siberian Railway.[62] Such a line would seem a logical continuation of past practice in widening the southern transport belt. What does not seem likely is relief of the railways by a growth of long-distance road traffic comparable with that in North America. Both the pattern of settlement and the composition of traffic in Siberia favour rail transport, and without a strong private road-users' lobby, it seems unlikely that the Soviet government would indulge in the kind of investment in roads which has characterised the United States and Canada.

NOTES AND REFERENCES

1. *BAM: stroitelstvo i khozyaistvennoe osvoenie* (Ekonomika, Moscow, 1984), p. 42.
2. Siberian estimated production figures for 1985 were: oil — 375m tons, natural gas — 380,000m cubic metres, coal — 271m tons (1983 figure, but probably little change thereafter). In 1965 the region produced about one million tons of oil and no natural gas. In 1945 it produced about 30m tons of coal. Annual movements westwards out of Siberia in the early 1980s were of the order of 300m tons of oil, 230,000m cubic metres of natural gas, and 80m tons of coal (or 116m tons including movements from Kazakhstan). T. Shabad, 'News notes', *Soviet Geography*, vol. 27, no. 4 (1986) pp. 252 and 258; L. Dienes, 'Economic and strategic position of the Soviet Far East', *Soviet Economy*, vol. 1, no. 2 (1985), pp. 150–1; R. North, 'Transport in Siberia: problems and perspectives' in B. Chichlo (ed.), *Sibérie I* (Institut d'Etudes Slaves, Paris, 1985), p. 270; V. Kontorovich, *Case study of transport in the Urals — West Siberia — North Kazakhstan region* (Wharton Econometric Forecasting Associates, Washington, D.C., 1982), p. 52, Central Intelligence Agency, 'USSR energy atlas' (CIA, Washington DC, 1985), p. 36.
3. Grouping enterprises in such complexes is claimed to reduce construction costs by 3–10%, operating expenses by 10–15%, and the length of communications by 15–20%. Yu. A. Sobolev, *Transport i razvitie ekonomiki Sibiri i Dalnego Vostoka*(Znanie, Moscow, 1980), p. 10.
4. Both in Kazakhstan for the most part, but the political boundary has no impact on the economic landscape or transport network: northern Kazakhstan is effectively an extension of western Siberia.

5. N. I. Savin, 'Morskoi transport v narodnokhozyaistvennom komplekse Dalnego Vostoka', in *Territorialnye aspekty razvitiya transportnoi infrastruktury* (Nauka, Vladivostok, 1984), p. 64.

6. In 1968 Siberian rivers accounted for 69.9m tons originated and 33,500m ton-kilometres. Corresponding figures for 1975 were 101.6m and 50,100m. J. N. Westwood, *Water transportation in the USSR* (Wharton Econometric Forecasting Associates, Washington, D.C., 1984), p. 9.

7. *Sibir v yedinom narodnokhozyaistvennom komplekse* (Nauka, Novosibirsk, 1980), p. 217.

8. North-western Siberia accounts for all Siberian oil and gas exports westwards. See note 1.

9. V. L. Krutikov and Ye. M. Makhlin, 'Rechnoi transport v yedinoi transportnoi sisteme SSSR', *Geografiya v shkole*, no. 5 (1982), p. 9.

10. About 1.2m cubic metres in 1980, of which 0.35m was sawn locally, the rest being brought in by river vessel from Lesosibirsk and Yeniseisk.

11. From 3.0 to 3.5m tons per annum. T. Shabad, 'News notes', *Soviet Geography*, vol. 22, no. 10 (1981), pp. 692–3.

12. Percentages vary from 70 to 85 in recent years, according to different authors. S. Ya. Zernov, 'K voprosu o prodlenii navigatsii na rekakh Yakutii' in *Transport v ekonomiko-geograficheskikh usloviyakh Yakutskoi ASSR* (Yakutskii filial SO AN SSSR, Yakutsk, 1976), p. 41; B. V. Belinskii and V. T. Lesnoi, 'Vliyanie form snabzheniya na velichinu proizvodstvennykh zapasov', in ibid., p. 6; Dienes, 'Economic and strategic position of the Soviet Far East', p. 158; B. V. Belinskii, 'Aspects of water transport in the Soviet northeast', *Polar Geography*, vol. 2, no. 1 (1978), p. 28. From *Problemy razvitiya transporta Severo-Vostoka SSSR* (Nauka, Novosibirsk, 1974). Since 1980 the movement north from Osetrovo has risen, probably to 5.5 m tons; total R. Lena traffic is about 10.0 m tons.

13. Belinskii, 'Aspects of water transport in the Soviet northeast', pp. 33–4.

14. I. N. Shtyrev, 'Vliyanie razvitiya zheleznodorozhnogo transporta na rabotu avtomobilnogo transporta v Yakutii' in *Transport v ekonomiko-geograficheskikh usloviyakh*, p. 52.

15. K. F. Shiyanskaya, 'Geografiya vodnykh perevozok sovetskimi sudami smeshannogo plavaniya', *Izvestiya Geograficheskogo Obshchestva SSSR*, vol. 117, no. 2 (1985), p. 12.

16. *Avtomobilnyi transport*, no. 4 (1983), pp. 5–6.

17. Dienes, 'Economic and strategic position of the Soviet Far East', p. 154.

18. For coal volumes see Note 2. Forest products shipments are of the order of 20m tons per annum.

19. Electrification is claimed to have raised freight-carrying capacity by 50%. See Kontorovich, *Case study*, p. 17.

20. *Sibir v yedinom*, p. 212.

21. Central Intelligence Agency, National Foreign Assessment Center, *USSR: Coal industry problems and prospects* (CIA, Washington, D.C., 1980), p. 12.

22. William Boncher, 'The current Soviet campaign to increase freight train weight', paper given at a symposium on 'Transport as a Problem in the Economic Development of the Soviet Union and the Communist Countries of Eastern Europe', Europäische Akademie, Berlin, May 1985.

23. Kontorovich, *Case study*, pp. 72–3.

24. A. I. Shrago, 'Kuzbasskii territorialno — proizvodstvennyi kompleks', *Izvestiya SO AN SSSR, seriya obshchestvennykh nauk*, no. 6, issue 2 (1980), p. 124.

25. S. S. Ushakov and T. M. Borisenko, *Ekonomika transporta topliva i energii* (Energiya, Moscow, 1980), pp. 133 and 136.

26. Yu. Bokserman, 'Freight can go by pipe', *Current Digest of the Soviet Press*, vol. 34, no. 51 (19 January 1983), p. 26. The latter project seems to have run into difficulties, and assistance has been sought from an Italian company.

27. Krutikov and Makhlin, 'Rechnoi transport', p. 7; A. I. Arikainen, *Transportnaya arteriya Sovetskoi Arktiki* (Nauka, Moscow, 1984), p. 174.

28. That growth of activity is surveyed in R. North, 'The Soviet Far East: new centre of attention in the USSR', *Pacific Affairs*, vol. 51, no. 2 (1978), pp. 195–215.

29. *BAM: stroitelstvo*, p. 48.

30. Paul E. Lydolph, 'Soviet maritime transport', paper presented at a symposium on 'Transport as a Problem in the Economic Development of the Soviet Union and the Communist Countries of Eastern Europe', Europäische Akademie, Berlin, May 1985, p.24.

31. Ibid., p. 23. TEU = Twenty Foot Equivalent Unit, roughly equivalent to 20 freight tons.

32. L. I. Kolesov, *Mezhotraslevye problemy razvitiya transportnoi sistemy Sibiri i Dalnego Vostoka* (Nauka, Novosibirsk, 1982), pp. 169–77; L. I. Kolesov, chapter 16 in *Sibir v yedinom*.

33. The debate is reviewed by Elizabeth M. Clayton, *Soviet rural roads: problems and prospects* (Wharton Econometric Forecasting Associates, Washington, D.C., 1984), p. 7.

34. T. Shabad, 'News notes', *Soviet Geography*, vol. 26, no. 4 (1985), pp. 296–8.

35. North, 'Transport in Siberia', p. 274.

36. Krutikov and Makhlin, 'Rechnoi transport', p. 8. More rivers would have possibly been brought into use but for the reluctance of the river transport authorities. Costs to the state are reduced by the use of small rivers, because other transport is more expensive. However, costs may be five times as high as on the large rivers, and this spoils the performance indices of the shipping companies.

37. Modules to be loaded at Tyumen will be 300-ton at first, rising to 1000 tons. Transport over the final 30 km will be by air-cushion vehicle. T. Shabad, 'News notes', *Polar Geography*, vol. 8, no. 4 (1984), p. 358.

38. Direct pipeline deliveries to Novyi Port from the West began in 1979, reaching 265,000 tons in 1983. In 1984, larger, 50,000-ton vessels were introduced and the first deliveries from Japan took place. Deliveries in 1985 appear to have been at least 500,000 tons. T. Shabad,

'News notes', *Polar Geography*, vol. 8, no. 2 (1984), p. 168; T. Armstrong, 'The Northern sea route, 1985', 'Polar Record', vol. 23, no. 143 (1986), p. 184.

39. Arikainen, *Transportnaya arteriya*, p. 147.

40. T. Shabad, 'News notes', *Polar Geography*, vol. 8, no. 3 (1984), pp. 259–60.

41. Ibid.

42. Kolesov, *Mezhotraslevye problemy*, p. 206.

43. S. Ya. Zavyalov, 'Neravnomernost gruzopotokov na rechnom transporte Yakutskoi ASSR', in *Transport v ekonomiko-geograficheskikh usloviyakh*, pp. 28–40.

44. Belinskii and Lesnoi, 'Vliyanie form snabzheniya', p. 6; Belinskiy, 'Aspects of water transport', p. 39.

45. Belinskii and Lesnoi, 'Vliyanie form snabzheniya', p. 6.

46. B.Kh. Krasnopolskii, *Infrastruktura v sisteme regionalnogo khozyaistvennogo kompleksa Severa* (Nauka, Moscow, 1980), p. 78.

47. *Izvestiya*, 12 Apr. 1985, pp. 1 and 6.

48. Westwood, *Water transportation*, p. 42.

49. Krutikov and Makhlin, 'Rechnoi transport', p. 10.

50. Sobolev, *Transport*, pp. 49–50; Zernov, 'K voprosu', p. 43.

51. T. Armstrong, 'The Northern Sea Route today', *Cold Regions Science and Technology*, no. 7 (1983), p. 255.

52. The first, the *Alexei Kosygin* of 35,000 tons deadweight, is in service with the Far Eastern Shipping Company. The second, *Sevmorput*, is under construction and will be a nuclear-powered vessel of 60,000 tons.

53. The SA-15 or *Norilsk* class of multi-purpose icebreaking freighter is built in Finland. It operates to a deadweight of 15,000 tons in winter in Arctic waters and 20,000 tons elsewhere. It can move through ice one metre thick, and can carry bulk, container, and roll-on, roll-off cargo, the last unloaded by a stern-ramp. Some have a refrigerated hold.

54. *Morskoi flot*, no. 6 (1985), pp. 36–7

55. *Polar Geography*, vol. 4, no. 1 (1980), p. 61; N. N. Gromov, V. F. Burkhanov and A. D. Chudnovskii, *Transportnoe obsluzhivanie severnykh raionov SSSR* (Transport, Moscow, 1982), p. 22.

56. *Izvestiya*, 12 Apr. 1985, pp. 1 and 6.

57. The modes most suitable for different volumes of traffic are discussed in *BAM: stroitelstvo*, pp. 43 and 47; and Gromov, Burkhanov and Chudnovskii, *Transportnoe obsluzhivanie*, p. 23.

58. Gromov, Burkhanov, and Chudnovskii, *Transportnoe obsluzhivanie*, p. 25.

59. Arikainen, *Transportnaya arteriya*, pp. 175–7; Kolesov, *Mezhotraslevye problemy*, p. 171; *Sibir v yedinom*, pp. 213–6.

60. A hovercraft track can be prepared for 85 rubles per kilometre, compared with 1,500 rubles for a winter road and at least 400,000 rubles for an all-weather road — *Sibir v yedinom*, p. 215. In the north-east, 70% of traffic not moving by water moves by winter road.

61. Gromov, Burkhanov and Chudnovskii, *Transportnoe obsluzhivanie*, pp. 29–55.

62. *Transport, Problemy Severa*, no. 20 (Nauka, Moscow, 1979), p.8.

6

The Baikal-Amur Railway (the BAM)

Violet Conolly

The 3,145 kilometres-long Baikal-Amur Railway involves too many geographical-geological, technical, construction and labour problems, *inter alia*, to be discussed in due detail in the following few pages. A book on the lines of Shabad and Mote's excellent initial survey of the BAM[1] would be required to deal adequately with this complicated subject, still partially covered as it is by official secrecy. The aim of this chapter is rather to provide a general conspectus of the construction difficulties and the aims of this greatest railway project of our times, running from Ust-Kut in East Siberia (Irkutsk *oblast*), to Komsomolsk-na-Amure and thence by the old railway to the Pacific port of Vanino.

In concept and design, the BAM of today largely originated in a Stalinist project of the 1930s, itself foreshadowed by various abortive tsarist Russian railway plans for Siberia. This early BAM was partly built until dismantled for its hardware during World War II. Work on it was subsequently resumed but ceased again in 1950. During these years, many exploratory studies of the line and its feasibility were made which would be modified as necessary for the BAM of today. Completely ignoring this background, Leonid Brezhnev announced the contemporary BAM construction in a major speech at the all-Union Youth Conference in Alma Ata in 1974 and called for 'volunteer' workers for the great task ahead. Thousands of young people responded enthusiastically to his appeal and were dispatched forthwith to the site of the Siberian track. Being mostly untrained, they were joined by more experienced Soviet railwaymen and many others all trained on the track under construction. Such was the onset of the new BAM.

After a decade of arduous construction work, the 'junction' of the eastern and western sectors of the railway at Kaunda in Chita *oblast* was jubilantly celebrated there and in Moscow on 29 October 1984. High-ranking Soviet medals were awarded to 'heroic workers' on the line, and in 1985, in recognition of the 'great contribution' made by members of the Leninist *Komsomol* (Young Communist League) in its construction, it was declared that in future the BAM would be named after them.

This *stykovka* or 'joining' of the eastern and western sectors of the BAM in 1984 did not imply its completion, as is sometimes assumed in English sources even though the word was never used in Russian accounts. Nor is it today: a great amount of work still remained to be done, including work on locomotive depots, wagon-repair points, unfinished sidings and stations, as well as housing, social, cultural and everyday facilities for the inhabitants of the BAM zone. Major tunnels, in the first instance through the Severobaikalsk and Kodar mountains, were also still far from completed, and bypasses were temporarily used to circumvent them. Nevertheless, in April 1985 *Pravda* announced 'the first through-journey' of a special train — 'the Science Express' — along the entire BAM track carrying scientists led by Academician Abel Aganbegyan on an itinerant mission to study BAM problems.[2] The terminal date for the completion of the BAM has been set back several times from the first years 1982–3 to 1984, and it was far from being 'fully operational' in 1985, as pledged in honour of the 27th party Congress in February 1986.

NATURAL HAZARDS

The laying of the BAM track was threatened extensively from the outset by daunting natural hazards. It had for the most part to be constructed for long stretches in areas where high seismicity and avalanches are endemic, and also hacked out of virgin *taiga* lacking settled population or any modern living facilities for the railway workers. It was also necessary to build 138 longer bridges and some 1,762 smaller ones over the many large and small rivers crossing the track, and eight tunnels, some of the greatest difficulty, had to be driven through high mountains blocking the railway's progress. Soviet scientists have long been studying technical means of coping with these hazards. The Yakut Permafrost Institute has been notably active in its research on

159

permafrost and seismic problems. Reassuring reports about these dangers have from time to time been published by Soviet scientists which cannot be confirmed until foreign observers have greater access to the BAM than at present. Meanwhile, it is interesting to note that Soviet experts in Tynda were in 1985 reported to have proposed simple and cheap methods for constructing railway beds and buildings in permafrost and now 'being used on the Baikal-Amur Railway'.[3] These new methods would allegedly obviate the need for track restoration caused by possible subsidence, and thus greatly reduce construction costs.

The Soviet decision to construct the costly and demanding BAM was never publicly discussed. It was undoubtedly motivated by both strategic and economic factors. At a time when Sino-Soviet relations were far from cordial, the establishment of a second rail link to the Pacific ports as an alternative to the old Trans-Siberian Railway (which in some stretches passes too close to the Chinese-Manchurian frontier for security), and facilitating the transport of troops, war material and so on must have weighed heavily with the Kremlin. Economically, in spite of the construction difficulties and the high costs, there was also much to be said in favour of the construction of the BAM. Heavy traffic pressure on the old Trans-Siberian line urgently called for alleviation by another regional railway. Moreover, within this proposed new railway zone Soviet geologists maintained that there existed great undeveloped mineral wealth: coal, iron, copper (at Udokan), tungsten, molybdenum and the 'largest synnyrite deposit in the world' apart from the 'noble minerals', gold and diamonds.

BAM: 'AN ALL-NATIONAL ENTERPRISE'

Both in regard to its equipment and construction labour, the Baikal-Amur Railway merits the official title of an 'all-national enterprise'. It is being built in the first place as a single-track line and planned as a completely modern railway, but designed primarily as a heavy-duty freight line. Owing to the extreme climatic conditions, mechanisation was regarded as essential to minimise the number of workers on the line. Track is reported to be laid on a 200 mm layer of sand covered with broken rock ballast to a depth of 250 mm. The BAM equipment originated in many plants located throughout the Soviet Union often thousands of kilometres from the construction. New industries were also established for special BAM requirements. Thus, experimental locomotives designed especially for harsh Siberian conditions of low temperatures and high seismicity have been tested. The most powerful type among them is reported now to be operating on the BAM track. Some sophisticated equipment has also been imported intermittently from abroad: German trucks, American bulldozers and Japanese excavators have received favourable but little publicised Soviet comment for their performance in BAM conditions.

Since the early days of the line's construction, many complaints have appeared in Soviet sources about the defects of some Soviet equipment for the BAM, notably regarding its vulnerability to severe Siberian climatic conditions, and the frustration caused to workers by delays in receiving badly needed machines. Sleepers necessary for the track construction were frequently reported to be lacking right up to October 1984 (the date of the 'joining' of the eastern and western sectors of the BAM) and later, to the general irritation of the workers concerned. BAM bridge detachments and mechanised groups of workers were also reported in the Soviet press to be discouraged by the fact that 'managements, chief specialists and supply services are located as formerly in Ust-Kut in the western sector, though track-laying was latterly more and more concentrated in the eastern sector' and 'are not interested in their daily needs' nor, allegedly, are their representatives seen by workers on the track.[4]

The scale and complexity of the engineering work required by this large construction project called for powerful industrial bases sited along the track and planned originally at Shimanovsk (on the Trans-Siberian Railway), Taishet and Zolotinka. Shimanovsk, the largest of these plants, proved entirely unequal to the major supply role designed for it while the long delays in completing the other smaller bases retarded their possible assistance to the BAM. The result was that industrial components and workers' housing which Shimanovsk was planned to supply had to be largely imported from far afield in the Soviet Union. Moreover, following poor planning, unnecessary costs were incurred for imports of timber, which exists abundantly in the surrounding *taiga*.[5]

Such apparently was the situation at Shimanovsk in 1983. In 1985, however, the Shimanovsk complex was highly praised by

Pravda for its large panel houses delivered for assembly to the
BAM track and its marble and granite sent for the first time to
BAM settlements. 'Stations, palaces of culture, dwelling houses
of the railway will be adorned with bluish granite and silver-white
marble.'[6] The truth may lie between the two accounts but it is
notable that local reports, being rather occupied with more
essential worker accommodation problems, do not dwell on
these grandiose adornments of buildings.

The BAM labour force, like the equipment, has been supplied
from all over the Soviet Union and is 'all-national' in composition. The provision of a reliable labour force, prepared to
withstand the harsh BAM construction and poor living conditions in spite of the relatively high wages and other privileges, has
throughout remained a problem for management. The situation
was eased in places by various expedients. Thus, a system of
shefstvo or patronage was early established by which various
Soviet nationalities deployed their native skills in the
construction of towns and settlements in the BAM zone. Thus,
the Muscovites were responsible for building Tynda, the Leningraders initiated the construction of Severobaikalsk, the
Georgians built Niya, and the Ukrainians the new town of Urgal
II. The contingents of Soviet military men, with their special
skills as engineers or mechanics, contributed valuably to the
work in hand whether in the western or eastern sector, and
notably in the latter where they had done very useful surveying
work in the 1970s.

The socialist countries of Eastern Europe, Cuba and
Mongolian People's Republic also participated to some extent in
the BAM construction work (though to what extent and how
successfully is not clear from Soviet sources). Some students
from the Patrice Lumumba University in Moscow spent summer
vacations working on the BAM. But no workers from non-
socialist countries seem to have been invited to participate in the
BAM, possibly owing to the harsh working and climatic conditions prevailing there. The various Soviet national and international groups working on the BAM construction appear to have
remained separate entities and not to have been integrated into
multinational groups while in Siberia.

In urging the need for a second track on the 'Little BAM' from
Bam station to Tynda, in view of the greatly increased traffic on
that line, the BAM chief, Valerii Gorbunov, commented on the
changed BAM labour force in 1984.[7] 'Construction workers have

162

left', he said, 'technical bases have been closed down. But the planners' assumptions that workers would only remain on the BAM for the period of their three year contracts and then depart had not been justified by the course of events.' In fact, he asserted, families had been formed and small children were growing up for whom there was a need for more kindergartens and other social services. It is however too early to say how far Gorbunov's special pleading for better conditions for workers on this second 'Little BAM' line will be implemented.

NEW SETTLEMENTS AND TOWNS

As the BAM moved forward in the western and eastern sectors, new urban-type settlements of lesser significance than the BAM capital town of Tynda appeared on the track. Soviet population estimates for the BAM zone, once the line is fully operational and latent resources start to be developed, range from one to one-and-a-half million inhabitants. Most of this new population will consist of railway workers established along the BAM; mining workers; and workers in the timber, fishing or other industries which may be established. The new farms to be organised in the zone to increase local food supplies should eventually have the effect of adding farm-workers to this population. In spite of the living-accommodation problems in the zone, the regional birth rate is reported by Soviet sources to be relatively high, with most of the zone's population being young.

Selected early to be the capital of the BAM zone, being the headquarters of the main BAM Construction Administration, and placed under the *sheftsvo* of Moscow, Tynda developed in a few years from an insignificant hamlet to its planned role as a relatively large modern city. However, the transition was marked by some typically Soviet blunders and constructional discrepancies making life exceptionally difficult for the inhabitants of the young town. Lack of co-operation between the various ministerial contractors building Tynda resulted in chaos on the work sites in the early stages, while the failure to provide even the minimum of social amenities, e.g. sewerage, plumbing or water supplies for the inhabitants, was described in gruesome detail by the Soviet media.

Little by little living conditions have improved in Tynda since the late 1970s, and it is now reported to enjoy the usual Soviet urban facilities including some high-rise buildings alongside humbler dwellings. The BAM chief Valerii Gorbunov stated in 1984 that he expected some 10,000 railway workers to be living in Tynda with their families in a couple of years time.[8] In spite of its civic progress since early days, however, Tynda can still lay no claim to architectural distinction or charm, judging from recent photographs in the Soviet press.

New towns of lesser significance than Tynda soon arose along the BAM track, both in the western and eastern sectors. The old settlement of Ust-Kut, as the western terminal of the BAM, is also expanding and is now the site of an important railway repair shop.[9] It is interesting to note that the first new towns to be built beyond Ust-Kut in the western sector — Niya, Magistralnyi, Ulkan and Severobaikalsk — were all long sparsely inhabited by natives and Russians. In the eastern sector, Urgan II, Alonka and Soloni are among the first new towns of some importance. More urban-type settlements will probably be built for the workers as timber and mineral resources are developed within the BAM zone.

It is useful to have some first-hand comments on these western sector towns from the respected *Pravda* correspondent, V. Orlov, who toured the entire BAM track in 1984. Orlov found Niya beautiful at any time of the year, being built by the Georgians of tuff and basalt with taste and foresight. Among the amenities for the inhabitants, he mentioned food shops, a general trade centre and a cinema. Nearby, there was also a school and a kindergarten to serve the children of two four-storey dwellings. Some time later (and not within Orlov's itinerary), the Georgians also started to build Ikabya, a new settlement in a wilderness between Chara and Khani destined eventually to be a main BAM local station when the rich mineral resources of the area are developed.

Further along Lake Baikal, Orlov was more critical of the flaws in the planning and construction of the important railway junction, site of the main locomotive electric depot and regional Lake Baikal port of Severobaikalsk. He found that the relevant ministries had evidently miscalculated the housing required for the town's increasing population, estimating that 80 per cent of the inhabitants would be bachelors, whereas four-fifths of them turned out to be married couples.

The Leningrad *sheftsvo* originally sponsored Severobaikalsk new town and provided it with a large school complex, a hospital precinct and a milk factory, all made from components from 'the city on the Neva'. However, when the Leningraders left at the expiration of their agreements in 1984, the citizens of Severobaikalsk learned that the Ministry of Transport Construction had not organised a building base to replace that of the Leningraders. Meanwhile, however, life seems to be rapidly improving in Severobaikalsk. In 1985, Soviet sources reported that many well-built houses had been constructed there. It is a young people's town built by young people from all over the Soviet Union and the birth rate there is now one of the highest in the USSR.[10]

For some years before Orlov visited the neighbouring town of Nizhneangarsk (also in the north Buryat ASSR), the central town boiler construction fell behind the terminal work date, thus in turn delaying construction of new housing and other new buildings needed by the citizens, while the temporary boilers which had been installed polluted the air. However, normal heating was not provided for this northern climate. In Nizhneangarsk, Orlov also notes that the new town plan 'forgot' to include a railway station, a house of culture, a sports complex or a trade-social centre, even though the town has been assigned a major role in regional development and BAM transport plans.

The new towns and settlements in the eastern sector have been favourably mentioned in other Soviet sources but relatively few have so far been built there. The most settled area here is the old Urgal coal mining area where a connecting line was built before 1950 to the Trans-Siberian-Railway town of Izvestkovyi (Izvestkovaya station), an important local limestone-mining area. Soviet military railway men have been surveying this region since the onset of the BAM and have built Urgal II, the largest new town, with the participation of Ukrainians and Moldavians. The new towns of Alonka and Chegdomyn, connected by rail with Izvestkovaya station, also belong to the Urgal coal-mining area.

Proceeding further east, across the Bureya river, the BAM reaches the new town of Soloni but there is blocked by the Dusse-Alin mountains. Tunnelling there has been frustrated by great environmental difficulties and unforeseen geological faults. The two kilometres-long Dusse-Alin tunnel was originally built in 1950 and then abandoned. When reopened for the BAM in 1976, it was found to have accumulated masses of heavy ice and dangerous rock fractures. Tunnelling was therefore suspended for a time but is now continuing again, though somewhat peril-ously. Meanwhile, a bypass is being used temporarily by the BAM trains until they can safely pass through the Dusse-Alin tunnel.

AGRICULTURE AND FOOD SUPPLIES IN THE BAM ZONE

The geologically proven mineral reserves of the BAM zone and its environs contrast sharply with the meagre extent of its agricul-tural crop-bearing land or potential. The local supply of food for the one to one-and-a-half million people officially estimated to be living in the zone in 'the near future' therefore presents considerable problems for the Soviet authorities. As of now, only a small percentage of the food consumed in the zone is locally produced by the 15 or so state farms (*sovkhozy*) established there. A comprehensive programme for the agricultural development of the BAM zone is now being officially prepared, and according to Soviet sources, the local food problem is under continuous study by agricultural experts. Until this programme is published, it would be idle to attempt to forecast how the Soviet government proposes to deal with these intractable problems of feeding (at least) over one million people with locally produced food.

THE FUTURE OF THE BAM

In spite of the daunting natural hazards facing the construction of the BAM and the maintenance of the track, the 3,145 km-long line was built by 1984 (with bypasses and gaps, and thus not fully operational). Some dangerous tunnelling remained to be carried out on the complicated Kodar and Dusse-Alin mountains around which the BAM trains used bypasses as a temporary expedient to facilitate their journeys eastwards, and a good deal of incidental work still had to be done on sidings, etc.

From the time the first section of the BAM track was completed from Ust-Kut in the late 1970s, trains started running carrying passengers, construction materials and other freight to the next construction side. Simultaneously, work was proceeding on the 'Little BAM', running from Bam station on the Trans-Siberian Railway to the Tynda junction of the 'Little BAM' and the future main BAM line. This line was completed in 1975. It had been originally built in the late 1940s under Stalin and then abandoned. From Tynda, the restored 'Little BAM' continued north-westwards towards Yakutia through the Nagornyi tunnel to Berkatit (reached in 1976), the transport base for the adjacent Yakut coal mines at Neryungri.

Since 1984–5, this line is being prolonged through southern Yakutia and the mica area of Tommot, on the Far Eastern highway, to the Yakut capital city of Yakutsk, a distance of 830 km. Thus, for the first time, the Yakut capital will be linked by rail with the Trans-Siberian and European Russia via the BAM. Owing to increased exports of coal, iron ore and apatites (among other minerals) Soviet sources anticipate that the high costs of this south Yakut line will be recouped within three years.[11] At the outset, 3,000 men were reported to be working on this 'Road to the North', the first kilometres of which were reported to be laid by 'warriors of the construction group of the Yakut Komsomols, headed by Deputy of the Supreme Soviet of the Yakut ASSR, Aleksei Ivanchenko'.[12] There is thus no doubt of the politico-economic importance attached by the Yakut government to the construction of this railway in their vast, hitherto rail-less republic. Some Soviet optimists now anticipate that this Yakut line may eventually be extended beyond the borders of Yakutia to the fast-developing port of Magadan in the far North. Whether this will prove to be an idle dream or a reality is currently difficult to assess.

Throughout the BAM construction period, Soviet experts and the Soviet media have constantly discussed the potential and actual mineral wealth of the BAM zone, where gold, coal, mica and iron are already being produced in the Aldan-Chulman area, as well as increasing quantities of coal from the new Neryungri coal mines. The distinguished Siberian expert, Academician Abel Aganbegyan, has no doubt about Yakutia's mineral wealth: 'As regards the diversity and reserves of natural riches, Yakutia probably has no equal', he declared in an *Izvestiya* interview in 1984; 'Virtually the whole of Mendeleev's table of elements is represented in Yakutia. The real pearl of this northern republic is the south Yakut Territorial Production Complex of the BAM.'[13] The huge Vilyui reserves of oil and natural gas, he continued, are most important sources of Yakut natural wealth, and a local refinery to obviate the present necessity of stocking up a year's supply of oil products everywhere in Yakutia (owing to the seasonal nature of transport) should be established. Aganbegyan, not for the first time, supported the oft-mooted idea of a regional metallurgical industry in the Chulman-Aldan mining area — a project which has been hanging fire awaiting an official decision for several years.

In view of the prevailing tight position regarding both investment funds and labour in the Soviet Union, the moment does not seem propitious for the promotion of major development projects in the BAM zone, most of them costly in terms of both investment and labour.[14] Rethinking is in progress at the highest level regarding the economic assimilation of the BAM in the light of the new state policies of accelerating the social, economic, scientific and technical progress of the Soviet Union as a whole. The *Basic Guidelines for the Socio-Economic Development of the Soviet Union* in the period of the twelfth five-year plan (1986–90) and the economic programme adopted by the 27th Party Congress in 1986 indicate some movement away from the high priority given to the BAM zone in recent years.

Significantly, Academician Aganbegyan, as Chairman of the Scientific Council on the BAM, had already stated in August 1985, 'We must of course work out matters of the economic assimilation of the BAM zone in a new way, the more so in that the twelfth five-year plan will, to a large extent, be a preparatory stage in the Party's economic strategy. We must seek ways and choose those versions which will bring the state the biggest return in the short term.'[15] Aganbegyan's statement suggests a shift from his former position as a strong protagonist of Siberian-BAM interests *vis-à-vis* those of the RSFSR and the Soviet state. He is an influential figure in this field and his future attitude to BAM development and investment is worthy of consideration.

The question also arises as to whether these tougher general Soviet economic policies have not also motivated the marked change in attitude to the BAM and its workers since the 'Golden Link' was achieved in 1985. In a trenchant article in *Pravda*, V. Orlov commented in August 1985, 'Today there is coldness to their concerns and needs where yesterday they received congratulations . . . The construction of the century is not finished. A most responsible and difficult stage lies ahead and support from central administrative and local Party and Soviet organs is specially important.' Among the BAM problems mentioned by Orlov was the 'alarming' situation on the 15 km-long Severomuisk tunnel brought about by faulty geological research and delays in materials essential for the full loading of the electrification of the main line from Lena station to Severobaikalsk.[16]

Nevertheless, even with its present 'gaps', the BAM is of no little importance to the Soviet Union for transport of passengers and freight. By Feburary 1985, the BAM had already carried 50m tons of freight and over five million passengers, though less than half the line is in permanent operation, with the remainder being used by occasional and works trains only, according to K. Mokhortov, head of the Baikal-Amur Railway construction main administration.[17]

The use of the BAM as part of the land-bridge for a new trans-continental means of container transport has also been stressed by the Soviet media. Great Britain and Japan are regarded as the countries most likely to benefit from access to the BAM from the Soviet Pacific ports (see also Chapter 5). It is pointed out that the BAM will offer Britain a new and shorter route to and from places such as Singapore and Hong Kong, while the attraction for Japan would be that the distance from Japan to the English Channel by the BAM route is nearly 40 per cent shorter than by other routes. So far, however, the Japanese seem to have shown little enthusiasm for the BAM route westwards. Like other foreign businessmen, they may be apprehensive of the serious natural hazards to be encountered, until Soviet assurances in this respect are corroborated by successful foreign experience of the BAM's effectiveness.

Finally, it must be recognised that the time is not yet opportune for a definitive assessment of the role of the BAM either regionally or in the Soviet transport system as a whole. The railway is still far from fully operational and the timetable for development of the economic potential of the line is now under discussion in Moscow. Nevertheless, in spite of many problems and difficulties, the creation of this long and arduous BAM track must be hailed as an 'heroic achievement' by the multinational Soviet work-force which faced many perilous natural obstacles and hundreds of kilometres of virgin *taiga* in the construction of this railway from Ust-Kut to Komsomolsk-na-Amura.

NOTES AND REFERENCES

1. T. Shabad and V. L. Mote, *Gateway to Siberian resources (the BAM)* (Wiley, New York, 1977).
2. *Pravda*, 23 Apr. 1985.
3. *Pravda*, 7 Aug. 1985.
4. TASS, in Russian for abroad, 1 Apr. 1985.
5. *Pravda*, 30 Aug. 1982.
6. *Pravda*, 26 Oct. 1983 and 7 Aug. 1985.
7. *Pravda*, 21 Feb. 1985.
8. *Dalnii Vostok*, no. 10, 1984.
9. Moscow Radio, 20 Apr. 1984.
10. *Pravda*, 25 Jul. 1985.
11. TASS, 12 Apr. 1985.
12. *Pravda*, 4 Apr. 1985.
13. *Izvestiya*, 23 Nov. 1984.
14. For example, *Pravda*, 12 Jul. 1985.
15. Moscow Home Service, 19 Aug. 1985.
16. *Pravda*, 7 Aug. 1985.
17. *Pravda*, 21 Feb. 1985.

7

Military and Strategic Factors

John Erickson

For the Soviet military command, as it was with its Imperial Russian predecessor, talk of what is increasingly coming to be called the 'Pacific shift' is neither new nor news. For more than 60 years Soviet strategic investment, command organisation and military deployments in eastern Russia — from the river Ob to the Pacific Ocean, embracing Siberia and the Soviet Far East — have undergone a wide variety of changes in response to an equally wide variety of threats, whether actual or perceived, though the scale of the current build-up in a vast potential theatre of war could well dwarf all previous efforts. On present evidence, for example, the Soviet Pacific Fleet is now the largest of the four Soviet fleet commands, surpassing in strength the key Northern Fleet and it could be argued that it is steadily becoming the most important: evidently the latest surface ships and submarines now go first to the Pacific Fleet, a complete reversal of former practice.

For both Imperial Russia and the Soviet Union this military-strategic nexus long embodied both an outpost (*forpost*) and a bastion, exemplifying at once both vulnerability and security. At the beginning of the century Japan inflicted a grievous defeat on the Russians in the Far East; but that was not to be the end of a serious conflict of interest between Japan and what became the Soviet Union, a relationship which may yet take a further crucial turn. In 1916 General Kuropatkin, enlarging on his earlier forebodings, pointed to the danger from a newly modernised China, which could strike through the Dzhungar Basin and thus cut the Russian Empire in half. He went on to argue that the best way to contain Chinese power would be to build up a buffer against it, and involving a border running from the Khan-Tengri mountain in the Tyan-Shan range to Vladivostok. Now the Soviet Union faces a China committed to the 'Four Modernisations', assisted by the United States, which has, from the Soviet point of view, intruded its military power into the Soviet margin of the Pacific. Superpower rivalry is clearly sharpening in the Pacific, bringing with it heightened Soviet fears of encirclement and the encouragement of an anti-Soviet coalition (or coalitions).

There are two problems to be considered here. The first is the process by which the Soviet authorities created a military system in these eastern reaches, what infrastructure was laid down, what threats such a system was intended to counter (or what security it was designed to guarantee) and what degree of effectiveness was derived from the 'management/command' arrangements for this outpost-cum-bastion. That the military investment and operational management (or co-ordination) of this region posed formidable problems for friend and foe alike is amply demonstrated by Colonel Saburo Hayashi's monograph, *Study of Strategical and Tactical Peculiarities of Far Eastern Russia and Soviet Far East Forces*,[1] a work which has by no means lost all its relevance. The panorama of exertion, anguish and achievement is also presented in an album of material published in Khabarovsk in 1973, aptly named *Outpost of Heroes* (*Forpost geroev*[2]) — but one item in a mass of material.[3]

The second aspect is concerned with developments in eastern Russia, Siberia and the Soviet Far East, in relation to the latest, quite radical transformations in the entire Soviet military system designed to provide an *integrated defence* for the Soviet Union at large, a programme pushed vigorously by Marshal of the Soviet Union N. V. Ogarkov during his tenure as Chief of the Soviet General Staff. Here the 'Pacific shift' is most obvious, though it could be more accurately described as a steady drift towards and along this strategic axis.

This inevitably widens the geographic scope of the discussion, beyond the physical confines of Siberia and the Soviet Far East and into the implications and ramifications of Soviet strategic thinking, operational planning and military preparation, but what does not alter — indeed, it appears to be amplified — is the double duty the region performs as outpost and bastion.

OUTPOST AND BASTION: FROM CIVIL WAR TO WORLD WAR II

The early military structures in Siberia and the Soviet Far East —
both the scene of savage fighting ranging over vast distances —
inevitably bore all the signs of having been built under fire.
Fighting off White counter-revolution and armed intervention,
which brought Japanese troops among others into Russian
territory, the Soviet authorities struggled to co-ordinate the
operations of a motley force of Red Guards, the first feeble
regular Red Army units and partisan bands in Siberia and the
Maritime provinces all splayed out over great stretches of
territory and pitted against a growing diversity of enemies.[4] At
the beginning of May 1918, on the orders of Lenin and
Sovnarkom, the East Siberian Military District (MD) was set up,
embracing the region of the Amur, the Maritime provinces,
Kamchatka and Sakhalin, with its headquarters in Khabarovsk.[5]
The life of the East Siberian MD proved to be brief, for it was
stripped of whatever manpower and resources it possessed in
order to man the 'Ussuri front', which may be accorded the
distinction of being the first recognisable 'command entity' in the
Far East under V. Sakovich as 'front commander', Flegontov on
his left flank, Zubarev at the centre and Shevchenko on the
right.[6]

In Siberia the increasingly powerful Siberian Revolutionary
Committee (*Sibrevkom*) set up the Omsk Military District on 3
December 1919, taking in the region of Omsk, Tomsk,
Chelyabinsk, Semipalatinsk and the Altai, only to have the
Revolutionary Military Council (*Revvoensovet*) of the Fifth Red
Army decide three weeks later on the designation of the Siberian
Military District. Within a matter of days, in January 1920, the
designation was handed yet again to the West Siberian Military
District and in the early summer, 'command and control' was
vested in the Assistant to the Commander-in-Chief of the
Republic Armed Forces in Siberia, the Assistant (V. I. Shorin)
joining the *Sibrevkom* and his staff (with that of the Military
District) forming the 'Military Section' of *Sibrevkom*, responsible for all military affairs in Siberia. Shorin had at his disposal
the Fifth Red Banner Army, the military commissariats of
western and eastern Siberia, military districts and 'fortified
districts' (URs).[7]

Under the pressure of the Japanese and White forces, the
'Ussuri front' buckled, though a successful action on 31 July 1918

is generally held to mark the foundation of the 'Far Eastern Military District',[8] even if the East Siberian Military District had provided the first command entity, based on Khabarovsk. At the end of 1919 the Red Army had effectively destroyed its opponents in Siberia, but the struggle in the Far East had yet to run its full course. The ensuing phase of partisan warfare ushered in yet more ferocity,[9] while the general 'breathing space' (*peredyshka*) enjoyed by the Soviet Republic did not bring pacification in the east. While the Fifth Red Banner Army, having destroyed Kolchak, pushed on to Lake Baikal and approached the frontier with Mongolia, Moscow decided on the creation of a buffer state in the Far East, the 'Far Eastern Republic' (DVR), 'bourgeois-democratic' in aspect but with the Communist Party as the 'ruling party'. By the declaration of April 1920 the DVR took in the regions of the Trans-Baikal, the Amur, the Maritime provinces, Sakhalin and Kamchatka; the National-Revolutionary Army (NRA) was formally subordinated to the Far Eastern Republic, but in practice it was counted as one of the field armies of the Soviet Republic.[10]

Meanwhile the East Siberian Military District was re-established on 18 March 1920 with its headquarters (HQ) in Irkutsk and taking in the region of the Trans-Baikal and Yakutia. At the same time, the National-Revolutionary Army of the DVR was struggling to its feet, drawing in the Revolutionary Army of the Maritime provinces, sundry Soviet units and the Baikal/Trans-Baikal 'national-revolutionary armies' as well as the partisan detachments of the Amur and eastern Trans-Baikal. At the end of 1920 the unification of these forces had begun to take shape, with S. G. Lazo placed in overall command and plans laid to raise eight rifle brigades, 17 regiments and 16 independent battalions.

In October 1920 the NRA succeeded in taking Chita: G. Kh. Eikhe, the new commander of the NRA, split his forces into two armies, the First Trans-Baikal Army and the Second Amur Army, total NRA strength now approaching 100,000 men.[11] However, the temporary truce between the NRA and the Japanese, concluded in 1920, was on the point of breaking down as the forces of Ataman Semenov and General Kappel utilised Japanese cover to infiltrate NRA positions, taking Spassk in May 1921. Aware of the growing danger, Moscow ordered not only reinforcements for the east but also the speedy transfer of V. K. Blyukher, an outstanding Civil War commander, to the Far East. On June 27 1921 Blyukher assumed the position of Commander-in-Chief of the NRA and the post of War Minister in the DVR. Blyukher was already a name to conjure with, a name which was also to stamp itself on many years of military-political developments in the Soviet Far East, and 1921 was no exception, — indeed, it marked a new beginning and a splendid climax the following year.

Blyukher set to work at once and with a will to reorganise the NRA, as well as pulling the whole military structure into shape.[12] In September 1921 the Amur Military District was set up, covering the Amur region and the 'liberated' areas of the Maritime province. On 3 November, Blyukher brought the First Trans-Baikal and the Second Amur Armies under the newly created Trans-Baikal Military District (*ZabVO*) and its first commander, S. M. Seryshev;[13] *ZabVO* replaced the 'East Trans-Baikal district military administration' which had been established in August (1921).[14] This newly consolidated group, the First Trans-Baikal Army in particular, operated not only against Kappel but also supported the actions to eliminate Baron Ungern's force which had taken Ugra and advanced on the Tran-Siberian Railway, intent on cutting off the Far East from Soviet Russia. Joint action by Mongolian 'national-revolutionary' detachments' under Sukhe-Bator and Choibalsan, assisted by the Fifth Red Army and the Partisans of Eastern Siberia, checked this drive, captured Ungern and his fellows, bringing them to Novosibirsk to be shot.[15]

In May 1922 the Trans-Baikal Military District was disbanded and its forces subordinated directly to the Military Soviet of the NRA. At this time the tide was turning strongly in favour of the NRA. In February 1922 Blyukher's troops stormed the White positions at Volochaevka; Spassk fell early in October and at the end of the month the NRA was driving on Vladivostok, steadily expelling Japanese troops, finally bringing the Far East into the Soviet Republic as one of its Soviet constituents in mid-November 1922. At the end of November the NRA was redesignated the Fifth Red Banner Army and on 2 December 1922 the administration of the Maritime Province Corps took up its station in Nikolsk-Ussuriisk, the *first* Red Army operational staff to be set up in the Far East.[16]

The Soviet Far East was not short of military talent. I. P. Uborevich, another distinguished Civil War army commander, had already assumed command of the Fifth Red Army and troops in the East Siberian Military District in August 1921, taking over from Blyukher as C-in-C of the NRA in August 1922, then resuming command of the Fifth Red Army in November 1922, all at the close of his successful campaign in the Maritime provinces. Short of flushing out the remnants of White forces, the time had come to demobilise the bulk of the Red troops in the east, who in their turn could not escape the effects of the 'military reform' which at the behest of Frunze swept through the whole of the Red Army. This reorganisation did not leave the Far East unscathed: the military establishment was brought under the administration of the 19th Rifle Corps, consisting of the First Pacific Rifle Division (with its HQ in Vladivostok), the Second Amur Rifle Division, an Independent Cavalry Brigade, two aviation detachments, some armoured trains and rear support elements.[17]

Other changes, however, were more fundamental. Under Order no. 757/138 of the Republic *Revvoensovet* (RVSR), dated 12 June 1924, the Siberian Military District was brought into existence, the largest military district ever to enter the Soviet military scene, running from the Urals to Chukotka and Vladivostok and from the East Siberian Sea to the Soviet-Chinese border. The Fifth Far Eastern Red Banner Army was disbanded and its units transferred to the newly established Siberian Military District, with two corps — the 18th based on Irkutsk and the 19th on Khabarovsk — deploying throughout the region,[18] with the new commander, Robert P. Eideman responsible for all Soviet forces in Siberia and the Soviet Far East.

The creation of the Siberian Military District must be accounted the earliest creation of a *theatre command* in the most expansive geographic context, covering both Siberia and the Soviet Far East. Coherent though this was as a *theatre* command, its very amplitude proved to be less than effective when it came to handling operations on a specific and narrower military-geographic axis, which proved to be the case in dealing with the infringement of Soviet rights with respect to the Chinese Eastern Railway in 1929. Events in the Far East were again on the boil, the turmoil in China involving a substantial presence on the part of Soviet advisers, including none other than Blyukher under his *nom de guerre* 'Galin',[19] the same Blyukher who was hurriedly seconded to the Far East for a second time to take command of the Special Far Eastern Army (ODVA), an *operational command* set up on 6 August 1929.

Here we come to basic and long-term *order of battle* for both

Siberia and the Soviet Far East. In its first form the ODVA consisted of five rifle divisions and two cavalry brigades, supported by a Buryat-Mongol cavalry squadron, five companies manned by Volga Germans, a battalion made up of Koreans, reinforced by two rifle divisions (21st and 12th) drawn from the interior, a company of MS-1 tanks and latterly four armoured trains, coastal artillery, signals and engineer units, plus aircraft and Amur Flotilla; three frontier guard detachments were also subordinated to the ODVA.[20] The 'Trans-Baikal Group of Forces' was formed from S. S. Vostretsov's 18th Rifle Corps (with three rifle divisions) supported by cavalry, a tank company, two armoured trains and an aviation detachment — in all some 7,500 men, 88 guns, 9 tanks and 32 aircraft.[21]

ODVA operations against Chang Hsueh-liang ended in mid-November 1929. In this successful limited action, Chinese threats to the Chinese Eastern Railway (a vital link for the Soviet Union) were deflected, while the Japanese officers with the Kwantung Army in Manchuria were both impressed and troubled by this obvious revival of Soviet military power in the Far East.[22] The Soviet-Japanese *détente* did not last long; for many Japanese Siberia still beckoned, its lure undimmed, while the 'Manchurian Incident' in mid-September 1931 loosed the Kwantung Army on its private conquest of Manchuria and brought it face to face with Soviet Far Eastern forces. The Soviet government (which is to say, Stalin), while not abandoning caution, was not slow to react. During the period of the first major Soviet military build-up in the Far East, between 1931 and 1935, ground strength virtually tripled, with corresponding increases in air and naval forces.[23] Reinforcement of divisions east of Lake Baikal proceeded apace. For all practical purposes the ODVA became a *theatre* command, or a command with theatre responsibilities with respect to the Soviet Far East, though this was further rationalised in 1935. For the moment, Soviet forces in 1932 went to work on their frontier defences, setting up concrete pill-boxes in the Ussuri, Amur and Trans-Baikal area (along the Borzya river). On 30 March 1932 the staff of the 'Far East Naval Forces' under M. V. Viktorov was set up, the precursor of the Pacific Fleet; the First Naval Brigade, with its minesweepers and minelayers, took shape under A. V. Vasilev, with S. G. Gorshkov as Fleet navigator;[24] a squadron of MTBs was also transferred from the Baltic to the Pacific station.

The focus of Soviet attention was the Ussuri area, coupled with

177

the development of an infrastructure which included basing for the TB-5 bombers (capable of striking Japan): even in February 1932, 160 aircraft had been sent to the Far East to form the 78th Fighter and the 105th Heavy Bomber Squadrons.[25] Troop strength in the Amur region remained at two divisions, as it did in the Trans-Baikal, though a mechanised brigade (one of the latest Red Army mobile units) was brought in. However, the Ussuri area was turning into the main Soviet *place d'armes*: by the end of 1934 Japanese intelligence assumed that the ODVA had some 500 aircraft (including about 170 heavy TB-5 bombers), 650 tanks, and submarines going to the Pacific Fleet. In the Far East all Soviet rifle divisions were also being assigned an independent tank battalion with 60 tanks, equipped with the latest T-26s, BT-5s and BT-7s. The new mechanised brigades were also being introduced to the Far East.

The Soviet command was seriously concerned about the vulnerability of eastern Siberia, wide open to a Japanese outflanking movement, advancing across the Mongolian plains. As early as February 1932 the 'Trans-Baikal Group' had been reorganised under its commander, B. S. Gorbachev, bringing in the Ninth Rifle Corps, two rifle divisions and two cavalry divisions, plus a tank brigade, but in 1935 the whole Far Eastern command structure was reorganised. In May 1935, the 'Trans-Baikal Group' was transformed into the Trans-Baikal Military District under the command of I. K. Gryaznov: with its HQ at Chita, the new MD now covered eastern Siberia and Yakutia. At the same time the Far Eastern Military District was established on the basis of the Special Red Banner Far Eastern Army (OKDVA), though on 2 June 1935 the OKDVA was again reconstituted.[26] In effect, the Soviet command set up a dividing line at the Great Hsingan range, with the OKDVA holding the eastern reaches. Chief of Staff in the OKDVA was K. A. Meretskov, chief of the Operations Section was P. A. Rotmistrov, while Blyukher himself was appointed a Marshal of the Soviet Union, all at a time when the Japanese General Staff reckoned that Soviet strength in the Far East had quadrupled since 1931, bringing it up to 16–20 rifle divisions, four cavalry divisions, 1,200 aircraft (the Far Eastern Air Force was actually set up on 22 February 1937) and 1,200 tanks.[27]

In 1937 Japan turned on China, momentarily diverting Japanese strength from the Soviet borders, but this did not preclude serious, escalating clashes in 1938 and 1939. On 1 July

1938, the OKDVA went operational as the *'Far Eastern Front'*, committed to the fighting at Changkufeng (Lake Khasan) in July/ August 1938, when two Soviet divisions (32nd and 40th) with tank and air support took on a Japanese division.[28] These actions brought about yet another change in command structures, with the disbanding of the Far Eastern Front (and the abolition of the OKDVA), bringing in a double command — the First Red Banner Army (HQ Ussuriisk) and the Second Red Banner Army (HQ Khabarovsk), both armies being under the direct control of Moscow. In addition, the 'Northern Army Group' was set up and the 57th Special Rifle Corps stationed in Mongolia.[29] As for Blyukher, he was flown to Moscow to be shot in the devastating military purge.

The Japanese now estimated Soviet strength at 24 rifle divisions. Four separate commands — 57 Corps, the Trans-Baikal MD, Second and First Red Banner armies — were presently under direct control from Moscow. Now the Far Eastern forces were thrown into action with a vengeance, committed to the heavy, sustained fighting at Khalkin-Gol (Nomohan).[30] A relatively unknown corps commander, Georgii Zhukov, took command of the 'First Army Group' at Nomohan, pulverising Japanese attempts to intrude on Soviet-Mongolian territory. The Japanese were stamped into the ground, much to their discomfiture and dismay. Brutal though this fighting was, with quite extraordinary implications for Japanese policy and Soviet-Japanese relations, war — worldwide war — was in the offing, putting the Far Eastern forces on full alert. In 1940 Soviet Far Eastern Forces consisted of two major commands, the Far Eastern Army responsible for the Amur-Ussuri area and the Trans-Baikal forces holding both the Trans-Baikal and Outer Mongolia. The Far Eastern command deployed three subordinate elements, the First and Second Red Banner armies, plus the 15th Army, while the Trans-Baikal after July 1940 was deploying the 16th and 17th Red Armies (plus the 36th raised in July 1941) — in all some 38–40 divisions available to the Soviet command.

In June 1941, the worst fears of the Soviet leadership did not materialise. Though the *Wehrmacht* ripped into the Red Army in the west, the Far East remained at peace, though the Kwantung Army's 'special manoeuvres' doubled Japanese combat strength, bringing it up to 700,000 men, while Soviet divisions from the Far East had already been moved westwards as early as the late spring of 1941. Local mobilisation, however, offset these losses in field strength, furnishing some eight rifle divisions and one cavalry division by the end of 1941. In September 1941 the Trans-Baikal Front was established as an operational entity: the front from Khabarovsk to Vladivostok, previously the entire responsibility of the First Red Banner Army, was split into three commands — the 25th Red Army holding the left, the 35th Red Army deployed on the northern sector and the First Red Banner Army at the centre. According to Japanese General Staff estimates the Soviet Far East was now fully mobilised, fielding 800,000 men and at least 23 rifle divisions with 1,000 tanks and 1,000 aircraft.[31] Faced with the Japanese threat, however, the Soviet command was obliged to hold the equivalent of 32–59 divisions in the Far East, 10–29 aviation divisions and six air defence divisions — one million men, 8,000–16,000 guns, 2,000 tanks and SP guns, 3,000–4,000 aircraft and a hundred warships, no less than 15–30 per cent of the Red Army's total combat capability at various times kept back from the deadly struggle in the west.[32]

At this critical juncture Siberia's time had come. Many years ago, in January 1920, in the midst of heated debates about future Soviet defence requirements, the former Bolshevik C-in-C Vatsetis insisted that the European segments of the Soviet Republic were open to attack, thus making it prudent to think of strategic dispersal, shifting the 'military-administrative centre' from west to east, into the Urals and setting up a 'state military-technical base' in the area of Vyatka-Perm-Yekaterinburg-Chelyabinsk-Ufa-Simbirsk. However, what had not been done by deliberate strategic planning (the dispersal of Soviet war industry) had now to be done under the most arduous conditions, exacting a tremendous toll on men and machines alike. From July to November 1941, of the 322 factories sent eastwards, 244 went to West Siberia and 78 to East Siberia: the majority of the plants were in operation within three to four months of being relocated, while such a massive shift required a huge expansion in sources of electrical power and urgent improvement of the rail nets and systems. The indigenous labour force had been substantially depleted by the demands of the army, leaving the *oblasts* of Novosibirsk and Tomsk short of some 280,000 workers by the beginning of 1942. Intensive training courses and the system of 'labour reserves' finally provided 340,000 skilled workers for the industries and railways, more than 16 per cent of the total labour force trained during the war. Women and adolescents were recruited into the industry, including metal-working and mining, war-time pressure bringing substantial changes in the structure and composition of the Siberian labour force.[33]

The 'Siberians' made their presence felt on the Soviet-German front almost at once. Already in 1940, in the Soviet-Finnish war, two Siberian divisions (91st and 119th Rifle Divisions, plus ski battalions) had moved west. Troop movements in the spring of 1941 brought more units westwards, but war demanded whole armies — the 24th from Siberia, and 16th Army from the Trans-Baikal in the beginning, with Siberians making their distinctive mark on almost every battlefront and in the air.[34] Further east the Trans-Baikal MD went on to a war footing as the Trans-Baikal Front, with the Far Eastern Front similarly alerted, the latter anticipating a Japanese attack in 1941 — an attack which never materialised — but then reacting strongly to the Kwantung Army build-up in 1942, strengthening the fortifications around Vladivostok and Voroshilov. Much to the dismay of the Germans, Soviet divisions continued to flow westwards; pleas for Japanese 'activisation' went unanswered.[35] In all, the Far East and Trans-Baikal sent more than 400,000 men, 5,000 guns and in excess of 3,300 tanks — in total, 3 field armies, 39 divisions (23 from the Far Eastern Front), 21 brigades and 10 independent regiments.[36] Overhead US aircraft were also ferried from Alaska to Yakutsk and Krasnoyarsk, with a peak traffic of 300 planes per month, most of which then went westwards to the Soviet-German front.

In 1944 Stalin issued secret orders to bring the Far East fronts up to war readiness for operations — obviously against the Japanese. The tide was reversed, ground and air units moiled eastwards accompanied by the latest equipment: Fifth, 39th and 53rd Red Armies came from the west, reinforced by Sixth Guards Tank Army, in effect virtually doubling the strength in the Soviet Far East and the Trans-Baikal. Under conditions of great secrecy the Far Eastern High Command under Marshal Vasilevskii was installed, while on a daily average ten troop trains together with five carrying munitions and equipment passed along the Trans-Siberian Railway. Three Fronts (Trans-Baikal, First and Second Far Eastern) were mobilised, together with the Pacific Fleet and the Amur Flotilla, air defence forces and three NKVD Frontier Border districts, plus a powerful air component: eleven field armies, one tank army, a Soviet-

Mongolian Mechanised Cavalry Group (under Live), three air defence armies (Trans-Baikal, Maritime provinces and Amur), the Chuguevka Operational Group, three air armies (Twelfth, Ninth and Tenth), plus the Kamchatka 'Fortified Region', the Pacific Fleet with the North Pacific Flotilla and the Amur Flotilla made up the general Soviet order of battle.[37] The Soviet air and naval forces also set up their own theatre High Commands, Novikov for the air force, Kuznetsov for the navy: both of these senior officers acted as deputy commanders to Marshal Vasilevskii.

On August 8 1945 the Soviet government informed Japan that as of August 9 the USSR would consider itself in a state of war with Japan. The next day the 'August storm' broke over the Kwantung Army, a giant, high-speed offensive which rolled across a 5,000-km front to a depth of 600–800 km.[38] On the conclusion of this lightning war, the Far Eastern High Command was disbanded in October 1945: the Trans-Baikal Front was redesignated the Trans-Baikal/Amur Military District with its HQ in Khabarovsk, the First Far Eastern Front became the Maritime Provinces MD with its HQ in Ussuriisk and the Second Far Eastern front was organised into the Far Eastern Military District with its HQ in southern Sakhalin.[39]

OUTPOST AND BASTION: FROM WORLD WAR II TO THE PRESENT

In May 1947, at a time when Mao Tse-tung had committed the Chinese Red Army in what proved to be the final offensive against Chiang Kai-shek's Nationalist forces, the Soviet Far East High Command was re-established under Marshal A. Ya. Malinovskii. In view of events in China, this was scarcely a coincidence. Based on the Trans-Baikal/Amur Military District (redesignated the Trans-Baikal MD in July 1947), Malinovskii's command with its HQ at Khabarovsk assumed control of the Far Eastern, Trans-Baikal and Maritime *krai* MDs, together with the Pacific Fleet and the Amur Flotilla. In this respect it differed little if at all, both in geographic spread and organisation, from its 1945 war-time predecessor, save for the presence of Military Districts as opposed to operational 'Fronts'. Colonel-General N. I. Krylov took over the Far Eastern MD, K. A. Koroteyev the Trans-Baikal (succeeded by D. N. Gusev in 1949) and S. S.

Biryuzov the Maritime *krai*.[40] Already in July 1945 the Siberian MD had been redesignated the West Siberian and the East Siberian MD reactivated in September 1945, taking over the region of Krasnoyarsk and the Tuvinskaya *oblast*; in April 1953, when the East Siberian MD was wound up, these regions again reverted to the West Siberian MD.

With the Korean War ended, uneasy though the truce was (and is) and Soviet-Chinese amity seemingly cemented, the second Far Eastern High Command was disbanded on 23 April 1953, the prelude to yet another restructuring of Soviet forces in the Far East and eastern Siberia. In June, Marshal Malinovskii assumed command of a newly configured Far Eastern MD, with its HQ in Khabarovsk and its boundaries covering the region of the Amur, Kamchatka, Sakhalin, the Maritime *krai*, the Khabarovsk area and the Jewish Autonomous Republic (Birobidzhan). The Trans-Baikal MD reverted to its autonomous status,[41] with the Siberian MD coming back into the overall eastern structure in 1956.

The 'core' command, however, and the 'core' area consisting of the Amur region, the Maritime *krai* and the Pacific, remained with the Far Eastern MD. This special significance was underlined by the quality (and seniority) of commanders assigned to the MD, beginning with Malinovskii himself (who became Defence Minister, taking a young colonel, Nikolai Ogarkov, to Moscow with him from his Far East command staff), V. A. Penkovskii (formerly chief of staff in the Trans-Baikal and Far Eastern MDs, promoted to full general and a future Deputy Defence Minister), Tolubko (until recently C-in-C Strategic Missile Forces), E. F. Ivanovskii (C-in-C, Ground Forces), V. I. Petrov (First Deputy Defence Minister) and a whole generation of officers, graduates of the senior academies in the 1950s who had been assigned to the Far Eastern command — S. F. Akhromeev (now Chief of the Soviet General Staff), Yu. F. Zarudin (Group of Forces commander), M. I. Sorokin, A. M. Mayorov, F. F. Krivda (rising to divisional commander in the Far East, Group of Forces commander and now returned to the Far East as chief of combat training in the revived Far Eastern High Command). In this sense, the Far Eastern command can be compared in status and importance with the other key command, Group of Forces in Germany (GSFG) with its own C-in-C, a 'dumb-bell' arrangement of vital commands between east and west.

After the death of Stalin and at the prompting of Khrushchev, Soviet policy appeared bent on 'rediscovering' Asia, wooing India, encouraging and sponsoring neutralism and advertising Soviet influence.[42] This 'Asian shift', however, enjoyed only modest success and already in 1959 the Sino-Soviet relationship was in serious disarray, developing into outright public acrimony in the early 1960s and culminating in armed clashes in the east.[43] Strengthening the Soviet-Indian relationship was hardly full strategic compensation: the link with Vietnam assumed greater significance after 1964, but the impasse in Soviet-Japanese relations and the prospect of a Sino-Japanese *rapprochement*, even if limited, together with the re-entry of American military power on mainland Asia, signalled a growing deterioration in the strategic environment, raising once again the contingency of a two-front war.

Sino-Soviet clashes on the Ussuri in 1969 triggered off the alarm bells. Tolubko was sent hot-foot to the Far East command and there was carefully inspired talk of a possible Soviet nuclear response — a pre-emptive strike. More serious was the acceleration of the military build-up in the Soviet Far East, resulting in the doubling of Soviet troop strength from 15 to 30 divisions in the first instance. To rationalise an increasingly complex defensive problem, the Central Asian Military District was created in 1969 by carving up the Turkestan Military District: General N. G. Lashchenko held this command (with its HQ in Alma-Ata) until 1977, when he was replaced by Colonel-General Lushev (now General, C-in-C Group of Forces in Germany), followed in turn by General D. T. Yazov, who took over this key 'frontier' command linking the Far East with the southern tier of the Soviet defensive system. Yazov had already served in the Far Eastern command: in the Central Asian district he was heavily involved with operations in Afghanistan and he has now returned to the Far Eastern command.

By the beginning of the 1970s it was becoming apparent that the 'core' command was too constricted, both in terms of geographic spread and potential operational commitments. Siberia, in addition to the growing pace of investment, exploration and exploitation,[44] assumed singular importance as the first Soviet ICBMs were first deployed — in 'soft' sites — along the land-strip of the Trans-Siberian Railway. That importance for and to the Strategic Missile Forces expanded as the exploitation of the unfrozen subsoil of southern Siberia facilitated extensive hardening of missile silos and command posts. North and south of the Trans-Siberian Railway some 26 missile fields accommodate Soviet strategic missiles (ICBMs), supplemented by 171 SS-20 medium-range missiles deployed throughout Central Asia and the Soviet Far East, covering targets in east Asia from deployment in the Maritime *krai* and the Silka valley west of Manchuria — a 'theatre' force capable of striking Harbin, Shenyang and the Taching oilfields (as well as Chinese nuclear installations and objectives in Japan, in the first instance).[45] Eastern Siberia is also a home for the long-range naval reconnaissance BACKFIRE-B aircraft.

There are some grounds for believing that in 1972 plans were afoot to activate command arrangements for possible operations in Manchuria, turning the Far East command in the direction of an operational theatre, or rather a TVD (theatre of military operations). In addition to Manchuria-Korea, however, other operational axes suggest themselves — from the extremity of the Central Asian MD in the direction of Sinkiang, the north and central China axis and, moving much further afield, Vietnam and south China; or yet again Japan and bases in the Philippines. The military anatomy (in terms of ground forces) in the east does display both the scale of effort and the burden involved.

From west to east, the Central Asian MD (also committed to supporting operations in Afghanistan) with its First Army deploys some seven divisions (with two combat-ready divisions up on the Chinese border);[46] the Siberian MD also has some six divisions; the Trans-Baikal, ten divisions; the Mongolian 'operational group' with 39th Army, five divisions; and the Far Eastern MD itself with two army HQs (5th and 15th) and corps administrations comprising 22–24 divisions (including artillery and air assault formations, plus a reinforced naval infantry — *morskaya pekhota* — division). For the whole gamut of force from west to east (including the Central Asian MD which could 'swing' east or into the southern theatre, depending on operational contingencies), the grand tally of over 50 divisions is undeniably impressive (even more impressive considering that the cost of maintaining a division in the east is estimated to be three times that for European Russia and East Europe), though not all formations are at full readiness and those at lower states would need to be 'fleshed out'. However, greater combat readiness has been the order of the day in the Far East for some time.

The 'core' command in the Far East can reckon on having

some 40 divisions to hand (not including Siberia), though the command has been pushing out. Reversing the trend of 1960, Soviet garrisons have been reinforced on the islands of Kunarshiri and Etorofu, with new Soviet contingents accompanied by armour, artillery, air defence systems and supported by tactical aircraft using refurbished and extended runways. Keeping pace with the ground force build-up, Soviet air strength now amounts to some 1,700 aircraft (excluding the BACKFIRE-Bs),[47] an increase of more than one-third over a decade. The Pacific Fleet is yet another case in point, since 1981 the most powerful in the Soviet Navy, tripling its force of ballistic missile submarines and bringing in the latest surface units: protection of Soviet SSBNs and the defence of the Sea of Okhotsk 'bastion', together with countering American SSBNs and carrier groups is a prime mission, though the Pacific Fleet has been instrumental in furthering the outlines of an 'Indo-Pacific' strategic commitment.[48]

The strategic problems of the Soviet Far East (in its widest sense) continue to multiply and not all factors are in the Soviets' favour. The potential enemy is not only the United States with its allies but also Communist China, not to mention the problem of military action on the part of an anti-Soviet coalition or indeed, escalating operations on the part of a pro-Soviet coalition. The year 1978 was, from this point of view, an illuminating period for the Soviet authorities: Hanoi and Peking drifted apart; Hanoi and Moscow enjoined formal friendship; Vietnam joined COMECON (there were even hints of Soviet pressure on the Warsaw Pact states to 'extend' the Pact eastwards); and in Afghanistan a *coup* seemed to favour Soviet interests, although 'encirclement' loomed even larger with the Sino-Japanese agreement and the Sino-American *rapprochement*. The security of the Asian power base, the co-ordination of increasingly diversified forces over an expanding geographical area, increased combat readiness and improved 'command and control' (C_3), as well as the need for greater responsiveness in the event of hostilities — all of these factors clearly prompted the re-establishment of the Far East High Command in 1978, a decision which had its immediate justification in view of the Sino-Vietnamese conflict.

Significant though this change was (and continues to be), it can also be viewed against an even grander design, the *integrated defence* of the Soviet Union promoted by Marshal N. Ogarkov during his tenure as Chief of the Soviet General Staff (1977–84).

Put briefly, over the past decade, the Soviet Union has been given a military-geographic facelift, with three major *theatres of war* (TVs) — the Western (under Ogarkov himself), the Southern (under Zaitsev) and the Far Eastern (under Tretyak). With the dividing line between east and west set more or less on a line running from the Caspian to the Urals, each theatre is divided into main operational 'sub-theatres' ('theatres of military operations' — TVDs), the Western theatre having three (plus the Arctic and Atlantic 'maritime TVDs'); the Far East theatre comprises all eastern commands; while the Far Eastern TVD is, essentially, the 'core' command, with its naval component. The 'theatre staff' under Tretyak,[49] to whom Yazov in the Far Eastern MD and Postnikov in the Trans-Baikal are subordinated in the first instance, embraces naval representation, air commander and air defence commander, combat training and a political directorate — an 'all-arms' integration, while integration and co-ordination with the Strategic Missile Forces is handled by the latter's Far Eastern operational directorate. Given also air defence forces (*PVO Voisk*), air elements, KGB Border Troops and MVD internal security units, not to mention logistics and 'rear services', the Far East theatre C-in-C has (given the full geographic expanse) manpower much in excess of the half million or so men quoted from the nominal order of battle.[50] He has also a brand new rail link, the Baikal-Amur Railway (BAM), a triumph of engineering which links central Siberia with the ports and bases at Sovetskaya Gavan, Vladivostok and Nadkhodka (see Chapter 6). While BAM is available to move the products and resources of south-eastern Siberia, such transportation is directed towards eastern ports on the Sea of Japan and thence the utilisation of the 'Southern Sea Route', passing from the Far East into the Indian Ocean, the Arabian Sea, the Suez Canal and to the Black Sea — a key link which imposes its own burden on Soviet maritime strategy, defending 'an elongated, externally exposed Soviet SSR' (Southern Sea Route), a sea line-of-communication which impinges on all three main dedicated 'theatres of war' — Western, Southern and Far Eastern.[51]

CONCLUSION

Talk of the 'Far Eastern build-up' is certainly dictated by

JOHN ERICKSON

inspection of numbers and nominal order of battle, but this hardly tells the whole story. Even the 'Pacific shift' has to be placed in a specific Soviet context, given the geographical constraints and the less-than-favourable balance of forces, numbers notwithstanding. Turning the outpost into a bastion, continuing the process of the permanent garrisoning of the whole theatre begun in 1969, providing not only the command and co-ordination of a vast theatre but also co-ordinating *theatres* in a country spread across two continents — all of these aims add up to a long-term task. All we presently have is an outline of what Siberia and the Far East may look like, or how the Soviet command might like it to look, in the twenty-first century.

NOTES AND REFERENCES

1. Japanese Special Studies on Manchuria, Vol. XIII: Military History Section, H.Q. Army Forces Far East (1953–5); see also S. Hayashi, *Kantōgun to Kyokutō Sorengum*, Tokyo, Fuyō shobō (1973) (on Kwantung Army-Soviet Red Banner FE Army); and S. Hayashi with Alvin D. Coox, *Kōgun. The Japanese army in the Pacific War* (Quantico, Va., Marine Corps Assn., 1959).

2. N. K. Kiryukhin (ed.), *Forpost gereov: Geroicheskie povestvovaniya o podvigakh dalnevostochnikov* (Khabarovsk Knizh. Izd., 1973).

3. For example, G. S. Chechulina (ed.), *Taezhnye pokhody* (Khabarovsk Knizh. Izd., 1972); *Vremya i sobytiya* (Khabarovskaya kraevaya nauchnaya biblioteka, Khabarovsk, 1972), and *Amurtsy v gody Velikoi Otechestvennoi voiny* (Blagoveshchensk, 1975), which contains a bibliography/recommmended reading-list.

4. For a recent study, see Yu. I. Korablev and V. I. Shishkin (eds), *Iz istorii interventsii i grazhdanskoi voiny v Sibiri i na Dalnem Vostoke 1917–1922 gg.* (Akad. Nauk, Sibirskoe otdelenie, Novosibirsk, 1985); see also *Partizanskoe dvizhenie v zapadnoi Sibiri (1918–1920 gg.): Dokumenty i materialy* (Novosibirsk Knizh. Izd., 1959).

5. See *Sovetskaya voennaya entsiklopediya* (hereafter SVE) (Voenizdat, Moscow, 1976), vol. 2, p. 382, under 'Vostochno-sibirskii voennyi okrug (VO)'.

6. See Kiryukhin, *Forpost geroev*, pp. 58–9, on the 'Ussuri front' (and also the 'Grodekovo front').

7. See *V plameni i slave: Ocherki istorii sibirskogo voennogo okruga* (Zapadno-sibirskoe knizh. izd., Novosibirsk, 1969); G. Kh. Eikhe, *Oprokinutyi tyl* (Voenizdat, Moscow, 1966); V. I. Shishkin, *Revolyutsionnye komitety Sibiri v gody grazhdanskoi voiny (1919–1921)* (Akad. Nauk, Sibirskoe otdelenie, Novosibirsk, 1978); *and V. A. Demidov, Oktyabr i natsionalnyi vopros v Sibiri 1917–1923 gg.* (Nauka, Sibirskoe otdelenie, Novosibirsk, 1978).

8. See collective authorship, *Krasnoznamennyi Dalnevostochnyi: Istoriya krasnoznamennogo dalnevostochnogo voennogo okruga* (hereafter *KDVO*), 3rd edn (Voenizdat, Moscow, 1985), p. 36.

9. See Chechulina, *Taezhnye pokhody, passim*; see also N. Ilyukov and I. Samusenko. *Partizanskoe dvizhenie v Primore (1918–1922 gg.)* (Voenizdat, Moscow, 1962).

10. See L. M. Papin, *Krakh Kolchakovshschiny i obrazovanie Dalnevostochnoi Respubliki* (Moscow Univ. Izd., Moscow, 1957); see also P. M. Nikiforov, *Zapiski Premera DVR* (Politizdat, Moscow, 1963).

11. See *KDVO* p.60.

12. *V. K. Blyukher: Stati i rechi* (Voenizdat, Moscow, 1963), pp. 79–81 (report on military situation in DVR, 18 December 1921).

13. See collective authorship, *Ordena Lenina Zabaikalskii: Istoriva ordena Lenina Zabaikalskogo voennogo okruga*, (hereafter *ZabVO*) (Voenizdat, Moscow, 1980), p. 33.

14. *SVE*, vol. 3, p. 356.

15. See *Sovetsko-mongolskie otnosheniya 1921–1966: Sbornik dokumentov* (Nauka, Moscow, 1966), Doc. no. 8 and Doc. no. 11, Award of Red Banner to Sukhe-Bator, Choibalsan, Khalan-Bator/ Maksarzhar, 31 December 1921–10 January 1922.

16. *KDVO* (Chronology), p. 345.

17. *KDVO*, p. 86.

18. *ZabVO*, p. 49.

19. See A. I. Cherepanov, *Zapiski voennovo sovtnika v Kitae*, 2nd edn (Nauka, Institut vostokovedeniya, Moscow, 1976), pts. 1–2; see also A. S. Perevertailo (ed.), *Sovetskie dobrovoltsy o pervoi grazhdanskoi revolyutsionnoi voine v Kitae: Vospominaniya* (Izd. vostochnoi lit., Moscow, 1961); and M. F. Yurev, *Revolyutsiya 1925–1927 gg. v Kitae* (Nauka, Moscow Univ. Institut Vostochnykh yazykov, Moscow, 1968).

20. *KDVO*, p. 91; also N. Bagrov and N. F. Sungorkin, *Krasnoznamennaya Amurskaya flotiliya* (Voenizdat, Moscow, 1976), pp. 87–102. For Soviet order of battle/Far East, see Iwanow (?), *Kurze Zusammenstellung über die Russische Armee* (Berlin, 1929).

21. *KDVO*, p. 97 for figures/order of battle.

22. On the 1929 operations, see J. Erickson, *The Soviet High Command. A military-political history 1918–1941* (Westview Press (Encore Reprint), 1984), pp. 239–46; *KDVO*, pp. 97–102; and *V plameni i slave*, pp. 69–76.

23. Saburo Hayashi, *Study of strategical and tactical peculiarities*, Vol. XIII, Japanese Special Studies, tables of Soviet strength (Chart no. 3), p. 46, also pp. 50–1.

24. Collective authorship, *Krasnoznamennyi Tikhookeanskii flot*, 3rd edn (Voenizdat, Moscow, 1981), p. 111.

25. *KDVO*, p. 106; see also Erickson, *Soviet High Command*, p. 360; see also German files, *Auswärtiges Amt/Geheim-Akten/Military Attaché Moscow-Kovno*, Rpt. no. 164/33, (17 October 1933), Beilage III, *Luftnachrichten*.

26. *KVDO*, p. 113; *ZabVO*, p. 63

27. Saburo Hayshi, *strategical and tactical peculiarities*, p. 53, on Soviet strengths.

28. Undoubtedly the most comprehensive and best researched work is Alvin D. Coox, *The anatomy of a small war: the Soviet-Japanese struggle for Changkufeng/Khasan, 1938* (Greenwood Press, Westport, Conn.); see also 'Small wars and border problems', in Japanese Special Studies on Manchuria series.

29. *KDVO*, p. 127.

30. Nothing can rival Dr. Coox's latest two-volume study, *Nomohan: Japan against Russia, 1939*, 2 vols. (Stanford University Press, California, 1985). For a recent Soviet work, see P. A. Zhilin (ed.), *Pobeda na reke Khalkin-Gol*, (Nauka, Moscow, 1981); see also 'Nomohan' in Japanese Special Studies on Manchuria series; and Edward J. Drea, *Nomohan: Japanese-Soviet tactical combat, 1939* (US Army Command/General Staff College, January 1981).

31. Saburo Hayashi, *Strategical and tactical peculiarities*, p. 66. There is also much detailed information on Soviet Far East forces in the reports of US Military Attachés/ Russia (US National Archives, Record Group no. 165, *Military Intelligence Division Files: Russia*).

32. *KDVO*, p. 136.

33. For details, see *Sibir' v gody Velikoi Otechestvennoi voiny (iyun 1941 — sentyabr 1945 gg.): Bibliograficheskii ukazatel* (Akad. Nauk, Sibirskoe otdelenie, Novosibirsk, 1976); Conference Report, *V groznye gody* (Trudy nauchnoi konferentsii 'Sibiryaki-frontu', Omsk, 1973); A. Dokuchaev, *Sibir v Velikoi Otechestvennoi voine* (Akad. Nauk, Novosibirsk, 1972) — bibliography, works published 1941–72; *Sibir v Velikoi Otechestvennoi voine* (Nauka, Sib. Otdelenie, Novosibirsk, 1977) (Conference materials); G. A. Dokuchaev, *Rabochii klass Sibiri i Dalnego Vostoka v gody Velikoi Otechestvennoi voiny*, (Nauka, Moscow, 1973); see also E. S. Kotlyar, *Gosudarstvennye trudovye rezervy SSSR v gody Velikoi Otechestvennoi noiny* (Vysshaya shkola, Moscow, 1975).

34. For extensive details of Siberian formations and units, see *Istoriya Sibiri* (Nauka, Leningrad, 1969), vol. 5, pp. 130–41; on Far Eastern forces, S. S. Bevz *et al.*, *Dalnevostochniki v Velikoi otechestvennoi voine: Ocherki* (Khabarovsk, 1973).

35. The German command submitted operational plans to the Japanese for a thrust on Vladivostok and the Trans-Baikal: in 1943 a German *démarche* was accompanied by German tabulation of Soviet troop movements; see *OKH/GenStdH/Abt. Fremde Heere Ost*. Nr. 668/ 43 g. Kdos. *Betr: Fernost*, 1 April 1943, with list of Soviet formations moved westwards since 22 June 1941, Soviet formations encountered since September 1942.

36. For detailed Soviet figures on troop movements, see S. Isaev, 'Vklad voisk Dalnego Vostoka v razgrom nemetskofashistskikh zakhvatchikov', *Voenno-istoricheskii zhurnal*, no. 8 (1979), pp. 73–7 (text and tables).

37. Soviet order of battle, deployment and command systems in Marshal M. V. Zakharov (ed.), *Final: Istoriko-memuarnyi ocherk o razgrome imperialisticheskoi Yaponii v 1945 godu*, 2nd edn (Nauka,

Moscow, 1969); also in English translation, *Finale*, (Progress Publishers, Moscow, 1972); of particular interest is Marshal Vasilevskii's own narrative in *Delo vsei zhizni*, 5th edn (Voenizdat, Moscow, 1984), pp. 453–82.

38. For operational narrative, see Zakharov, *Final*. Among a very extensive Soviet literature, see also V. N. Bagrov, *Yuzhnosakhalinskaya i kurilskaya operatsii (Avgust 1945 goda)* (Voenizdat, Moscow, 1959); *Osvobozhdenie Korei: Vospominaniva i stati* (Nauka, Moscow, 1976); L. N. Vnotchenko, *Pobeda na Dalnem Vostoke* (Voenizdat, Moscow, 1966 and 1971 edns.); an indispensable work by LTC David M. Glantz, *August storm: The Soviet 1945 strategic offensive in Manchuria* (Leavenworth Papers nos. 7–8, US Army Command and General Staff College, February 1983); 'The USSR and the defeat of Imperial Japan, 1945', *Soviet Studies in History*, vol. XXIV, no. 3 (Winter 1985–6) — Introduction by John Stephan, and Soviet essays by Pegov, Achkasov, Yurev and Rzheshevskii.

39. *KDVO*, p. 245.

40. *KDVO*, pp. 248–49.

41. *KDVO*, p. 252.

42. See discussion in Geoffrey Jukes, *The Soviet Union in Asia* (Angus & Robertson, London, 1973).

43. Amidst a mass of Soviet publications, see O. B. Borisov and B. T. Koloskov, *Sovetsko-kitaiskie otnosheniya*, 2nd edn (Mysl, Moscow, 1977); O Borisov, *Iz istorii Sovetskokitaiskikh otnoshenii v 50-kh godakh* (Mezhdunarodnye otnosheniya, Moscow, 1981); the serial publication *Opasnyi kurs* (Politizdat, Moscow, 1971–1980); and Gilbert Rozman, *A Mirror for Socialism: Soviet Criticisms of China* (I. B. Tauris, London, 1985).

44. See Theodore Shabad, 'Siberia and the Soviet Far East: exploitation policies in energy and raw material sectors; an economic assessment', and James P. Lister, 'Siberia and the Soviet Far East: development policies and the Yakutia Gas Project', both in *Regional development in the USSR: trends and prospects* (Oriental Research Partners, Newtonville; NATO, Economics Directorate, 1979).

45. See Robert P. Berman and John C. Baker, *Soviet strategic forces: requirements and responses* (The Brookings Institution, Washington 1982) pp. 12–13 and 13–18 (also Figures 1–3).

46. These and the subsequent figures generally follow those presented by Mark L. Urban, *Soviet land power* (Ian Allan, London 1985), under 'The Muscle — The order of battle', pp. 42–56.

47. See Lt. Col. Ralph A. Cossa, USAF, 'Soviet Eyes on Asia', *Air Force Magazine*, vol. 68, no. 8 1985), p. 54.

48. See Dr. Geoffrey Till, 'The Soviet Pacific Fleet', *Armed Forces*, London (August 1985); Yasunobu Somura and Hirosato Asonuma, 'Die sowjetische Seemacht im Nord-Pazifik', *Marine Rundschau*, no. 5 (1979), pp. 289–96; A. J. Hinge and N. Lee, 'Naval developments in Southeast Asia', *Naval Forces*, vol. VII, no. 1 (1986), pp. 30–43.

49. See Richard Woff, 'Soviet Far East forces; command changes to July 1984', in *Soviet Command Changes and Policy Implications* (Papers presented in association with Defence Studies, University of Edinburgh

and Center for Strategic Technology, Texas A&M University).

50. For a lengthy and well-informed discussion, see Michael Sadykiewicz, 'Soviet Far East high command . . .', *Asian Perspective*, vol. 6, no. 2 1982), pp. 29–69.

51. Fully explored in James T. Westwood, 'Soviet maritime strategy and transportation', *Naval War College Review* (November–December 1985), pp. 43–9: see also his important article, 'The Soviet Union's southern sea route', *Naval War College Review*, January-February (1982).

Addendum: As of 1986, Army General Voloshin replaced General Tretyak as Far East Theatre Commander (C-in-C).

8

Siberia and its Far Eastern Neighbours

Stuart Kirby

Siberia is a slightly vague appellation. Specifically it consists today of the three major Soviet Economic Planning Regions of West Siberia, East Siberia and the Soviet Far East. Separately or together, these do not conduct foreign relations on their own account. They are just regions of the RSFSR, much the largest of the republics of the USSR, and the most heterogeneous. The whole country and its constituent parts are fully integrated, with ultimate decisions, down to a detailed level, highly centralised in Moscow. This also affects the availability of information; essential data (econometric or sociometric), if given at all, are rarely disaggregated to local levels, notably on such vital aspects as imports and exports, national income and other matters pertaining to national security in the Soviet mentality. Fundamental indicators, readily to-hand in the case of other countries, are thus largely lacking. Analysis is nevertheless possible, but only by collecting and collating scraps of information and pointers that are produced much more plentifully in other and more incidental ways.

The USSR embraces the whole northern half of Asia, and Siberia fronts on all of East Asia, thrusting far into the Pacific Ocean to within sight of the United States and Japan — a prodigious confrontation that can only be treated here in drastic summary. Siberia borders on Mongolia, China, North Korea and Japan (as well as the United States in the Bering Strait and the Aleutians). Two of these need be given no space here. The Mongolian People's Republic is so closely linked with the USSR as to be practically an adjunct in all respects, including the stationing of Soviet forces. North Korea is also in close nexus — though it is within the gravitational field of China as well as that of the USSR — and is more truly a 'buffer state' in view of the division between North and South Korea.

The important question therefore concerns relations with the two Asian giants, China and Japan, of which those with Japan are by far the more important. Relations with China are at present (and will evidently be so for the near and more foreseeable future) comparatively limited — indeed, for the most part negative. Relations with Japan, on the other hand, are very extensive and extremely portentous. Furthermore, Japan has become extensively and systematically engaged in participating in the development of Siberia, while other 'developed capitalist' nations have involved themselves only in more occasional, sporadic or marginal ways.

In the complex enmeshment of contemporary international relations it is of course impossible to examine the relationships between any two countries in total isolation, one by one or two by two, as the particular case of Siberia and the nations of the Pacific Basin will illustrate. The Soviet Union has taken up the position vacated by the USA in Vietnam, and discharges this function mainly through Siberia. A powerful and energetic movement has also recently arisen for the conjoint development of the Pacific Basin as a whole by all the countries in it or on it.[1] The Soviet Union stands apart from this movement, which has impetus from North America, Pacific-coast Latin America, Australasia and South-East Asia to the extent of envisaging a Pacific Community. China also currently lies outside the movement, but in its current stance of openness to the world in its quest for modernisation and development, it could well become associated with it. The looming quandary for Siberia lies not only in sets of state-to-state relations; it is that of confrontation, subjective as well as material, with a vastly dynamic, swiftly changing Asian and Pacific world in which Siberia appears conservative — in the sense of adhering to given circumstances — and essentially distinctly slow-moving, even relatively primitive or backward.

The resultant scenario must be presented in two main parts. Firstly it is necessary to be as clear as possible regarding Siberia's nature today and what it means in particular to its neighbours in East Asia. Secondly, one may then proceed to analyse the case-history inferences and prospects which flow from that, mainly and most actively, the connection with Japan, but also relations with China and other lesser powers.

The following account draws mostly on Soviet materials and

viewpoints. Those of the Japanese (which take a much wider perspective) and those of the Chinese should also ideally be incorporated within this study, but lack of space precludes any such detailed consideration. It may justifiably be presumed that readers are more familiar with American and other Western materials.

PERCEPTIONS OF SIBERIA

What constitutes Siberia today, and precisely what destinies are canvassed for it? That vast and rich area has always had a great 'tomorrow', which as of yet does not seem to have arrived, though it may be about to dawn. To Asia and the world, it is the largest remaining under-utilised storehouse of natural resources in the northern hemisphere, with minerals and other materials, fuels, fish, agricultural potentials, and even water being rapidly depleted elsewhere. To East Asia it is — in terms of economic geography and common sense — highly complementary. However, Soviet autarchism, together with an insistence on material rather than spiritual values, resembles a 'bear in the manger' stance from Asian points of view (though the latter, frenetically bent on industrialisation, are willing to concede a good deal to material considerations).

The resource potential, always of course a weighty aspect in Russia's past, has now also moved to a high priority in Soviet calculations. In the last 20 years the development of Siberia has been postulated as a main condition for the success and prosperity of the country and the system as a whole. At the extreme, it may not be too much to assert that it has been viewed by some as a *sine qua non*, essential to the Great Futurity, 'the building of Communism'. Certainly that is not a unanimous or whole-hearted view; though Mikhail Gorbachev tends largely and explicitly to sustain it in his determined policy of raising all levels of performance in the Soviet Union, as he has made clear in both speech and action during his first two years in power. Far beyond simply cutting down on vodka and tightening work-discipline, the Gorbachevian regeneration depends upon acquiring resources from Siberia to make up for the many avowed deficiencies, shortages, shortfalls and shortcomings in the Soviet economy and society; and upon finding in Russia's 'Great East' clear ground and open space for new plants and

195

fresh stimuli for innovation with an infrastructure that is not inefficient or obsolescent (as is that of the older-industrialised parts of the country).

Thus would argue the 'Siberianists', and other detractors or critics of the older (European) Russia; but they are not unopposed. The Gorbachev 'line' rests heavily, however, on the acquisition of the newest and highest technology, for the raising of efficiency throughout, in both industrial and organisational spheres, conjoined with calling in the resources of Russia's New World, Siberia, to redress the imbalance of its Old.

There are, however, intrinsic stresses and strains within Siberia, as well as in its external setting; the 'contradiction' with China rating as fully antagonistic, while feelings in Japan and the rest of Asia and the world are very mixed. Gorbachev's Herculean task entails formidable difficulties. The environment, climate and conditions in Siberia are harsh, and the distances vast; development is costly and cannot be instantaneous. Human and social problems abound; the extent, expense and complexity of the infrastructure needed to cater for those problems have come to be realised in recent years. (Formerly, Marxism tended to consider the whole services sector, including even transport, not to be fully part of the 'productive' process.) Investment has to be substantial, long-term, slow-yielding and all the inter-sectoral linkages complex. The forceful or Procrustean methods of Stalin are no longer applicable.

Local and other vested interests both abound and conflict — most broadly between the well-entrenched big bureaucracies on the European side of the Urals where decision-making is still almost completely centralised, and 'upstart' Siberia. Beyond this, however, there are more ubiquitous rivalries in and between all the regions and other subdivisions, sectoral and special enterprises and lines of activity, each of which must constantly pressure and lobby for priorities on an almost unimaginably broad scale.

Such, then, is the condition on the home front, which must be clearly understood if problems of foreign relations are to be cogently assessed.

THE MAIN PARTNERS

China

Relations with China can be treated most briefly at this juncture — on the one hand because they are already abundantly presented in the Western literature and discussions, and on the other because they are limited, and even negative in some respects. Negotiations have been sporadic for a quarter of a century, with a background of minimal and far from amicable diplomatic relations, vituperations and armed clashes on the border (most alarmingly in 1969, and most recently in the summer of 1986). Essentially the two powers have only normalised such matters as navigation on the frontier rivers and some limited exchange of local products in an agreement with the adjoining north-eastern provinces of China. The acrimony still continues with the Soviet Union being described in China as 'the worst imperialism', or at least a dire 'hegemonist'. The dimensions are shown by the low level of trade between them (Table 8.1). Cultural and other exchanges are practically non-existent.

The extent and venom of the Sino-Soviet split is well known and extensively documented. The media worldwide are eager to seize on any contacts or utterances that might be interpreted as indicating a *rapprochement*. In the present writer's view, reconciliation is impossible — at present or in the immediately foreseeable future — for very powerful reasons, all of them, whether historically or in the tensions of the present day, being causes of conflict rather than conciliation.

The swift Russian annexation of Siberia in the seventeenth century easily overrode the hapless aborigines, but it precipitated clashes with China, which diverted the Russian impetus to the north-east — as far as Alaska and into northern California. The latter proved to be an over-extension, even after considerable consolidation of Siberia during the eighteenth century, and meant confrontation with Britain (in Canada), the United States, Spain and France. Consequently Russia sold Alaska cheaply to the United States and withdrew to concentrate more fully on the development of Siberia.

In the meantime the tsarist Empire developed trade with China through Siberia (Kyakhta), together with political, cultural and missionary efforts. The Chinese annals record that a

Table 8.1: Soviet Trade with China and North Korea, 1956–83 (million rubles)

	China		North Korea	
	exports to	imports from	exports to	imports from
1956	2932	3057	215	205
1957	2176	2952	240	250
1958	2536	3525	232	188
1959	3813	4401	297	206
1960	735	763	36	67
1961	331	496	69	71
1962	210	465	73	79
1963	169	372	74	79
1964	122	283	75	73
1965	173	203	81	80
1966	158	129	77	63
1967	45	51	99	97
1968	53	33	155	109
1969	25	26	181	114
1970	22	20	207	122
1971	70	71	330	122
1972	100	110	252	128
1973	101	101	224	133
1974	108	106	194	149
1975	187	151	93	108
1976	182	119	180	135
1977	118	130	165	164
1978	164	175	177	202
1979	175	157	235	256
1980	170	147	288	284
1981	83	94	279	250
1982	120	103	319	363
1983	256	233	262	325

Source: *Vneshnyaya torgovlya*, Statistical Yearbooks (Moscow, 1956–83).

Russian regiment served the Manchu Emperors in those days. It is worth noting that Russia has thus had a continuous presence in China, closely under Moscow's control, for three centuries, in contrast to the other Europeans, who appeared more sporadically from over the sea, in diverse scattered groups. This is not to say, however, that the one group, the 'big noses' from Russia, was loved more than the other, the 'red-haired' barbarians of the Western Ocean.

By the twentieth century, the Russian Empire was poised to join with the other powers in the scramble for position and profit in China, particularly in its own corner in the north-east, seeking dominance in Manchuria and Korea. It also looked to Japan, after having joined in the Western pressure on that country, to open its doors to the world. Although the clash with Japan brought ignominious defeat to tsarist Russia in 1904–5, China continued to consider itself the main victim, as the Russians had annexed from it territories as large as Western Europe in the Amur and Ussuri areas, and on its other flank, had seized similar expanses of Central Asia.

On coming to power, Lenin had proclaimed that all the tsarist annexations should be given up, but the Soviets have never followed that precept, particularly in the case of China. (Their latter day revisers of history aver, in fact, that Lenin made exceptions in this and other instances.)[3] Twenty-five years after Lenin's death, another cycle of Cathay was completed; China became the second Communist Great Power, the natural ally of the USSR. That alignment lasted hardly more than a decade — an insignificant time in the Chinese reckoning — before turning into the present estrangement and antagonism. The reasons are highly relevant to the question of Siberia's relations with its neighbours.

China requires independence, not a merger. Chairman Mao, on his accession to power in 1949, spoke of 'leaning to the side of' the Soviet Union; that metaphor meant keeping his feet on his own home ground. Soviet methods proved highly unsuitable for China's development — mechanisation and heavy-industrial investment in a country abounding with labour (the opposite case to Siberia, where labour-shortage is the greatest practical problem). What China needs is access to Siberia's natural resources; what it was offered was the methods of development applied in Siberia by Stalin.

The ideological breach is fundamental, of the quality of a religious war — a conflict for the leadership in the Communist faith of the liberation of the world between a richer established 'Vatican' in Moscow and a 'Protestant', more puritanical, do-it-yourself Asian peasant and populist Communism in Peking. Great cultural differences are also involved together with (unfortunately) an element of racial feeling. The upshot is that present-day China, after the turmoil of its Cultural Revolution, has taken a very different path from Russia — more different than that of Yugoslavia or any other Communist country — pursuing the course of modernisation and industrialisation on the basis of complete openness to, and collaboration with, all other countries.

Japan

Turning next to the more positive case of Japan, the account can rely upon more factual data, figures and examples. In 1965 Japan was invited to participate, on a large and systematic basis, in the development of Siberia, and has done much in that direction in the following 20 years. It was most remarkable that this *démarche* came from the Soviet side. The difficulties in the case of China also apply largely to that of Japan. There is even a territorial issue, dismissed by the Soviets as irrelevant and malevolent, inspired by 'revanchist' elements in Japan sustained by United States imperialism, but very real to the Japanese. It is the question of the Kuril Islands. Japan asks for the return of only four of those 'thousand islands' (as they are called in Japanese — in reality there are 56) annexed by the Soviet Union in 1945 from a prostrate Japan a few days after the atomic bombs were dropped. These are the four tiny islands nearest to the Japanese coast and in full sight of it, constituting the Habomai group. The Soviets refuse even to discuss the question. The Soviet Ambassador to Japan characteristically assured a meeting at Hokkaido University in 1979, in his role as the guest speaker, that 'these islands are Soviet territory, inhabited by Soviet people' (which is true, the Japanese population having been deported) 'and we shall never give them up.' The Soviet Union flaunts its military power in those waters, and even shot down a Korean passenger plane that strayed over Sakhalin in 1983.

As with China, much of the preceding history has been troubled. There was the trauma of the Russo-Japanese War (followed by the 1905 revolutionary situation in Russia), the shock of the 1917 overturn presenting a 'red menace' to imperial Japan, which responded by participating extensively, protractedly, and none too gently in the subsequent Allied Intervention in Siberia. The 1930s were stressful, with conflict in Manchuria, Japan establishing Manchoukuo and joining the Axis, followed by armed clashes on the borders of Japan's Korea (Lake Khasan) and Mongolia (Khalkin Gol). During World War II in the Sea of Japan, the delivery of American supplies to the ports of the Soviet Far East was blocked by Japan, and finally, in 1945, the USSR seized the Kuriles and southern Sakhalin. There is still no full peace treaty between Japan and the Soviet Union, only a normalisation of trade and diplomatic relations (since 1956).

The territorial issue still remains. Japan's persistence on it, though not rudely pressed, is sufficient to complicate, hamper and protract all their negotiations, whether on Siberia or on any other issue. The main and related area of practical friction is fisheries. Fish and marine products are important to the Japanese livelihood, and also to that of the Siberians and other Russians. Japan's fisheries are operated by some large capitalist concerns with huge cannery ships and a large number of distinctly more 'proletarian' Japanese operators in small vessels with simple equipment. The Soviets deal fairly smoothly with the former, and harass the latter.

The conflict is complicated, but in sum the picture is as follows. The North Pacific is divided fairly equally for fishing between United States and Canadian, and Soviet, areas of dominance. The Soviet domain is divided into five main zones: the Okhotsk Sea side of the Kuriles, the Pacific side of the Kuriles, the east side of the southern part of Sakhalin, part of the Sea of Japan off the Maritime and Khabarovsk region's coast, and the La Perouse Strait between Hokkaido and Sakhalin. Those were the areas of controlled access for Japanese fishing, with the remainder being (in principle) wholly or predominantly for Soviet use. There are manifold differences in types of fish (including shellfish, sea kale etc.) and in the procedures and equipment used in catching and processing them, as well as the seasonalities involved and the location of processing facilities.

All these matters are governed by voluminous rules, including the keeping and inspection of detailed records on everything that is done. A new dimension of complication was added in 1977 with the ubiquitous introduction of the 200-mile (i.e. nautical miles) zone on all coasts. The results are summarised statistically in Table 8.2. It shows a notable variability in quotas, catches and conditions (hence considerable insecurity for the Japanese operators) on a generally declining trend. The strongest justification on the Soviet side is the need to conserve the fish stocks, necessitating restrictions and controls. This matter is vital to Siberia and Japan, a joint sphere of activity between them. It is however not only of local significance, but part of a world-wide question (with whaling also, as well as the aspects mentioned above), with many countries expanding their operations in all the oceans.

Ideology is also involved — though not as fiercely as with Communist China — since Japan is a highly developed capitalist nation, 'catching up and outstripping' America in a way neither

Table 8.2: Japanese and Soviet fisheries in their 200-mile zone, 1977–85 (thousands of tons)

	Japanese in Soviet zone		Soviet in Japanese zone		Total	
	quota	actual catch	quota	actual catch	quota	actual catch
1977 (July–Dec)	455	302 (66%)	335	63 (10%)	790	365 (46%)
1978	850	466 (55%)	650	360 (55%)	1500	826 (55%)
1979	750	537 (72%)	650	457 (70%)	1400	994 (71%)
1980	750	535 (71%)	650	331 (51%)	1400	866 (62%)
1981	750	526 (70%)	650	209 (32%)	1400	735 (53%)
1982	750	478 (64%)	650	188 (29%)	1400	666 (48%)
1983	750	427 (57%)	650	200 (31%)	1400	627 (45%)
1984	700	441 (63%)	640	119 (19%)	1340	560 (42%)
Total	5755	3712 (65%)	4875	1927 (40%)	10630	5639 (53%)
1985	600	. . .	600	. . .	1200	. . .

Khrushchev nor Gorbachev surely ever dreamed of. Japan too has been subjected to a spate of Soviet abuse, being variously described as feudal, reactionary, revanchist, a colony and lackey of American imperialism, on a scale and at a level of vituperation little realised in the West.[4] This is not just a feature of the past, for it continues today. Instance Soviet Defence Minister Sokolov, writing on the fortieth anniversary of Japan's defeat in the *Red Star* of 3 September 1985 of the 'revanchist' intentions of the Nakasone government and the 'danger' from the 'militarist alliance of Washington-Seoul-Tokyo'; and another Marshal of the Soviet Union, First Deputy Defence Minister and former Commander-in-Chief of the Far East High Command Petrov writing in the same paper on 1 September 1985 that 'the Soviet people cannot ignore the increasing attempts to turn Japan into an American nuclear base and increase her role in the alliance system with the USA . . . Obviously, not everyone drew the correct conclusions from the lessons of World War II and the Hiroshima and Nagasaki nuclear bombings.' Petrov also attributed to Gorbachev himself a suggestion of possible pre-emptive action: 'to stop the aggressor in time is the most important duty of all peaceloving countries.' On the same tack *Izvestiya* on 28 August 1985 approved of a new book, *The Armed Forces of Japan: History and the Modern Day*, for writing that 'Japanese military and political circles are working to . . . expand the ANZUS bloc to a scale comparable to that of NATO. In the event of a world military conflict . . . Japan plans to be the leading military power in that warlike alliance.'

The older generation in Japan has not forgotten the traumatic ending of the war, which involved the capture by the Soviets of one million Japanese, many of them held for a long time in Siberia, subjected to hard labour and attempted indoctrination. Younger Japanese could have forgotten the past, but the Soviet Union takes care to remind them of it persistently.

Nevertheless, Japanese participation in Siberian development was inaugurated in 1965, with very substantial results. The experience of this, the joint Soviet-Japan Siberian Development Scheme (the largest and most solid component in their present relationship), must be summarily quantified here. Before doing so it should be noted that a great deal was involved besides just scheduling and signing a compact; a great development of shipping, credit, financial and foreign exchange facilities, communications, documentation, control, exchange of informa-

Table 8.3: Soviet trade with Japan, 1960–82

	1960	1965	1970	1975	1976	1977	1978	1979	1980	1981	1982
(i) Million rubles											
Soviet imports from Japan	55	160	311	1254	1372	1444	1584	1654	1773	2213	2926
Soviet exports to Japan	69	166	341	669	748	834	736	944	950	817	757
Balance	+14	+6	+30	−585	−624	−610	−848	−710	−823	−1396	−2169
(ii) Index (1965=100)											
Soviet imports from Japan	34	100	194	784	858	903	990	1034	1108	1383	1829
Soviet exports to Japan	42	100	205	403	451	502	443	569	572	492	456
(iii) Share (%) of Japan in USSR's total:											
imports	1.1	2.2	2.9	4.7	4.8	4.8	4.6	4.4	4.0	4.2	5.2
exports	1.3	2.3	2.9	2.8	2.7	2.6	2.1	2.2	1.9	1.4	1.2
of USSR in Japan's total:											
imports	1.9	2.9	2.6	2.0	1.8	2.1	1.8	1.7	1.3	1.4	1.3
exports	1.5	2.0	1.8	2.9	3.3	2.4	2.6	2.4	2.1	2.1	2.8

Source: *Vneshnyaya torgovlya*, Statistical Yearbooks (Moscow 1960–82)

tion, accounting and registration was also involved. All of this must be considered, but the primary overall indicator is again the trade figures (Tables 8.3 and 8.4).

These are the official Soviet figures. Japanese sources give other sidelights from their various angles. The trade has leapt forward mightily since the early 1970s, especially through Japanese deliveries to the USSR, accumulating a very large adverse balance for the USSR which has to be repaid in the future out of increased production, largely from Siberia. The amounts have to be heavily discounted for the great increase in prices during the period, but they do show the trend and the relative proportions. This reflects of course the massive Japanese supply to the Soviet Union under the joint Siberian Development Scheme which continues, but may now be faltering. According to the Japanese side, Japan's exports to the USSR declined by over 27 per cent in 1983 over 1982, and her imports from the USSR by over 23 per cent. While the Japanese government constantly stymies over the territorial issue, Japanese business circles, especially the suppliers of hardware (iron and steel and heavy engineering) still press the scheme. However, the 'Siberia fever' which gripped Japan at the begining of the scheme has now abated — to be replaced by 'China fever'. This, too, has had its difficulties and disappointments, but is powerful; and it is significant that the same persons and interests that head and direct the movement for trade with Russia figure as leaders of the movement towards China. China has cultural affinities with Japan and is politically more accommodating. It is also less abrasive and has made a Treaty of Peace and Friendship (1972) and actually offers a long-term basis of substantial sequential deals, whereas the Soviets deal rather on a project-by-project or sectoral basis.

The composition of the trade (Table 8.4) shows clearly the high 'specific gravity' of machinery of all kinds and the Soviet emphasis on heavy industrialisation. Consumer goods now figure much more largely, but still constitute a small proportion in relation to the demand for them. A notable feature in the tables here is the very large residual entry, 'other', representing one-quarter of the USSR's imports from Japan and of Japan's exports to the Soviet Union. Much of this goes really to the heading 'machinery etc.' for such things as the refurbishment of the fine port of Nakhodka, the creation of another at Vostochnyi on the same bay, container terminals at each, other port works,

Table 8.4(i): Composition of Soviet-Japanese trade, 1960–82 (million rubles)

To USSR from Japan	1960	1965	1970	1975	1976	1977	1978	1979	1980	1981	1982	Total	(1975–82)
(A) *Machinery, equipment and means of transport*													
ships and maritime	11	35	7	15	24	24	42	55	21	5	14	187	(1%)
metallurgical	0[a]	3	24	6	7	22	49	31	35	28	34	212	(1%)
chemical	4	6	36	31	115	286	233	337	90	52	84	1228	(9%)
oil	–[a]	–	–	–	–	26	167	6	9	15	105	328	(2%)
forestry and pulp	–	3	1	2	3	6	10	1	3	3	2	30	
light industry	1	11	5	23	17	5	24	21	17	14	20	141	(1%)
laboratory equipment	–	4	7	4	12	14	15	16	15	21	37	134	
other (A)	0	4	27	361	321	284	277	226	135	534	861	2669	(19%)
total (A)	17	66	107	442	499	685	830	649	575	672	1157	5509	
(B) pipes	10	23	19	208	241	207	309	481	341	640	922	3349	(12%)
rollings and sheet metal	9	7	23	242	264	162	105	152	241	247	234	1647	(3%)
chemicals and plastic	1	13	15	30	30	30	40	48	72	72	55	377	
textiles and clothing	4	10	133	218	223	259	156	167	281	311	273	1888	(13%)
others (other than (A) and (B))	14	41	14	114	115	101	144	157	263	271	535	1570	(4%)
Total	55	160	311	1254	1372	1444	1584	1654	1773	2213	2926	14,220	

Note: a. '0' denotes less than 0.5 million; '–' denotes zero.
Source: *Vneshnyaya torgovlya*, Statistical Yearbooks (Moscow, 1960–82).

Table 8.4(ii): Composition of Soviet–Japanese trade, 1960–82 (million rubles)

To Japan from USSR	1960	1965	1970	1975	1976	1977	1978	1979	1980	1981	1982	Total	(1975–82)
Machinery, equipment and transport	0[a]	2	2	2	4	6	2	4	6	3	6	34	
lathes and forge equipment	–[a]	0	2	2	2	2	1	2	2	2	3	16	
coal	5	13	31	109	112	105	77	73	70	57	66	669	(10%)
oil and oil products	14	36	30	68	113	63	74	95	109	126	113	761	(12%)
iron ore	–	–	4	8	7	8	7	4	0	–	–	34	
pig iron	13	26	15	–	–	–	–	–	–	–	–	–	
scrap iron	–	3	8	9	10	15	10	10	15	13	19	101	(2%)
chrome ore	1	2	2	8	7	4	–	–	–	1	4	24	
aluminium and other non-ferrous	0	5	17	30	12	15	4	7	9	10	8	76	
potash salts	5	6	5	10	10	10	9	8	20	17	12	96	
chemical products	2	1	3	6	7	10	11	11	13	21	18	97	
timber, logs	10	39	129	46	237	323	270	406	375	264	214	2335	(36%)
timber, sawmill	–	1	–	4	5	7	6	9	13	6	5	55	
chips or pulp	1	–	4	8	18	–	6	9	14	17	14	86	
cotton thread	6	6	16	95	86	138	83	93	77	122	99	515	(8%)
other textile materials	0	3	2	8	–	1	3	5	3	2	4	26	
fish and marine products	–	5	4	5	8	6	23	27	24	27	15	135	(2%)
other	12	18	64	51	110	35	150	271	200	126	157	1445	
Total	69	166	341	669	748	834	736	944	950	817	757	6505	

Note: a. '0' denotes less than 0.5 million; '–' denotes zero.
Source: *Vneshnyaya torgovlya*, Statistical Yearbooks (Moscow 1960–82).

communication facilities and many other similar items. The Japanese accounts suggest that gold (a highly secret item on the Soviet side) figures distinctly among the repayments by the USSR. It represented less than one per cent of Japan's imports from the USSR between 1974 and 1979 (nil between 1965 and 1973) but increased to 2.3 per cent in 1978, 2.2 in 1979, 2.6 in 1980, soared to 26.5 in 1981 and 21.9 in 1982, and then falling back to 7.4 per cent in 1983. One may infer that the Siberian projects were not yielding pay-back fully according to plan at the beginning of the 1980s.

The figures reveal marked fluctuation in trade, demonstrating that business with the USSR is not the regular, reliably increasing affair producing all-round mutual benefits that is suggested in the propaganda surrounding it. The relationship is, in the Leninist term, a 'colonial' one, of industrial goods from Japan in return for materials from the USSR. This trade is in any case only a small percentage of the total world-wide activity of either country (Table 8.3 (iii)). The procedures and negotiations, though comprehensive and finely detailed, are cumbersome (in comparison with those with other countries) often overrunning the deadlines. All the matters concerned are generally operated — within the sovereignty, of course, of the governments on each side — by Economic Co-operation Committees (of government, industry, trade and provincial representatives) in each country, a Japan-Soviet Economic Relations Committee in Japan and a Soviet-Japan Committee in the USSR. The Japanese one is accordingly heterogeneous, but the Soviet one is obviously of a State complexion. This has functioned with annual meetings of the said committees, or special extra ones, in each country, and joint ones of the Soviet and Japanese committees together. In that respect there is currently unease only as regards fisheries. In this sphere also negotiations were on an annual basis until 1984, but ceased to be so in 1985 when the quotas for Japan were sharply reduced and the conditions tightened.

Naturally, some interests are affected more than others, and all are vociferous accordingly. A change by a decimal point of one per cent can mean a million-dollar gain to some firms or individuals, and a crippling loss to others. The media and government hear from them accordingly, in the case of Japan and other countries where press and comment are free. Overall, certainly, there has been much growth. Shipping increased prodigiously, the East Asian and Pacific component for the

USSR rising by large percentages, the network of financial links broadened and deepened, and the USSR gained much in technical and organisational know-how.

The foregoing discussion has been couched in terms of relations between Japan and the USSR as a whole. This is necessarily the case because that is the basis on which the information is given, but also because that is the pattern into which Siberia in particular fits, not being autonomous but rather, being completely geared to the national entity. It is therefore necessary to understand that pattern as the framework, the very blueprint that fixes Siberia's role. From that basis it is possible to proceed, as far as one can, to analyse the role of Sibera as such.

The figures given in Table 8.5 are in rubles; the unit of account on all foreign dealings is however US dollars. Apart from the Siberian Development Scheme, the part most specific to Siberia is the 'coastal' (*priberezhnaya*) trade with its own account, established by a special agreement in 1975 and run since 1978 by the *Dalintorg* corporation set up for that very purpose. This is the more local trade between the Soviet Far East and East Siberia with Japan, particularly the west-coast prefectures of Japan, though Australia and North Korea also figure here. This is a small part of the total trade, much more moderately developed but useful (see Table 8.5).

More than 40 local products are involved: principal Soviet exports to Japan are fish and marine products (about 50 per cent), timber and sawings (another 40 per cent), with the rest

Table 8.5: Coastal trade between USSR and Japan, 1976–82 (million rubles)

	1976	1977	1978	1979	1980	1981	1982	Total
To USSR from Japan	21	23	24	28	36	50	36	218
% of all USSR imports	1.5	1.6	1.5	1.6	2.0	2.2	1.3	
To Japan from USSR	23	26	27	33	35	39	35	218
% of all USSR exports	3.1	3.0	3.7	3.5	3.7	4.8	4.5	
Balance	+2	+3	+3	+5	−1	−11	−1	0
Total	44	49	51	62	71	89	71	436

Source: Ya. A. Pevzner and Yu. S. Stolyarov (eds), *SSSR-Yaponiya: problemy torgovli i ekonomicheskikh otnoshenii* (Moscow, 1984), chapter 8.

being composed of small amounts of coal, fluorspar, scrap mica, peat, gravel, salted fern (*paporotnik*), syrup from berries, and scrap iron. In exchange Japan sends textiles, knitwear, shoes, vegetables and fruit, but also some producer goods: fishing gear, processing equipment for food or woodworking, varnish, paint, tanning and packaging materials. These are partly on the 'compensation' basis, to be paid out of the resultant product; a récent example is plant for drying peat, another some decorative stonework. Though constituting only one-fortieth of Soviet-Japanese trade, it does brighten up the consumer goods scene in Siberia, providing about three per cent of the whole turnover of such goods in Khabarovsk *krai*, including 7.1 per cent of the textiles, 5.6 per cent of clothing but 20 per cent of the knitwear and 41.7 per cent of the chinaware.[5] In some such proportions, it links especially the Sakhalin, Khabarovsk and Maritime *krais* with Hokkaido and west-coast Japan, benefitting the latter's small enterprises.

The coastal trade quadrupled in the 1960s (from a very low base) and trebled in the first half of the 1970s, thence increasing in the 1970s by 13.6 per cent a year. It includes few innovations, though syrups from Siberian berries are used by the Japanese confectionery industry, and there are cargoes of opportunity, such as a sale of iron scrap from Magadan (believed to come partly from the dismantled camps on the Kolyma).

Overall, the Soviet Far East furnishes 44 per cent of all the USSR's exports of timber in the round, but only four per cent of the sawings and about eight per cent of the cellulose — so much more processing could be carried out. It provides 23 per cent of the exports of fish, but in contrast, 77 per cent of those of fish in cans. Seventy per cent of the Soviet Far East's exports go to Japan, the rest going to some 50 other countries. (The discussion refers to value terms throughout.) The coastal trade represents 80 per cent of all Soviet exports to Japan, but only 25 per cent of all Soviet imports from Japan — representing, however, only about five per cent of all Soviet exports to capitalist countries and four per cent of Soviet imports from them. Some 300 enterprises in eight provinces of Siberia take part in the coastal trade.

In physical terms, Siberia has gained most from the Siberian Development Scheme — new port facilities, shipping (the Far East Navigation organisation now has over 400 vessels totalling three million tons), complete plants and production units, communications systems, and constructional and other gear. The heavy machinery and automotive 'park' is an impressive component, of which only a few examples can be given here. A huge amount of big earth-moving and tunnelling equipment went to build the BAM. The general agreements on mining in south Yakutia and on forestry provided more than 80 billion yen worth of vehicles and road-making equipment, including 2,500 log-transporters, 1,200 dump-trucks, 22 water-transport adjuncts (hydraulic dredgers, floating cranes, tug-barges and piledrivers). Of the total, forestry accounts for 15 billion yen. Reference in this chapter is mainly to East Siberia and the Soviet Far East. Practically all the pipeline material and a large part of the chemical-industry and other plant goes to West Siberia from Japan. The chemical industry has been the main domain for the provision of complete plants or processes by Japan: 74 chemical factories and installations worth 2.8 billion dollars, including five fertiliser works, two for urea, one for chloroprene rubber, three for benzol, other facilities for industrial washing, nylon film and texturised polyester thread. About 40 of these plants were completed by 1984, with some production for export as well as use within the USSR. For the Sakhalin oil and gas search, the basis was rather the leasing of good modern equipment (on a smaller scale, of course). The new port of Vostochnyi, opened in 1974 (first phase completed in 1979), had 80 million dollars in credits from Japanese firms covering pier and wharf construction, dredging operations, etc.[6]

CONCLUSION

These are but fragments of a large story. Much has been done in and for Siberia, especially by Japan — but this has not merely benefitted Siberia *per se*, because it is part of the highly integrated Soviet totality. Indeed, in a wider sense this also applies to the whole Soviet bloc, including Eastern Europe which supplies much to Siberia and also draws on it (though to a far lesser extent than Japan) and other areas of Soviet influence. Though Siberia's development is relatively small and not the most spectacular in comparison with the fundamental and dramatic changes proceeding elsewhere in East Asia and the Pacific Basin, Siberia — with one-twelfth of the Earth's surface and a larger proportion of the most-needed natural resources — obviously has a great future, most immediately for its neighbouring countries but also for the world as a whole. Those larger prospects for Siberia's involvement in the global economy form the subject of the final chapter by John Stephan.

NOTES AND REFERENCES

1. For a more extensive exposition of the present author's view of the Asian-Pacific setting, see S. Kirby, *Japan's role in the 1980s* and *Towards the Pacific century: economic development in the Pacific Basin* (Special Report nos. 81 and 137, Economist Intelligence Unit, London, 1980 and 1983); and annually in the *Far East and Australasia Yearbook* (London).

2. The present author's assessment of the area may be found at greater length in S. Kirby, *Siberia and the Far East*(Special Report no. 177, Economist Intelligence Unit, London, 1985).

3. For a detailed analysis, see S. Kirby, *Russian studies of China* (London, 1975), and *Russian studies of Japan* (London, 1981).

4. During the fortieth anniversary of Japan's defeat in 1945, the Soviet media repeatedly carried accounts of, for example, their airborne military successes against the enemy; see *Pravda*, 18 Aug. 1985.

5. Details from Ya. A. Pevzner and Yu. S. Stolyarov, (eds), *SSSR-Yaponiya: problemy torgovli i ekonomicheskikh otnoshenii* (Moscow, 1984).

6. V. A. Aleksandrov, in ibid., ch. VIII.

9

Siberia and the World Economy: Incentives and Constraints to Involvement

John J. Stephan

Western press coverage of the 'Russian problem' between 1918 and 1922 periodically featured speculative discussion of Siberia's economic future. The so-called Vanderlip affair of 1920 elicited animated, if not always informed, commentary on this subject. Washington B. Vanderlip arrived in Moscow in October amid much fanfare. He described himself as a well-connected Californian entrepreneur, representing a consortium of wealthy American investors and Ohio Senator Warren G. Harding, the Republican Party's presidential candidate. The Soviet leaders received Vanderlip and accorded him an audience with Lenin. On 22 October, the Commissariat of Foreign Affairs announced that Vanderlip was being offered an exclusive 60-year concession for all natural resources in Soviet territory east of the 160th meridian, an area of over a million square kilometres stretching from Kamchatka and the Kolyma Basin to the Bering Straits. The announcement did not mention Vanderlip's assurances to Lenin that in the event of a Republican victory in the November elections, the new administration would extend diplomatic recognition to the Soviet regime.[1]

The Republicans duly won the election. Vanderlip hailed Lenin as a 'Russian Washington', but heady visions of Siberia's entry into the world economy evaporated, leaving a residue of disclaimers. Harding could not remember having met or corresponded with anyone named Washington Vanderlip. The consortium proved to be largely imaginary. Vanderlip turned out to be a Hollywood promoter whose greatest asset was a surname shared with a prominent Wall Street banker.* This coincidence

* Frank Arthur Vanderlip (1864–1937), president of the National City Bank of New York

accounted for Moscow's hospitality, the 60-year concession, and the meeting with Lenin. When the mists cleared, Vladimir Ilich summed up the affair with sardonic humor in a speech to bewildered comrades: 'Unfortunately, our VChK [*Cheka* — author] counter-intelligence has not yet seized the North American states, so we still can't get all these Vanderlips straight.'[2]

This episode retains more than anecdotal significance. It illustrates the chronic discrepancy between the promise and the reality of Siberia's international economic profile. Rooted in geography, domestic and international politics, this discrepancy has plagued Siberia throughout its modern history.

Since the 1960s, however, forces have been at work that may change Siberia's traditional isolation from the world economy. Firstly, there is a growing awareness of the magnitude and implications of Siberia's natural endowments: 90 per cent of the USSR's (15 per cent of the world's) fossil fuels, 75 per cent of the USSR's (15 per cent of the world's) forests, and vast marine and mineral resources which make the USSR the only country in the world capable of supplying its own raw material needs.[3]

Secondly, the USSR's own economic future is ever more clearly tied to Siberia. Exploitation of Siberian resources will be a mainspring propelling the development of the country as a whole. At the same time, the speed and effectiveness of this process will depend significantly upon imported technology and equipment, thereby underlining the international dimension of Siberia's future.

Thirdly, Siberia is adjacent to the Pacific Basin, economically the most dynamic region in the world today. Many Pacific-rim countries are not only developing rapidly but forging multilateral ties of regional economic interaction. While market economies such as the United States, Japan, Canada, Australia, South Korea, Taiwan, Hong Kong, New Zealand, and the ASEAN nations* play a leading role in this process, the People's Republic of China has, by stressing a comprehensive modernisation programme, demonstrated that a communist country can participate in an emerging Pacific 'community'. These dramatic and far-reaching integrative trends have not escaped the attention of Soviet observers, and it is probably safe to assume that they will figure in the new Soviet leadership's deliberations about economic reform.

To what extent will these forces enhance Siberia's role in the

* Malaysia, Singapore, Indonesia, Thailand, the Philippines, and Brunei

world economy? This question will be addressed by: (1) reviewing the record of Siberia's international economic ties from the sixteenth century until the present; (2) identifying current geographical, economic, and political constraints to greater Siberian involvement in world (and particularly Pacific Basin) markets; and (3) sampling Soviet and foreign prognoses of Siberia's future in the global economy.

PAST PATTERNS

Siberia's entry into international commerce dates from the sixteenth century and for nearly 300 years revolved around the export of furs. A portion of pelts collected by Yermak and his Cossack successors along the Tobol, Irtysh, Ob, Yenisei, and Lena rivers was exported from Russia to Western Europe where sartorial fashions made them prized possessions of aristocrats and wealthy merchants. After the regularisation of Sino-Russian trade through Mongolia in the aftermath of the Kyakhta Treaty (1728), Siberian furs and other animal products found their way into the Celestial Kingdom. From the late eighteenth century, American traders started frequenting the North Pacific littoral, acquiring Siberian and Alaskan pelts and re-selling them in Canton.

Until the middle of the nineteenth century, Siberia's international economic ties were severely curtailed. A harsh climate, immense distances, poorly developed overland transport, and the absence of an ice-free port on the Pacific all discouraged commerce. The population of Siberia was too small and scattered to generate significant internal markets. Neither Japan (locked in self-imposed isolation) nor China (restricting trade through Kyakhta and barring Russian ships from Chinese ports) offered realistic commercial opportunities. Most tsarist administrators, aware of Siberia's role as a receptacle for exiles and convicts, and alert to possible sources of unrest, discouraged regional contacts of any kind with the 'outside' world. As the governor-general of Western Siberia wrote in 1849: 'It is important above all to keep the inhabitants of Siberia away from immediate contact with foreigners, contact which could easily turn into fatal propaganda.'[4] Not surprisingly, foreigners such as John Ledyard (1751–89), who tried to interest St Petersburg in linking Siberia with a Pacific regional trade network, met a cold reception.

215

Events in the 1850s and 1860s challenged Siberia's insularity. A new generation of administrators and naval officers, represented by the Governor-General of Eastern Siberia, N. N. Muravev (1809–81), and Captain G. I. Nevelskoi (1813–76) regarded the establishment of economic links with Asia and the Pacific as a fulfilment of Russia's imperial destiny. The Crimean War (1854–6) exposed Russia's strategic vulnerability in north-east Asia, casting doubt on the conventional bureaucratic wisdom of preserving Siberia as 'a great slop pit . . . into which is poured everything base and revolting from all of Russia'.[5]

Acquisition of 500,000 square kilometres of north-eastern China in 1858–60 gave Russia access to the only major waterway connecting Siberia and the Pacific — the Amur river. It also extended Siberia's eastern coastline southward several hundred kilometres along the Sea of Japan and paved the way for the founding of a new port — Vladivostok (1860) — which since the 1870s has been Russia's gateway to the Pacific.

Mid-century changes in the political geography of north-east Asia coincided with a sharp rise in American commercial interest in Siberia. During the 1850s American merchants opened thriving import businesses at Nikolaevsk on the Amur. In 1858, the president of the United States appointed a 'Commercial Agent on the Amoor' in anticipation of new opportunities for American enterprise in Siberia.

Siberia's participation in the international economy received a strong impetus from construction of the Trans-Siberian Railroad (1891–1904), the Ussuri Railroad (1891—98) and the Amur Railroad (1906–16). The need for steel, rolling stock, and bridge materials for these projects generated hefty orders from British, German and American manufacturers.

Improved overland transportation and the establishment of a regular steamer service from Odessa to Vladivostok facilitated massive peasant migrations from European Russia to Siberia between 1891 and 1914. A smaller but significant flow of foreign immigrants, notably from Scandinavia, gave Siberia an international complexion. Danes helped to create a flourishing dairy industry in western Siberia. Between 1894 and 1912, Siberia exported half a billion rubles worth of butter, much of it shipped directly to London in special refrigerator railway cars.[6] Demand for American agricultural machinery at the turn of the century outpaced supply, in spite of the fact that hardly a village between the Urals and the Pacific lacked a local representative of International Harvester or John Deere companies. Small wonder that even such a sober observer as Henry Adams wrote of the 'Americanization' of Siberia[7] or that catch-words such as 'New California' and 'land of the future' should crop up in journalistic discourse.[8]

Japanese, Chinese and Korean enterprise contributed to the internationalisation of Siberia's economy. Korean immigrants settled in the southern Maritime province around Lake Khanka, engaged in rice farming and ginseng collecting, and moved back and forth across the Russian-Korean frontier. Chinese traders, ginseng collectors, and gold smugglers linked the Russian Far East with Manchuria. Japanese importers, shop-owners, barbers and prostitutes established themselves in Vladivostok, Khabarovsk, Nikolaevsk, Chita and Blagoveshchensk, served by Japanese chambers of commerce, Japanese banks and Japanese-language newspapers. Vestiges of their presence can be seen today in Japanese cemeteries of several Soviet Far Eastern cities.

At the turn of the century Vladivostok personified Siberia's new-found cosmopolitan exuberance. As the Pacific gateway to Asiatic Russia, it served as a transhipment port for cargoes and passengers travelling between Europe, the Far East, and the American West Coast. Ships from Odessa, Hamburg, London, Hong Kong, Yokohama, and San Francisco found shelter in Vladivostok's Golden Horn. Rail transport was available to Europe via the Chinese Eastern Railroad across Manchuria which linked up with the Trans-Siberian. Undersea cables built by a Danish firm secured Vladivostok's telegraphic communications with Nagasaki and Shanghai. Dozens of foreign firms, such as Brynner & Company of London, which developed Amur timber resources and the Tetiukhe lead mines, located their regional headquarters in Vladivostok. France, Germany, Italy, Great Britain, Turkey, Greece, China, Japan, the Netherlands, Norway and the United States maintained consulates in Vladivostok. Of the city's 29,000 residents in 1897, nearly 12,000 were Chinese, Japanese or Koreans.[9]

Neither the Russo-Japanese War (1904–5) nor revolutionary unrest derailed Siberia's growing involvement in international markets. More and more Siberians, notably merchants, manufacturers, the professional classes and members of the Siberian peasant co-operatives, perceived the advantages of freer trade and greater regional interaction with Asian and Pacific nations. As an English visitor noted in 1912: 'Siberia is beginning to discover her needs, is gradually forming a public opinion of her own, and is shaping her own policies, not infrequently definitely opposed to those of European Russia.'[10] Such centrifugal tendencies aroused some disquiet in St Petersburg. Even such an enlightened advocate of freer economic enterprise as Prime Minister P. Stolypin warned in 1910 that Siberia must be dealt with or it would produce a 'rough democratic society' that would some day 'crush European Russia.'[11]

A world war, two revolutions, civil war and foreign intervention buffeted Siberia between 1914 and 1922, creating vicissitudes for, but not interrupting, Siberia's international economic ties. By immobilising Baltic and Black Sea Ports, the European War made Vladivostok one of Russia's principal gateways, through which large quantities of commodities and military ordnance from America and Japan flowed *en route* across Siberia to European Russia. The Allied Intervention (1918–22) strengthened the international colouration of eastern Siberia's economy by bringing with it heavy doses of American and Japanese capital investment and commercial enterprise. Soviet allegations notwithstanding,[12] it is debatable whether the United States sought to impose economic control over Siberia between 1918 and 1920. Some concessions were awarded to American firms by 'White' (anti-bolshevik) authorities, but these concessions were no more grandiose than those conferred on Washington Vanderlip (1920) or on the Sinclair Oil Company (1922) by the Soviet regime.[13] Russia's Far Eastern fisheries, to which the 1905 Portsmouth Treaty had guaranteed Japanese access, did come under Japanese domination between 1918 and 1925.

The establishment of Soviet rule from the Urals to the Pacific between 1920 and 1922 curtailed but did not eliminate Siberia's participation in the international economy. The Far East was allowed by Moscow to maintain trade links for pragmatic reasons with Manchuria (nominally part of China but in fact controlled by a regional warlord, with extensive Soviet and Japanese railroad concessions), Japan and the United States. A shortage of capital, equipment and managerial skills led Moscow to allow selected Russian and foreign entrepreneurs to continue their pre-revolutionary enterprises, albeit under strict supervision. Exports of Siberian furs, minerals and marine products (27 per cent of US crabmeat imports came from the Soviet Far East in

1930)[14] enabled the region to support itself without capital allocations from European Russia during the early and mid-1920s. Oil and coal concessions on northern Sakhalin, awarded to Japan in 1925, also provided capital for imports such as American agricultural machinery and canning equipment.

The relative importance of foreign commerce for capital accumulation in the Soviet Far East may account for the fact that the New Economic Policy (NEP) was permitted to continue there even after the beginning of the first five-year plan in 1928. As late as 1930, *Gosplan* chief Gleb M. Krzhizhanovskii could affirm that 'the question of utilising the resources of Siberia is not one for the USSR alone but for the world order as a whole.'[15]

Krzhizhanovskii's statement was belied by events. The 1930s brought Siberia isolation from, not integration with, the world economy. Flanked by hostile and expansionist regimes in Germany and Japan (the latter's occupation of Manchuria in 1931–2 posed a direct threat to eastern Siberia and the Soviet Far East), Stalin opted for rearmament and autarky. Stalin was obsessed with the spectre of a Japanese invasion.[16] He also believed, or pretended to believe, that certain Party oppositionists were plotting with Japan to detach the huge Far Eastern Maritime *krai* from the USSR.[17] Indeed, there *were* such thoughts among Japanese military and civilian leaders at this time. The future foreign minister, Matsuoka Yōsuke, wrote to President Franklin D. Roosevelt in 1938 suggesting a Japanese-American joint purchase of Siberia 'to the Urals'.[18]

Siberia's insulation from foreign commerce during the 1930s also derived from the Soviet regime's determination to shield harsh internal realities from international publicity. Although hundreds of American and European youth volunteered to take part in the construction of a giant metallurgical complex at Magnitogorsk in West Siberia in the early 1930s, projects in the arctic (Norilsk), East Siberia and the Far East were closed to outsiders, except on an involuntary basis, such as Polish deportees working in the Kolyma mines under the auspices of *Dalstroi* (Far Eastern Construction Trust), an organ of the NKVD.*[19] Construction work on the Baikal-Amur Railway (BAM) during the second and third five-year plans (1932–42), suspended after the German invasion in 1941, drew upon

* NKVD: People's Commissariat of Internal Affairs, appellation of the secret police between 1934 and 1944. From 1944 until its dissolution after Stalin's death, *Dalstroi* was administered by the Ministry of Internal Affairs (MVD).

thousands of forced labourers[20], but unlike the current BAM 'project of the century' (see Chapter 6) involved no visible foreign corporate participation. The forced resettlement in 1937 of an estimated 250,000 Soviet Koreans from the Maritime *krai* to Central Asia underlined Moscow's nervousness about any kind of unofficial regional contacts with neighbouring states.[21]

Germany's invasion of the USSR forced Soviet leaders to reopen Siberia — a bit. As in World War I, the Far East became a vital maritime gateway for desperately needed war *matériel* and foodstuffs. Fully 75 per cent of US Lend-Lease tonnage to the USSR between 1941 and 1945 passed through Vladivostok.[22] Other cargoes were flown from Alaska to Yakutsk. Siberia's new economic and geopolitical significance in an air age, dramatised by Lend-Lease and by Vice President Henry A. Wallace's visit in 1944, was popularised in upbeat literature hailing what was then perceived as the birth of a new Pacific era.[23] Some American writers envisioned an upsurge of trade between the Soviet Far East and the US West Coast in the post-war period.[24]

Siberia's highly touted international prospects withered in the face of post-war Soviet-American rivalry. The termination of Lend-Lease, the advent of the Cold War, the Korean War, and Japan's emergence as an American ally all reinforced Siberia's economic insulation from international markets. After sustained pressure from senior naval officers, Vladivostok was made a military port off-limits to foreign commercial traffic. The Japanese and US consulates there closed in 1945 and 1948 respectively. A new commercial port at Nakhodka took shape some 55 miles east of Vladivostok, but its facilities remained quite modest through the late 1940s and early 1950s.

Siberia's international ties throughout the 1950s centred around neighbouring communist states — Mongolia, China and North Korea. Siberian timber, fish, and some manufactured items were exchanged for animal products, various foodstuffs and textiles. In 1954, Nikita Khrushchev discussed with Mao Tse-tung the possibility of 200,000 to one million Chinese coming to work in Siberia.[25] No agreement was reached, but the question re-surfaced in 1985 on Moscow's initiative.[26]

Notwithstanding the deterioration of Sino-Soviet relations during the 1960s and the resulting decline in Sino-Soviet trade, Siberia's international economic ties proliferated throughout the decade. Soviet-Japanese economic co-operation, negligible in the 1950s, assumed a leading place among Siberia's international links, a place that has not been relinquished since. Bilateral trade with Japan made impressive annual gains (see Chapter 8). Starting in 1963, Siberian and Japanese enterprises engaged in 'coastal trade', a form of regional bartering conducted outside the formal bilateral trade framework. Since 1968, Japan has concluded agreements with the USSR for five major joint projects in Siberia: the exploitation of Amur timber resources, wood chip production, construction of a container port at Vostochnyi (near Nakhodka), the exploration of offshore Sakhalin petroleum and the development of south Yakutia coal. In 1967 the Trans-Siberia land-bridge of container shipments between the Far East and Europe went into operation (see Chapter 5). In 1968, a coastal trade agreement was concluded with North Korea. Largely as a result of war in Vietnam, maritime traffic between Vladivostok and Hanoi dramatically increased during the 1960s, developing firm economic links between Siberia and South-east Asia.

During the 1970s, as the Soviet Union moved decisively away from autarky towards integration with the global economy, Siberia shed its vestigial isolation. Several conditions and policies underlay this shift. Firstly, geological exploration during the 1960s had uncovered vast quantities of oil, natural gas, coal and minerals in Siberia, the magnitude of which greatly enhanced the region's global 'visibility' as a major potential source of raw materials. Secondly, Siberia's natural resources assumed new value in the international market as a result of rising prices for raw materials in the wake of the 1973 Arab oil embargo. Thirdly Soviet planners recognised that exports of Siberian resources could earn hard currency for the purchase of Western technology and equipment necessary to maintain the pace of the USSR's economic development. Fourthly, the advent of *détente*, signalled by the 1972 Nixon-Brezhnev summit and resultant arms control, trade, and scientific and technical agreements, created a political atmosphere conducive to Soviet participation in the world economy. Fifthly, the economic dynamism of Pacific Basin nations appeared to raise prospects for regional markets for Siberian resources. Finally, in 1974 resumption of work on the Baikal-Amur Railway committed the USSR to making East Siberia's untapped resources available to international markets and to preparing the Soviet Far East for more active economic participation in the Pacific Basin.

By 1984, the USSR had become the world's leading exporter

of energy.[27] This achievement is largely a result of exporting Siberian oil, gas and coal. The USSR exports about 15 per cent of all primary energy which it produces: 27.4 per cent of oil, 12.3 per cent of gas and 3.8 per cent of coal.[28] Most of these exports are destined for socialist (COMECON) countries, including Cuba and Vietnam. Nonetheless, significant exports of energy are directed to Western Europe — namely to West Germany, France, Italy, Austria, Belgium, the Netherlands, United Kingdom, Sweden and Finland. The *Soyuz* natural gas pipeline from West Siberia's Urengoi field via Czechoslovakia to several West European countries dramatises this relationship.

Siberian energy exports to Japan have developed less rapidly than have those to Europe. Nonetheless, Soviet-Japanese joint development of south Yakutia coal and Sakhalin oil and gas, initiated in the mid-1970s, is proceeding.

The importance of Siberia's new links with the world economy may be gauged from the fact that Siberian exports now account for about three-quarters of the USSR's hard currency earnings.[29] Oil remains the single largest earner of hard currency for the country, but the proportion of natural gas — Siberian natural gas — is steadily increasing.

Not surprisingly, a large proportion of technology imports to the USSR is destined for Siberia. During the 1970s, Siberia received about one-seventh of all foreign investment in the USSR. Some 40 contracts for Siberian projects were concluded with European, Japanese and American firms. Historically East European countries have worked closely with the USSR to develop Siberia's energy resources. East Europeans contributed labour, equipment and hard-currency support for construction of the natural gas pipeline from West Siberia to Europe.

Siberia's role in the world economy does not depend on the export of energy resources alone. Siberian factories produce a wide variety of goods, from precision instruments to diesel engines, that are exported throughout the world. Offering comparatively rapid deliveries and favourable freight rates, the Trans-Siberian land-bridge has become a major international artery, accounting for 15 per cent of container shipments between Europe and Japan in 1980.[30] It is also worth mentioning the international economic significance of research in such fields as permafrost and aquaculture, conducted at the Siberian Department of the USSR Academy of Sciences at Novosibirsk and the Far East Science Centre at Vladivostok.

Siberia has also assumed growing significance in international aviation. Trans-Siberia flights offer the fastest service between East Asia and Europe. In 1985 Japan and the Soviet Union agreed to allow Japan Air Lines to fly from Tokyo to Western Europe non-stop over Siberia, covering in twelve and half hours what currently takes 15 hours via Moscow and 17 hours via Anchorage, Alaska.[31] Japan, the United States and the Soviet Union agreed late in 1985 to link Khabarovsk air controllers with existing North Pacific flight monitor systems in order to avoid a repetition of the Korea Air Lines tragedy of 1 September 1983.[32]

PROBLEMS

Siberia has moved towards greater integration with the global economy, yet it still faces formidable obstacles to further progress in this direction. These obstacles derive from geography, socio-economic problems, and political forces.

A harsh environment and remoteness seriously inhibit Siberia, particularly East Siberia and the Soviet Far East, from playing a larger role in the world economy. Geographical impediments are likely to increase rather than decrease in the future, as relatively accessible deposits of raw materials are exhausted and development of new deposits moves northwards into even more inhospitable climes located further from final markets. Geographical obstacles are especially a major consideration in East Siberia and the Soviet Far East. Remote from the country's economic core in European Russia, these areas might be expected to establish economic links with Pacific-Basin countries, notably Japan. Yet major deposits such as Yakutia coal and natural gas are separated from the Pacific littoral by several hundred kilometres of rugged mountains and untamed *taiga*.

A variety of economic forces and conditions impede Siberia's participation in the global economy. Soviet investment policies have, according to one observer, polarised rather than integrated the economies of Siberia and European Russia.[33] Renovation of European Russian industry absorbs a growing percentage of capital investment, leaving an ever smaller portion to be allocated to Siberia. What is allocated to Siberia tends to be concentrated in developing the area's natural resources. By channelling available investment capital into resource extraction, Moscow has narrowed Siberia's industrial specialisation and neglected the region's transport and social infrastructures, paticularly in East Siberia and the Soviet Far East whose international economic ties are primarily with nations of the Pacific Basin. The construction of the BAM and a container port at Vostochnyi are designed (among other things) to afford greater access to and across these regions.

External economic trends beyond Moscow's control further complicate Siberia's participation in the global economy. Declining world prices for oil and other raw materials since 1981 have adversely affected Siberian exports. While West Siberia's oil and gas continue to flow to Western Europe, the Japanese market for East Siberian and Soviet Far East raw materials may actually be shrinking. Structural changes in Japan's economy (a smaller role for resource-consuming manufacturing industries), as well as strict conservation measures since the early 1970s, have reduced Japanese interest in Siberia's raw materials.[34] Meanwhile, Soviet-Japanese trade declined by 21 per cent between 1982 and 1984 as Japan dropped over the course of a decade from first to sixth place among the USSR's capitalist trade partners.[35]

Siberia is taking part only marginally in the upsurge of international economic activity among Pacific-Basin nations, notably the United States, Japan, Canada, New Zealand, South Korea, Hong Kong, Taiwan, and ASEAN. This upsurge has witnessed a shift in the geographic structure of US foreign trade away from the Atlantic to East Asia and the Pacific (which accounted for 31 per cent of total US foreign commerce in 1984). No such shift has occurred in Soviet foreign trade. Between 1968 and 1984, the percentage of Soviet trade with East Asian and Pacific countries hovered around 9 per cent of total USSR trade.[36]

Siberia's role as a land-bridge between East Asia and Western Europe did not grow during the first half of the 1980s. Container shipments by western firms across Siberia declined between 1981 and 1984.[37]

State planning and administrative policies play a decisive role in encouraging or inhibiting the formation of economic ties between Siberia and the rest of the world. Centralised planning precludes regional economic autonomy and can negate commercial possibilities arising from, for example, the Soviet Far East's geographical propinquity to Pacific-Basin nations. In 1981, only 20 per cent of Soviet Far East exports originated within the region.[38] Regional coastal trade along the Pacific littoral with Japan is small-scale and strictly limited. On the other hand, West Siberia's international economic links are given high priority by Moscow. Exports of West Siberian oil and gas to Western Europe account for a hefty portion of the USSR's hard currency earnings. Mindful of these advantages, Moscow allocates about one-third of all Siberian investment to the Tyumen region alone.[39]

International politics obviously influence Siberia's relations with other countries. Political factors reinforce West Siberia's links with socialist nations of Eastern Europe and East Siberian/ Soviet Far East ties with Mongolia and Vietnam. Conversely, political forces constrain Siberia's economic relations with China, Japan and the United States.

Soviet-American rivalry diminishes Siberia's economic ties not only with the United States but also with Japan. Washington's embargoes on capital and technology transfers in the wake of events in Afghanistan (1979) and Poland (1981) have slowed the momentum of Soviet-Japanese co-operation in Siberia. Washington has not, however, been able to exercise a similar restraining influence over West European participation in construction of the *Soyuz* natural-gas pipeline from West Siberia.

Superpower rivalry also hardens Soviet attitudes towards Siberia's international economic ties. The heavy military investment in Siberia (discussed in Chapter 7) detracts from international commercial possibilities by reducing available resources and intensifying inhibitory security precautions. International tensions have deepened Soviet suspicions about the Sino-American and Sino-Japanese *ententes* and have fuelled Moscow's attacks on the Pacific Community concept as a device to exclude the USSR from — and ensure Japanese-American domination of — the Pacific Basin.[40] These suspicions feed upon the pronounced reluctance of the United States and Japan to include the USSR in discussions about emerging forms of multilateral economic co-operation among Pacific Basin nations.

Analogous forces constrain Siberia's economic ties with China. To these are added specific obstacles arising from an extraordinary Soviet preoccupation with frontier porosity and real or imagined internal political consequences of such porosity. Circulation in Siberia of anti-bureaucratic literature emanating from the People's Republic of China has been a source of concern since the 1970s.[41] Peking's current experiment with market mechanisms in a bold modernisation programme also contributes to the high level of cautionary obstacles to Siberian regional ties with China.

PROSPECTS

Opinions vary widely about the prospects for Siberia's role in the global economy. Among the many forecasts, two broad categories can be distinguished: 'optimistic' (envisioning a progressive enhancement of Siberia's international economic profile); and 'pessimistic' (emphasising the persistence of Siberian insularity).

Soviet commentators tend on the whole to be optimistic about Siberia's economic future. As a corollary, they see a real potential for greater international participation in Siberian development in the form of 'compensation' agreements (long-term co-operative projects where foreign firms provide capital and technology in exchange for deferred payment in the form of raw materials or a resultant product). Considerable attention has been accorded to pipelines, the BAM and the construction of a new port at Vostochnyi as projects enhancing Siberia's international profile. Soviet writers describe these international ties as helpful but not indispensable to Siberia's development. The Soviet Far East is portrayed as having a significant potential for economic interaction in the Pacific Basin, as Mikhail Gorbachev underlined in a highly publicised speech delivered at Vladivostock in July of 1986.[42]

A number of foreign observers also foresee greater Siberian participation in the world economy. In addition to citing factors adduced by Soviet writers, they identify incentives for making Siberian resources increasingly available to foreign customers: the need for hard currency, foreign technology and more efficient access to Siberian raw materials. Some see a greater role for Siberia as a link between Pacific Asia and Europe.[43] One Japanese writer goes as far as to evoke the scenario of massive Japanese participation in the development of Siberia's north-east (Yakutia, Magadan), involving large-scale Japanese immigration and the formation of a special Soviet-Japanese economic zone.[44]

Less sanguine prognoses, emphasising Siberia's enduring insularity from world markets, cite:

(1) central planning policies aimed at keeping the Soviet Far East economically dependent upon the rest of the country;

(2) a concentration of resource extraction to the detriment of infrastructure development that might contribute to broader international ties;

(3) declining Japanese interest in Siberia (one observer calls the Sakhalin oil and gas compensation agreement 'likely to be the last of such huge ventures in this century');[45]

(4) sustained insularity of the Soviet Far East from the economic vigour of Pacific Basin economies; and

(5) long projected delays in BAM's impact upon international trade.[46]

While pessimistic about short-term Siberia-Pacific connections, a number of forecasters see a shift in Soviet investment priorities from the Far East to West Siberia.[47] In this scenario, Siberia-European ties will grow as Siberia-Pacific ties stagnate. Nonetheless, total Siberian energy output (the region's biggest export) is not expected to expand 'at a pace sufficient to enable the USSR to become more than a minor factor in world energy markets'.[48] (But see also Chapters 3 and 4.)

Siberia's future in the world economy will ultimately depend upon many complex variables: the global and regional political climates (especially the interrelationships of the USSR, USA, Western Europe, Japan and China); global economic trends (notably prices of raw materials and the state of the Pacific Basin economies); the development of new technologies (such as alternative sources of energy; arctic technologies opening the Northern Sea Route to year-round navigation); and internal Soviet policies (the spatial distribution of investment, the discretionary conferral of limited regional economic autonomy, and diversification of the Siberian economy away from extractive industries). The distinguished Siberian economist, Academician Abel Aganbegyan, has called labour productivity the key to Siberia's future.[49]

These variables will all come under consideration by the new Soviet leadership, making the late 1980s a watershed in Siberia's long, oft-interrupted emergence onto the world scene.

NOTES AND REFERENCES

1. Albert Parry, 'Washington B. Vanderlip, the "Khan of

Kamchatka"', *Pacific Historical Review*, vol. 17, no. 3 (August 1948), pp. 311–30. Vanderlip recently made his debut in the Soviet novel: see D. I. Yeremin, *Zolotoi poyas* (Sovetskii pisatel, Moscow, 1972).

2. V. I. Lenin, *Sochineniya*, 2nd rev. edn, edited by N. I. Bukharin, V. M. Molotov, M. A. Savelev, vol. 25 (Gos. sots. ekon. izdat., Moscow, 1931), p. 502. The full text of this speech has not been published in subsequent editions of Lenin's collected works.

3. For details, see Kirby, *Siberia and the Far East: resources for the future* (Special Report no. 177, Economist Intelligence Unit, London, 1984), p. 46; Robert G. Jensen, Theodore Shabad and Arthur W. Wright (eds), *Soviet natural resources in the world economy* (University of Chicago Press, Chicago, 1983), pp. 5 and 11; A. Aganbegyan and Z. Ibragimova, *Sibir na rubezhe vekov* (Sovetskaya Rossiya, Moscow, 1984), pp. 63 and 77.

4. Mark Bassin, 'A Russian Mississippi? A political-geographical inquiry into the vision of Russia on the Pacific, 1840–1865' (unpublished PhD dissertation, University of California, Berkely, 1983), p. 142.

5. N. M. Przhevalskii (1839–88) as quoted in Mark Bassin, 'The Russian Geographical Society, the "Amur Epoch", and the Great Siberian Expedition 1855–1863', *Annals of the Association of American Geographers*, vol. 73, no. 2 (1983), p. 252.

6. Nikolaus Poppe, 'The economic and cultural development of Siberia' in Erwin Oberländer, *et al* (eds, *Russia enters the twentieth century, 1894–1917* (Temple Smith, London, 1971), p. 147.

7. Henry Adams, *Letters of Henry Adams*, ed. W. C. Ford (Houghton-Mifflin, Boston, 1930), vol. 1, p. 511.

8. S. M. Williams, 'A new California', *Munsey's Magazine*, vol. XXVI (1902), p. 761; *The Nation*, vol. LXI (1895), p. 165; Albert Bordeaux, *Sibérie* (Librarie Plan, Paris, 1904), p. 138.

9. Yurii Muravin, Gordian Dmitriev and Pavel Demidov, *Vladivostok: gorod u okeana* (Planeta, Moscow, 1980), pp. 9 and 20; Yurii Ligin, *Na Dalnem Vostoke* (Zadruga, Moscow, 1913), p. 94.

10. Morgan Philips Price, *Siberia* (Methuen, London, 1912), pp. vii–viii.

11. Quoted in Paul Dotsenko, *The struggle for a democracy in Siberia, 1917–1920* (Hoover Institution, Stanford, 1983), p. 4.

12. M. I. Svetachev, *Imperialisticheskaya interventsiya v sibiri i na Dalnem Vostoke, 1918–1922* (Nauka, Novosibirsk, 1983), pp. 8–9, 22, 59 and 166; S. Grigortsevich, *Amerikanskaya i yaponskaya interventsiya na sovetskom Dalnem Vostoke i ee razgrom* (Politizdat, Moscow, 1957), p. 35; V. S. Flerov, *Stroitelstvo sovetskoi vlasti i borba s inostrannoi ekspansiei na Kamchatke, 1922–1926* (Tomsk. Knizh. izdat., 1964).

13. Floyd J. Fithian, 'Dollars without the flag: the case of Sinclair and Sakhalin Oil', *Pacific Historical Review*, vol. 39 (May, 1970), pp. 205–22.

14. *Handbook of the Soviet Union* (Amtorg, New York, 1934), p. 309. *Statistical Abstract of the United States, 1934* (GPO, Washington, 1934), pp. 428–9.

15. Quoted in Kirby, *Siberia and the Far East*, p. 44.

16. See a Far Eastern party secretary's memoirs of a 15 October 1941

audience with Stalin: N. M. Pegov, *Dalekoe-Blizkoe: Vospominaniya* (Politizdat, Moscow, 1982), pp. 110–13.

17. See Stalin's 3 March 1937 speech, 'O nedostakakh partiinoi raboty', in I. V. Stalin, *Sochineniya 1934–1940* (Hoover Institution, Stanford, 1967), vol. I (XIV) p. 200.

18. Hallet Abend, *Pacific Charter* (Doubleday, New York, 1943), pp. 241–56.

19. For details, see Robert Conquest, *Kolyma* (Viking Press, New York, 1968).

20. V. P. Artemev, *Rezhim i okhrana ispravitelno-trudovykh lagerei MVD* (Munich, 1956), p. 11, cited by Aleksandr Nekrich, *Utopiya u vlasti* (OPI, London, 1982), vol. 2, p. 235.

21. For details, see John J. Stephan, 'The Korean minority in the Soviet Union', *Mizan* vol. 13, no. 3 (1971), pp. 141–3.

22. V. P. Lomakin, *Primore* (Politizdat, Moscow, 1981), p. 24.

23. Henry A. Wallace, *Soviet Asia mission* (Reynald & Hitchcock, New York, 1946); Emil Lengyel, *Siberia* (Garden City Publishing, Garden City, New York, 1943); William Mandel, *The Soviet Far East and Central Asia* (Institute of Pacific Relations, New York, 1944); Owen Lattimore, 'New road to Asia', *National Geographic Magazine*, vol. 86, no. 6 (1944), pp. 643–76.

24. Robert Mossé (ed.), *Soviet Far East and Pacific Northwest* (University of Washington Press, Seattle, 1944); Foster Rhea Dulles, *Russia and America: Pacific neighbors* (Institute of Pacific Relations, New York, 1946).

25. *Khrushchev Remembers*, translated and edited by Strobe Talbott (Little, Brown, Boston, 1974), pp. 249–50.

26. *Japan Times*, 13 June 1985.

27. Central Intelligence Agency, *USSR energy atlas* (GPO, Washington, 1985), p. 6.

28. Ibid., p. 9.

29. Ibid.; Kirby, *Siberia and the Far East*, p. 45.

30. Victor L. Mote, 'The Baikal-Amur Mainline and its implications for the Pacific Basin', in *Soviet natural resources in the world economy*, p. 135.

31. *Japan Times*, 11 Feb. 1985.

32. *The New York Times*, 22 Nov. 1985.

33. Boris Z. Rumer, *Investment and reindustrialization in the Soviet economy* (Westview, London, 1984), p. 140.

34. Leslie Dienes, 'Economic and strategic position of the Soviet Far East', *Soviet Economy*, vol. 1, no. 2 (1985), p. 166.

35. Leslie Dienes, 'Soviet-Japanese economic relations: are they beginning to fade?', *Soviet Geography*, vol. 26, no. 7 (1985), p. 510. A slight (4%) upturn in Soviet-Japanese trade occurred during the first eight months of 1985 — *Japan Times*, 4 Oct. 1985.

36. *Vneshnyaya torgovlya SSSR v 1968* (Finansy i statistika, Moscow, 1969) and *Vneshnyaya torgovlya SSSR v 1984* (Finansy i statistika, Moscow, 1985), passim.

37. Kirby, *Siberia and the Far East*, p. 46. Allen S. Whiting and Victor L. Mote, *Pacific Basin transportation prospects* (Wharton,

Washington, 1984), p. 27.

38. N. L. Shlyk, 'The Far East and the international economy', in John J. Stephan and V. P. Chichkanov (eds.), *Soviet-American horizons on the Pacific* (University of Hawaii Press, Honolulu, 1986), p. 123.

39. Dienes, 'Economic and strategic position of the Soviet Far East', p. 166.

40. See for example N. Tripolsky, 'Plans to set up a "Pacific Community" — a fresh threat to peace', *Far Eastern Affairs*, no. 2 (1985), pp. 112–22.

41. Nekrich, *Utopiya u vlasti*, vol. 2, p. 334.

42. Boris N. Slavinsky, 'Siberia and the Soviet Far East within the framework of international trade and economic relations', *Asian Survey*, vol. 17, no. 4 (1977), pp. 311–29. Mikhail Gorbachev, 'A new stage in the development of the Soviet Far East' (Novosti, Moscow, 1986).

43. Allan Rodgers, 'Commodity flows, resource potential and regional economic development', in Jensen (ed.), *Soviet natural resources in the world economy*', p. 211.

44. Fujita Sadao, *Shiberia no yoake* [Dawn of Siberia] (Keizai bungei-sha, Tokyo, 1971), pp. 205–22.

45. Dienes, 'Economic and strategic position of the Soviet Far East', p. 166.

46. Mote, 'The Baikal-Amur Mainline', p. 182.

47. Dienes, 'Economic and strategic position of the Soviet Far East', p. 172; Dienes, 'Soviet-Japanese economic relations', p. 520; Mote, 'The Baikal-Amur Mainline', p. 170.

48. Robert G. Jensen, 'Soviet natural resources in a global context' in Jensen (ed.), *Soviet natural resources in the world economy*, p. 6.

49. Aganbegyan and Ibragimova, *Sibir na rubezhe vekov*, p. 71.

Index